Opening the Bible

Opening the Bible

Essays by Howard H. Charles

edited by
J. Robert Charles

Institute of Mennonite Studies
Elkhart, Indiana

Co-published with Herald Press
Scottdale, Pennsylvania
Waterloo, Ontario

Copyright © 2005 by Institute of Mennonite Studies
3003 Benham Avenue, Elkhart, Indiana 46517-1999
www.ambs.edu/IMS

Co-published with
Herald Press
616 Walnut Avenue, Scottdale, Pennsylvania 15683
490 Dutton Drive, Unit C8, Waterloo, Ontario N2L 6H7
www.heraldpress.com

Printed in the United States of America
by Evangel Press, Nappanee, Indiana
Institute of Mennonite Studies ISBN 0-936273-37-2

Library of Congress Cataloging-in-Publication Data

Charles, Howard H.
  Opening the Bible : essays / by Howard H. Charles ; edited by
J. Robert Charles.
     p. cm.
  Includes index.
  ISBN 0-936273-37-2 (alk. paper)
  1. Bible—Criticism, interpretation, etc. I. Charles, J. Robert.
II. Title.
  BS511.3.C43 2005
  220.6—dc22
                              2004030328

Book design by Ken Gingerich, Albuquerque, New Mexico

Dedication

To my mother and to the memory of my father

"For many years now I have found in the scriptures the wellspring of my own faith and life. Poring over their pages I have repeatedly been enlightened, rebuked, exhorted, encouraged, and challenged. Above all I have been pointed beyond the book itself to God who is the living Word in whom I have found life. It has been my great joy also to help others listen for God's voice through serious and intensive Bible study and to observe what happens when such dialogue with the scriptures occurs. It is my constant hope that what goes on in the classroom may be not only an academic exercise but also a meaningful experience of growth in faith and in Christian discipleship."

—Howard H. Charles

Contents

Part 3 Opening the New Testament • 115

Foreword

For more than three decades, Howard Charles's *Builder* pieces were a monthly gift to the Mennonite church, nurturing Sunday school teachers and ably equipping their minds and spirits for their labor of love. I know of no other single educational resource then or now that has been so formative and so enriching; these study materials for teachers of adult Sunday school classes are arguably the most outstanding contribution a Mennonite professor has made to the life of this church.

Over several years in the 1980s and 1990s, I had conversations with Howard about publishing a collection of these essays. In his humble and perfectionist manner, Howard told me they needed more revision and updating. What a gift his son Robert now gives the church in at last making this selection of Howard's essays available.

Howard's writing is noted, as his teaching was, for penetrating precision. As one expects from a New Testament scholar, his work shows depth analysis of biblical theology and exposition. Moreover, his penchant for detail in both historical background and textual analysis shines through these essays, as it shone in his teaching, which many of his students respected deeply and remember fondly. These articles reveal Howard's characteristic depth of insight, clarity, and seasoned perspective.

Esteemed and loved as a teacher during his long career as professor of New Testament at Goshen Biblical Seminary, Howard possessed a remarkable ability to move from exacting detailed analysis to eloquent proclamation or meditative spiritual reflection on a text. His courses in inductive Bible study opened the eyes of many students to the richness of scripture.

Howard patiently pursued his pedagogical goal of bringing the horizon of the student's learning closer and closer to what he believed to be an adequate understanding of a text, one that was often spiritually moving. He doggedly pursued the teaching task so that his students would come to grasp the text's distinctive structure and literary features, its historical significance and its enduring meaning for Christian faith. This pedagogical style shows in these pieces, which combine solid academic scholarship with spiritual formation, to nurture heart and head.

At the 1980 celebration on the occasion of Howard's formal retirement from full-time teaching, his colleagues Millard Lind and William Klassen described Howard well: a man of humility and humor, steady, conscientious (he burned midnight oil to be well-prepared for class), not a flashy popular churchman but one who in both teaching and writing built a solid biblical foundation for the church. Colleague Jacob Enz rightly described Howard's *Builder* articles as a "tremendously significant ministry." My tribute emphasized Howard's reverence for scripture, combined with masterful scholarship. He knew that scripture has the power to shape, transform, and empower the life of the church.

I speak for many in expressing deep appreciation to Robert for making these essays accessible to the next generations of the church. Howard's words, recorded here, will continue to make the scripture the foundation of our faith, which none other than Jesus Christ—the Lord of scripture—can lay.

Willard M. Swartley

Editor's preface

From late 1950 until late 1984, my father, Howard Hess Charles, wrote background study materials and essays for Mennonite Publishing House in Scottdale, Pennsylvania. Published first in *Herald Teacher* and subsequently in *Builder*, these 1,500–2,500 word essays—numbering around 400 in all—were resources for teachers of adult Sunday school classes using the Uniform Series of Bible Studies.

These monthly essays were my father's principal literary output during his long career as a teacher of New Testament at Goshen Biblical Seminary and Associated Mennonite Biblical Seminary from 1947 until his final class in 1989.

I remember hearing, as a child, worried mentions of the "Scottdale deadline" that was looming as my father worked in his study late at night and early in the morning. Then would come the conjugal sigh of relief when Miriam, my mother, had deciphered my father's nearly illegible script well enough to type the manuscript and send it safely on its way east. Then a new month—and the same cycle would repeat. My own short experience as a writer of the 350-word "If I Were Teaching the Lesson" weekly column for *Builder* from 1999 to 2003 gave me a new, if belated, respect for what my father accomplished on a monthly basis over his thirty-four years of putting big thoughts onto paper in simple words and sentences.

A first collection of fifty-six of his essays published by Herald Press appeared in 1969 bearing the title *God and His People*. Introducing that volume, Paul M. Lederach noted that each article "is well within the grasp of the least educated and has a way of leading the more sophisticated into new insights." That collection was published because "on numerous occasions teachers have requested that these articles be made available in a more permanent and more usable form."

Similar requests continued to arise in the following decades. At the time of my father's death in March 2002, long-discussed ideas for publication of a further selection of his writings were finally moving forward, although, sadly, without his active participation in the project because of a combination of his poor health and his perhaps excessive modesty. The present collection has been culled from essays that first appeared in *Builder* during the final fifteen years that my father wrote for the Mennonite church community engaged in serious congregational Bible study.

Selecting fifty essays from nearly four times that number was not an easy task. But reading through them all gave me a new appreciation for the "seamless combination of scholarship and piety"—to quote one of his former students—with which my father opened the Bible not just for himself but for countless others. It is my hope that this volume will allow him to continue to open the Bible in an engaging way for a new generation of students and readers, as well as for those who valued his teaching, writing, and friendship during his lifetime.

I have attempted to wield a light editorial pen in revising and titling these essays, while making adjustments in style and contemporary references so that they would not appear dated. Because my father used The Revised Standard Version for his study and writing—as his well-worn and annotated RSV New Testament, pictured on the cover along with his reading glasses, attests—it seemed appropriate to use The New Revised Standard Version (1989) for all scriptural quotations.

Many people have encouraged me to undertake this project and have kept me or put me back on the path to its completion over the past decade. My special thanks go to Levi Miller of Mennonite Publishing Network; David S. Garber, former book editor at Herald Press; Willard M. Swartley of Associated Mennonite Biblical Seminary; Mary Schertz and Barbara Nelson Gingerich of the Institute of Mennonite Studies at AMBS; and Ken Gingerich, the book's designer and a former colleague at Mennonite Mission Network.

Family members also have played an important role in supporting and participating in this endeavor. To my mother, Miriam Stalter Charles; my brother and sister-in-law, Thomas and Kristine Kopp Charles; my wife, Sylvia Shirk Charles; my aunt, Anna Mae Charles Fretz; and my son, Daniel Christian Charles, who prepared the scriptural index, my deepest gratitude.

A final word of appreciation goes to The Hermitage in Three Rivers, Michigan, and the co-directors of its resident community, David and Naomi Wenger. During the early months of 2004 , they offered me a weekly quiet place to worship and work away from the distractions of e-mail and ringing phones, providing the spiritual and physical space in which this project could come to fruition.

J. Robert Charles

Part 1
Opening the Scriptures

How the Bible came to us

The Bible is a book from long ago. The story of its long journey to the present day is full of interesting details that we would never guess when we look at a Bible now.

Let us go back to the beginning of its fascinating story. It is well known, of course, that the Bible was written bit by bit over a very long period of time by many hands. The content of much of the Old Testament was passed on by word of mouth for generations before being written down. Some of our present books are based on older written sources: there are many references, for example, in 1 and 2 Kings to the "Book of the Chronicles of the Kings of Israel" and to the "Book of the Chronicles of the Kings of Judah." The preaching of some of the prophets may have been written down first by their disciples. The book of Psalms is a collection of poems of many Hebrew poets, and the book of Proverbs also draws together material from various sources.

The books now included in our New Testament were written over a much shorter period of time. The earliest were some of the letters of Paul written about the middle of the first century AD. The Gospels did not begin to appear until about AD 65–70, with Mark most likely the first to be written. The sayings of Jesus and the stories about him first circulated orally, but the desire for a more permanent record of these materials led to the writing of our Gospels. Most, if not all, of the remaining books of the New Testament were written before the end of the first century.

Most of the Old Testament was written in Hebrew, while the whole of the New Testament was written in Greek, the common language of the Roman world in the first century AD. The writing was sometimes done on treated animal skins. More often, something much like paper, papyrus, was used. These materials were cut and rolled into a scroll. Instead of turning pages, readers unrolled and rerolled the scroll as they read. The longer books needed more than one scroll; several of the shorter ones were written on the same scroll. Because scrolls wore out through use and age, new copies had to be made. Unfortunately, none of the original copies of any of the books of the Bible are known to exist today. The oldest copy of any part of our New Testament is a small piece of manuscript with thirty words from John 18 that dates from about AD 130. The oldest remains of the Old Testament were discovered in the late 1940s in some caves on the west side of the Dead Sea; these manuscripts were made during the three centuries before the destruction of Jerusalem in AD 70.

> The church did not so much select the books that finally got into the Bible as the books selected themselves. These books agreed with the living faith of the church in a way the others did not.

There was a very long period of time between the writing of the biblical books and the coming of the printing press, which was not invented until about AD 1450. During these centuries, many copies of the Bible were made by hand. Thousands of such handwritten copies still exist; many of them, of course, contain only a portion of the Bible and belong to the latter part of this period. As we might well expect, the frequent hand copying of the Bible by hundreds of people over hundreds of years resulted in variations of text. Some of these were the result of unintentional mistakes on the part of the copyist. At other times, scribes made what they thought of as improvements in the reading. Occasionally, some materials were added and others were dropped. These differences, however produced, can easily be seen when various copies are compared.

It is only natural that when such differences are found, the question arises: what was the original text? If we use only one English translation of the Bible, we likely will not be much aware of the problem of differences of text. Occasionally, however, especially if you have a New Revised Standard Version (NRSV), you may find a note in the margin calling attention to another reading. If you compare this translation at some length with the King James or Authorized Version (KJV), you will see the problem more readily!

Perhaps an example will make the point clear. Here is Matthew 5:22a in the KJV: "But I say unto you, that whosoever is angry with his brother without a cause shall be in danger of the judgment." Let us put the NRSV text alongside of this: "But I say to you that if you are angry with a brother or sister, you will be liable to judgment." What is the difference? You will see that the word "liable" in the NRSV replaces "danger" in the KJV. This is not a very important difference, because both words have about the same meaning. More important is that the phrase "without a cause" in the KJV is left out in the NRSV. This change gives another meaning to Jesus' statement, does it not? All anger against a brother or sister, even if we think it is justifiable, is forbidden by Jesus. The statement as found in the KJV would allow anger in some circumstances.

How are we to account for this difference? Behind both of these versions lie older English translations, until we get back to the first printed English New Testament by William Tyndale in 1526. In their concern for revisions and new translations, Bible translators have two things in mind: changes in English language usage and the use of older texts of the scriptures.

It is a long way back from 1526 to the first century. As we have already seen, during this period the Bible was being copied, in whole and in parts, again and again, by an untold number of people. The Old Testament was copied in Hebrew and the New Testament in Greek. Furthermore, from the second century onward, the New Testament and later the Old Testament were translated into Latin. The great Latin translation known as the Vulgate was made by Jerome at the end of the fourth century. It also was copied many times, often only in parts, with many differences occurring.

To keep from getting lost in too much detail, let us limit our attention to the New Testament. You will remember that our illustration above is taken from the Gospel of Matthew. From what has been said, it is clear that Matthew 5:22a was not originally written in English, but in Greek. And Tyndale did not have the original copy of Matthew 5:22a in hand when he made his translation.

We may liken the original text of the New Testament to the head of a river that later divides into many branches. These branches are the later copies either in Greek or Latin of the original text. We don't know how many such copies were made between the first and the fifteenth centuries. Almost five thousand handwritten copies of the New Testament (or parts of it) in Greek are known to us today. In addition there are many thousands of Latin manuscripts. Many of this large number, of course, have been discovered only in modern times.

The first attempt to bring some of these branches of the original stream together again was made by a Renaissance scholar named Erasmus, who published his first Greek New Testament in 1516. It was based on several incomplete manuscripts, together with some material from the Latin Vulgate. The oldest and best of his Greek manuscripts came from the tenth century; unfortunately, he used this one the least. Erasmus published several later editions of his Greek New Testament in which he made some corrections. But the text of Erasmus became the basis for Tyndale's English New Testament and also the King James Version of 1611. Since the KJV was made, many older Greek manuscripts of the New Testament have been discovered in the libraries of Europe and the Middle East. These have been brought together and studied by scholars. Out of their work has come the Greek New Testament which now underlies the more recent English editions of the New Testament, such as the American Standard Version (1901), the Revised Standard Version (1946), the New English Bible (1961), Today's English Version (1966), the New International Version (1978), and the New Revised Standard Version (1989).

Let us return again to the passage in Matthew 5:22a. It is clear that the oldest and best Greek manuscripts do not have the phrase "without a cause" in them. It likely was not part of the original text. Probably the phrase "without a cause" was introduced by some scribe who wanted to soften the words of Jesus a bit.

What then shall we say about using the familiar King James Version? We may continue to use it, especially if we have become accustomed to it, for it has great literary beauty and we can certainly come to an understanding of the way of salvation through it. Millions have done so since it was first published. The differences of text between it and modern English versions are minor and do not affect the basic message of the Bible. But it is well to compare the KJV with the more recent versions mentioned above. These will throw light on such problems as we have illustrated from Matthew 5:22a; they will also make many passages clearer, because they reflect more up-to-date English usage than the KJV.

We must now look briefly at one more problem. We have seen that the Bible was produced gradually over a long period of time. Can we be sure that we have all the writings that ought to be a part of it? Or we might put the question another way: is there any book now in our Bible that should not be there? Other books similar to some of the books in the Bible are in existence. They are called the Apocrypha. The present collection of sixty-six books was arrived at gradually. The early church took over the Jewish Bible, which was composed of our present Old Testament and which had been finalized early in the second century AD. Already by AD 200 the collection of New Testament books had been essentially made, agreed on, and was being circulated in the church.

Our present New Testament took final shape somewhat later. The important point to remember is this: the church did not so much select the books that finally got into the Bible as the books selected themselves. That is, there is a quality about these books that clearly distinguishes them from the rest. The best way to understand this is to read both the Bible and the Apocrypha. The books that were finally selected agreed with the living faith of the church in a way the others did not.

Two testaments, one Bible

The Christian Bible contains two parts, commonly referred to as the Old Testament and the New Testament. Why should there be such a division? Should it have been made where it was? How are the two parts to be related to each other? These are important questions whose answers will have far-reaching implications for our understanding of the Bible.

It is common knowledge that our Bible took shape gradually over a long period of time. However, the mere passage of time is not sufficient to explain the presence of the two testaments in our Bible. On this basis the division might not have been made at all or, if made, might have been made at some other point along the time line. Again, the division has not been made on the basis of literary forms or theological ideas. Although there are differences between the testaments in each of these areas, there are also similarities that might argue for no division—or one of another sort.

The division of the Bible into two parts is the result of something that happened in history. It should not be forgotten that the New Testament is not the only sequel to the Old: Judaism has its Talmud, which also stands in a relationship of continuity to the Old Testament. Both Jews and Christians accept the Old Testament, but then the road forks: Judaism traveled one literary road while Christianity traveled another.

The point of divergence was occasioned by the Christ-event. The Talmud accords no significance to Jesus Christ; it has taken shape and can be understood without reference to him. The opposite is the case with the New Testament: it owes its origin to Christ. He fills its pages and is its chief glory.

The New Testament beyond question is the book of the Christian church. All branches of the church regard it as basic to Christian faith and life. But what can be said about the Old

Testament? It might be argued that because we now have the New Testament, we can dispense with the Old. In the second century AD, Marcion regarded the Old Testament as a book wholly unworthy of acceptance by the church. It seemed to him to speak of another god than the Father of Jesus Christ; it had nothing helpful or important to say to the Christian church. Marcion's view was rightly rejected by the church of his day. It must be said, however, that more or less distinct echoes of Marcion's voice continue occasionally to be heard in more recent times. But there is no indication that the church in any of its major branches intends to surrender its claim to the Old Testament as an essential part of its Bible.

Nevertheless, the firm decision to retain the Old Testament is not without its problems. Some of it seems remote from our world and irrelevant to our faith—indeed, parts of it seem to constitute a real liability. The difficulty is felt most keenly in the area of certain religious conceptions and moral practices. Some of these, which appear to have divine sanction, seem contrary to the teachings of Jesus and to modern Christian understandings.

Through the long centuries of church history the relationship between the testaments has been understood in various ways. Several of the more important of these methods are as follows. The first is what may broadly be called the allegorical approach to the Old Testament; in one form or another, it was commonly used from the time of the church fathers to the Protestant Reformation. Allegory was a way of "saving" the Old Testament for the church by reading Christian meaning into the text; in this way, what appeared on the surface to be trivial or even offensive could be forced to yield edifying spiritual truth. For example, the author of the epistle of *Barnabas* (early second century AD), by assigning certain Greek letters to the number 318 in Genesis 14:14, saw there a reference to the cross of Jesus. This, he maintained, was the real meaning of the passage. Again, the story told in Exodus 17:8-16 is also given a Christian meaning: Moses, by stretching out his arms, made the sign of the cross; by this sign Jesus (represented by Joshua) was able to overcome Amalek. Closely related to allegory is typology, which in its older form sees in persons (as above) types of later Christian figures or in events and institutions the foreshadowing of later Christian realities. A more recent example of this approach is the finding of typological meaning in the furniture and materials of the tabernacle.

The desire to find Christian meaning in the Old Testament is a legitimate one, and in a limited way the New Testament writers do make use of allegory and typology as they read and cite the Old. But this fact offers no justification for a free and unrestrained use of these methods; indeed, such an approach can only lead to a serious abuse of the Old Testament. Our primary concern must be with the pre-Christian historical meaning of the text. Only after that word is clearly heard can we inquire about its Christian significance. More will be said about this procedure.

We must hold to a genuine unity between the testaments without demanding uniformity. The unity is one of a dynamic divine purpose that is worked out in an ongoing and ever-changing historical situation; this dynamism not only allows for but demands a degree of diversity.

A second approach to understanding the relationship between the testaments is the liberal approach common around the beginning of the twentieth century. This way of relating the testaments finds the normative expression of truth in the New Testament—or more especially in the teachings of Jesus. What does not conform to this standard in the Old is then discarded. Associated with this view are certain assumptions that are important for understanding it. One is that there has been an evolutionary development from the crude and less spiritual to the more noble and exalted conceptions and practices; the other is that the normative element is to be found in the realm of moral and ethical principles. The result of this liberal approach is that Jesus is viewed primarily as a religious teacher who stands at the apex of a long incline of development.

It is true of course that the Bible does not offer a flat plain of truth: Jesus is God's final word to humanity in the light of which all else must be understood. But the liberals did not take Jesus in his wholeness seriously enough. He is more than a supreme ethical and religious teacher: in him, God was active in the establishment of God's kingdom. The liberals had no adequate conception of the eschatological nature of Jesus' mission. Furthermore, their application of the category of evolutionary development to the biblical materials badly distorted the true understanding of relationships both within the Old Testament and also between the testaments. There is movement—but it can hardly he characterized as a progressive, evolutionary one. This category is a modern rather than a biblical one.

A third way of relating the testaments is to equate the Old Testament with law and the New with gospel. The Old Testament is then regarded as a preparation for the reception of the message of the New. There is an element of truth in this view, but it is not an adequate statement of the theological relationship between the testaments. Yes, there is a sense in which the Old Testament, with its demand for response to covenant obligations that are not met, does serve to prepare men and women for hearing the good news of the gospel. But the Old Testament cannot be interpreted wholly in terms of law nor the New Testament wholly in terms of grace.

As Paul indicates in Romans 4, there is something much deeper in the Old Testament than the Mosaic law: the framework within which the Mosaic law is set in the book of Exodus is one of grace. God had acted in Israel's redemption. The law given at Mount Sinai was meant to provide a guideline for Israel's response to their redeemer. Grace and law are thus joined. A similar conjunction is found in the New Testament: the gospel of God's grace in the Beatitudes is followed by specific directives for practical conduct. Likewise in the letters of Paul, the powerful exposition of the gospel is followed by definite commands for the ordering of daily life. The indicative of God's action and the imperative of human response are constantly intertwined throughout both testaments.

Yet a fourth pattern of relationship is that of promise and fulfillment: whereas the Old Testament speaks of promise, the New Testament is the record of fulfillment. This formula is preferable to any of the preceding. It has genuine biblical support. The Old Testament is a book of unfulfilled hopes; the New affirms repeatedly that the age of fulfillment has dawned. Nevertheless the pattern cannot be pressed too rigidly. There is both promise and fulfillment in the Old Testament and fulfillment and promise in the New—indeed the New Testament ends on a note of promise. Furthermore, the relationship between promise and fulfillment is not one of exact equation. The New Testament fulfillment of the Old Testament promise frequently carries with it elements of novelty and surprise. It often clarifies by way of modification that which it fulfills.

How then should we think of the relationship between the testaments? We must hold to a genuine unity between them without demanding uniformity. Due recognition must be given to elements of both continuity and discontinuity. The unity is one of a dynamic divine purpose that is worked out in an ongoing and ever-changing historical situation; this dynamism not only allows for but demands a degree of diversity. The God of the biblical story is an actor, and each act—although consistent with God's ultimate goal—introduces a new situation that is no mere replica of the past.

The utterly unique and decisive act lying between the beginning and the end of the biblical story is the Christ-event: what precedes it is incomplete without it and all that flows from it. Likewise, the Christ-event and its sequel would be incomprehensible apart from what precedes it. But something more must be said: it is only from the vantage point of the Christ-event that the true significance of all that precedes it can be clearly seen. This conviction explains the difference between the Jewish and the Christian understanding of the Old Testament.

The interaction between the testaments may be expressed in an analogy: the river runs forward into the sea, but the sea, under tidal pressure, then backs up into the river. All the practical implications of this way of viewing the relationship between the testaments for interpreting the Bible—especially the Old Testament—cannot be pursued here. The guiding principle, however, may be stated simply: we must read the Old Testament both forward and backward, and in that order. The first reading allows it to speak its message honestly and clearly as a pre-Christian book. In the second reading, its message is then filtered through the lens of the New for whatever reaffirmation, correction, or completion it may provide.

The good news:
What God has done

William Taylor went to California during the gold rush of the nineteenth century as a Methodist missionary. Arriving in San Francisco, he was unable to find a church available to him as a place to preach. So he got a barrel and put it on a busy street corner. On Sunday morning, he stood on it and shouted, "What's the news?" He soon attracted a crowd about him. Having their attention, he began his sermon with the words, "Thank God I have good news for you this morning."

The good news to which Taylor was referring was, of course, the gospel. The word *gospel* means "good news." But it is not good news of just any sort, such as a pay raise or an unexpected visit from a friend. It has a restricted reference arising out of its New Testament usage. It is a religious term, indeed, a specifically Christian one.

To speak of the gospel as good news presupposes a bad situation to which it provides a welcome solution. Where no sense of need exists, no good news arrives; there are no unfulfilled expectations. For this reason, the gospel does not appear to be good news to many people. It offers something for which they are not looking.

The gospel, therefore, must not be understood only as supplying an answer to a problem; it frequently helps to clarify the problem itself. It must serve to make us aware of the true dimensions of our need that we may indeed see the gospel for what it is—great, glad good news. Seen from this point of view, the gospel may be said paradoxically to be both bad news as well as good; the one cannot be separated from the other.

If it is true that the gospel clarifies the problem, then we must begin by looking briefly at the human situation as seen from the biblical standpoint. The ugly but realistic word here is *sin.* We must be careful, however, to define it properly. It is often understood in a moralistic sense as the breaking of this or that law. The relative seriousness of sin and corresponding guilt then is rated according to the importance of the particular law that has been broken. But sin according to the Bible is not so much the breaking of laws as it is the rupturing of relationships.

Sin is living out of fellowship with God and our fellow humans. It is a self-centeredness that refuses to bow the knee in worship to God or to reach out in genuine love and concern to one's neighbor. Sin basically is to make a god of self; it is a denial of our continuity both with God and with other human beings, for which we have been made. Out of this stance flow a variety of specific attitudes and actions that corrupt human existence.

> **The gospel is not a timeless truth but is wrapped up in a person. It is a presence in one who was truly human but also one in whom God was uniquely present and active among us for our salvation.**

To describe sin is not to explain it, however, for there is mystery at the heart of it. It is deeply rooted in human nature and is all-pervasive. Why should we all want to live with our backs toward God and without genuine regard for the neighbor? To blame our problem on Adam or on the devil may momentarily be helpful, but it is not an ultimate answer to sin in the universe.

Our concern then is not with explaining sin but rather with removing it. How can the depravity that poisons human life in all of its dimensions be overcome? Here we need help from outside ourselves. We cannot extract ourselves from the predicament in which we live. All our efforts only seem to compound our awareness of our helplessness, for sin involves both guilt and power. We cannot compensate for the guilt of past sin by going beyond what is required of us today, in our relationship with God or with others. No plus achievement is possible in either of these areas, because nothing exists that is more than our duty. Furthermore, the guilt of past sin lives in our experience today as a paralyzing power.

Even if it were theoretically possible to go beyond what is expected of us in our God-ward and human relationships, how should we who have not been able to meet our obligations in the past now hope to exceed them? The burden of past failure can only further weaken an already failing will. The prospects, then, of dealing with our problem out of our own resources are not at all promising. What appear to be escape routes turn out to be dead-end streets. Are we shut up to live without hope of ever achieving our true destiny?

The gospel speaks precisely to such a situation. Indeed, it offers good news. There is help for us from beyond ourselves. God has come to our rescue. This is what the Bible is all about.

How then shall we describe the gospel? From the pages of the New Testament, it soon becomes clear that we must speak about Jesus. The gospel is inseparably tied to him. In the Gospels he is represented as preaching the gospel (Matt. 4:17; Mark 1:14). In Acts and in the letters of Paul, Jesus is himself the gospel (Acts 8:35; Rom. 1:3). The gospel, then, is not a timeless truth but is wrapped up in a person. It is a presence in one who was truly human but also one in whom God was uniquely present and active among us for our salvation.

To understand Jesus, however, we must see him as part of God's larger plan to meet our needs. The story began long centuries before his coming. We will pick it up at the point of the formation of the Hebrew people at the time of the exodus-Sinai event. There God delivered a people from the bondage of slavery and entered into covenant with them. He would be their God and they should be his people. To provide guidance in expressing their gratitude to their redeemer, God gave them the law. Israel was to be a unique people among the nations of antiquity, living with their face, not their back, toward God. God's purpose for humans appeared to be on the way to fulfillment in a small community and through it in the rest of the world.

But this fulfillment was not to be. The story of God's people is often a tale of disappointment. No fault was to be found with the law, the scaffolding intended to shape their response. The difficulty lay deeper, in the inner realm of motivation: Israel could not summon strength to love God with all their heart and to enlist all their energies in God's service. Until the will was healed, the relationship between God and humans and among people would remain broken.

Could this basic weakness be remedied? The prophets believed that it would be. The remedy would not come about, however, by a renewed effort on Israel's part: it would require a fresh act of God. Jeremiah looked forward to the day when God would write his law on the hearts of his people. Then they would truly be his people (Jer. 31:33). Ezekiel, likewise, spoke of God putting a new heart and a new spirit in humans that would enable them to respond to God as they ought (Ezek. 36:26–27). The fulfillment of this hope tarried long. Generations came and went, but the story remained monotonously the same—failure.

Then one day Jesus appeared, and suddenly the weary tale was altered. Here was one whose response to God was not traditional. The uniform witness of various strands of New Testament material is that where others failed, he succeeded. Paul, for example, contrasts the obedience of Christ to the sin of Adam (Rom. 5:19). He insists that Christ "knew no sin" (2 Cor. 5:21). To Paul's testimony we may add Peter's, that Jesus "committed no sin" (1 Pet. 2:22). The writer of Hebrews affirms that Jesus "in every respect has been tested as we are, yet without sin" (4:1a; see 7:26). Note also the witness of 1 John 3:5 that "in him there is no sin." Reference finally may be made to a passage where Jesus is said to have thrown down the challenge to his critics: "Which of you convicts me of sin?" (John 8:46).

Here at last was a new person in the human community whose response to God was one of complete openness, trust, and obedience. Of all people, he alone was able to say: "I always do what is pleasing to him" (John 8:29). Such obedience in a world where disobedience reigned ultimately cost him his life. The cross is not to be regarded as arbitrarily arranged or as mechanically executed. It is the product of unfailing obedience to the passion in God's heart to pursue men and women in their sin, even at the cost of death, in the hope of their salvation. And death was indeed the outcome but not the last word: God vindicated Jesus in raising him from the dead. And what is more, the Spirit that indwelt the obedient Son during the days of his earthly life has now been shared with all who, out of sense of need, identify in penitence and self-surrender with him. The Christ-event (the person, ministry, death, and resurrection of Jesus) is thus the place where our sin was judged by his perfect obedience. Here, too, forgiveness is offered to the penitent. Beyond that, new resources are made available to those who open their lives to the obedient Spirit of the ever-living Christ.

Paul sums up the good news of the gospel in a remarkably compact statement: "For God has done what the law, weakened by the flesh, could not do: by sending his own Son in the likeness of sinful flesh, and to deal with sin, he condemned sin in the flesh, so that the just requirement of the law might be fulfilled in us, who walk not according to the flesh but according to the Spirit" (Rom. 8:3–4). This carefully constructed sentence points not only to what God has done but also the way we can respond to that action.

The good news:
What must I do?

In ancient Phillipi many years ago, a frightened jailer asked a jailed missionary, "What must I do to be saved?" What he meant by that question is not entirely clear. He knew that matters were not as they ought to be. He also assumed that he had some responsibility in the situation. Paul's answer was prompt and forthright. It focused on what needed to be done. The jailer had to act (Acts 16:30–31).

Adolf Deissmann once remarked that all religious cults can be divided into two types: the acting and the reacting cults. An acting cult stresses human initiative. Humans make the first move and hope to influence the deity in their favor; the divine response is subject to human doing. This approach, the way of some ancient religions, is still a temptation to people. The Pharisee at prayer in the temple is a classic example (Luke 18:9–14). Over against this type of religion is what Deissmann called the reacting cult. This cult also has a place for human action, but our doing is no longer in first place. It does not try to tie God's hand. Action is a response to God's prior activity, whose action determines our doing. The scriptures in both the Old and the New Testaments point us to this religion.

Human effort, then, has a place in biblical religion. It is not a foe of grace but a complement, for apart from our action salvation is impossible. We must understand, however, both the character and the content of our responsibility.

To clarify this responsibility, we must give brief attention to the meaning of *salvation* in the religious sense in the Bible. Listening to much popular religious talk about salvation today, one might conclude that it is an impersonal gift, somewhat like a Christmas present. It is an objective "it" that is given to us to be enjoyed in its own right, more or less apart from the giver. This impersonal quality is not what the Bible intends as its content. Salvation is to be thought of in relational terms: to be saved is to enter into right relationships both with God and with our fellow humans. Salvation means existence that is characterized by wholeness and soundness. It is to realize that pattern of life for which we have been made.

This goal of wholeness cannot be achieved unless both God and we are actively involved in the process. Satisfactory interpersonal relationships cannot be worked at from only one side. Although God has taken the initiative in righting the wrong relationship between God and us, the process is not finished until we act. If we do not act, there is no salvation for us, because the relationship, its essential content, does not exist. We have thwarted it. But what is the character and shape of our response to God to be? Three elements must find a place in describing it.

First is the matter of penitence. No progress can be made toward establishing a right relationship until the wrongness of the existing one is acknowledged. But recognition of need is not enough. We must assume responsibility for the situation, for God has not turned his back on us. We have refused to respond to God's love and purpose for us. We have gone our own way, ignoring or defying God. But even willingness to assume responsibility for what we have done is not yet penitence. Penitence is present only when we express genuine regret for what we have done. It is sorrow for the wrongness for which we are responsible.

Second, if penitence lays the foundation for a new relationship with God, it is not all that he desires from us. God is looking for a new attitude toward him. Although this response might be described in various ways, at the heart of it is the biblical word *faith*. Paul told the Philippian jailer that he must believe in the Lord Jesus if he wished to be saved (Acts 16:31).

Perhaps a better or less ambiguous word than *faith* or *belief* to express what lies at the heart of this new response is *trust*. Trust involves the total person in relationship to another, not only head knowledge. Beyond changed understandings is a new openness, reliance on and commitment to God as known in Jesus. All of this is part of the reorientation of life that lies at the core of the relationship known as salvation.

Third, implicit in what has been said about belief or trust is another element in our response to God that needs explicit mention. It is obedience. So closely is obedience linked to faith that at times the former appears to be substituted for the latter (for example, John 3:36 when compared with 3:16; Acts 5:32 when compared with 15:7–9). Obedience suggests the master-servant relationship, which trust does not necessarily imply. Christian existence is not the same as spiritual democracy. Obedience lives in concrete forms and specific deeds. It speaks of discipleship in which no aspect of our daily living is excluded from God's lordship. If disobedience springing from distrust or disbelief is the response to God that the Bible calls sin, obedience born out of penitence and trust is the hallmark of the new relationship that is called salvation.

> **From popular religious talk, one might conclude that salvation is an "it," a Christmas present to be enjoyed more or less apart from the giver. But the Bible intends that salvation be thought of in relational terms. Salvation refers to wholeness and soundness, which cannot be achieved unless both God and we are actively involved.**

Such, then, in broadest outline is the shape of the response that the gospel anticipates from us. But we cannot stop here; to do so would invite despair. How can we respond as the gospel demands? How can we experience penitence, turn face about, and offer our trust and obedience to the one we formerly ignored or defied? Unless the gospel can help us make the offering it solicits, it is in the end no good news. We are left prisoners in our sin.

Thanks be to God, the gospel does provide help at this crucial point of need! First, at the heart of the gospel is the historical figure of Jesus—his life, ministry, death, and resurrection. Jesus was a fresh and unique in-break of God into the human community. In the life of Jesus we are allowed to glimpse the pattern of response to God that he intended for us to make. No longer is that ideal set out only in precepts; it has taken shape in flesh and blood. But to look full into Jesus' face is to become aware of the distance that separates us from him; he has a loveliness that makes us aware of our ugliness.

But that is not all. He is not only the model but also the concrete expression of the passionate love in God's heart for

The good news: What must I do?

us. God is saying in all that Jesus was and did that God loves us even though we have turned our backs on him. Calvary stands as a monument forever both to the depth of our sinfulness and to the greatness of God's love. Pondering the Christ-event in its totality as it is made alive, contemporized, and personalized by the Spirit is likely to tap the springs of penitence in our hearts.

Penitence, however, is not enough. How is faith or trust in God or in Christ born in a heart where it does not exist? Although we cannot banish all the mystery that surrounds the birth of trust, an analogy from our experience with other human beings may provide some help. Trust in other people is elicited in us when we discover that their conduct toward us is not conditioned by our attitude toward them. This attitude surprises us and suggests that another estimate of them may be possible if not indeed necessary. Again, we may be helped to change our attitude toward others by the testimony of a third party who has found them to be completely trustworthy.

Both of these common experiences are applicable to the birth of faith or trust in the religious sense. It is precisely the way God's attitude toward and treatment of people in Christ has not been shaped by their distrust and lack of faith in him that calls for a reexamination of our response to God. God loved people when they did not love him. When they heaped abuse on Christ, he did not respond in retaliating anger but in forgiving love. What Jesus said about God in words, he incarnated in deed and in spirit. And, what is more, there is the testimony of a countless multitude from the days of Jesus' ministry until now who have found God in Christ utterly worthy of full trust.

In ways such as these, then, faith may be provoked in our hearts. The total life and ministry of Jesus, however, is not only the catalyst for the birth of faith or trust in a Christian sense but also the agent for our response to God. It is God's gracious pleasure that Jesus, whose trust in and obedience were all that God desired, should be our representative before God. Our willing but imperfect response thus is caught up and perfected in his as we identify ourselves with him.

Finally, our positive response to God in Christ should not be thought of apart from the aiding ministry of the Spirit. The

Spirit calls us to penitence and trust. When we acknowledge our wrongness and turn in surrender and obedience to God in Christ, a new relationship is established between God and us. This new relationship means that we are now open to the presence of God through the Spirit in our lives in a way that will allow God to further his purposes in us and through us. God wants to reproduce the character of Jesus in us through the sanctifying work of the Spirit. God also wants to carry forward the ministry of reconciliation in our world by the Spirit working through us.

So from the beginning of our Christian life to its end, both what we are and what we do cannot be explained apart from reference to the Spirit of God. The gospel, then, both demands response from us and offers resources in meeting that demand. But we must decide whether we will meet that demand and lay hold of the offered aid.

The good news: What difference does it make?

The question the title poses may appear to be a pragmatic one, suggesting that the worth of the gospel is to be determined by its ability to produce results. This statement is not to be denied. What is important, however, is the criteria by which the changes wrought are evaluated. The gospel is good news only if the goal to which it is addressed is deemed important.

The thrust of the gospel has been expressed in various ways. One common way is to say that it has to do with our salvation. The term *salvation*, however, is capable of a variety of meanings. It may, for instance, be thought of in a wholly futuristic sense: the gospel then is viewed as a sort of insurance policy that guarantees escape from hell, but with no immediate cash value. Again, salvation may be interpreted as basically an inner spiritual experience of peace and joy, flooding the soul with light and raising the emotional temperature, but with little relevance to the patterns of external behavior that mark our daily living. In this case, the gospel is a kind of medicine for the heart, while outwardly we continue to bear the marks of the old order in which we live.

If salvation, however, is understood as dealing with the whole person in the entirety of life both personal and social, now and in the future, then the gospel takes on another shape. It then is seen to have relevance to our outward conduct as well as to our inner spirit. It can no longer be interpreted wholly in individual terms; it also has social dimensions. It speaks not only of well-being in some future age but of a different quality and pattern of life here and now. Indeed, salvation in this sense embraces a discipleship that is as broad, as long, and as deep as life itself.

It is this third view that best represents the New Testament understanding of salvation. On almost every page, it encourages us to believe that the gospel should make a difference now in our lives. Jesus, for example, referred to the meaning of his mission under the imagery of new wine in the process of fermentation (Mark 2:22). The old wineskins which had lost their elasticity would not be able to adjust to the new demands of the powerful dynamic at work in his ministry. The gospel presupposes change.

If salvation deals with the whole person in the entirety of life both personal and social, now and in the future, then the gospel has relevance to our outward conduct as well as to our inner spirit. It has both individual and social dimensions.

The evidence of the Acts of the Apostles is no different from that of the four Gospels. Some twenty years after Jesus' death, Paul and Silas arrived in Thessalonica on a preaching mission. The city was soon in an uproar. Some of the Jews told the city authorities that the reason for the disturbance was that those who "have been turning the world upside down" had come to their city (Acts 17:6). The gospel could not live with the status quo; the new order challenged the old.

No matter where we sample in the New Testament, we discover that the word *new* is inseparably related to the gospel. It is refreshing to turn the pages and note how often and in what contexts the word occurs. There is the "new covenant" (1 Cor. 11:25), the demand to be "born anew" (John 3:3), the "new humanity" (Eph. 2:15), the ongoing process of renewal (Rom. 12:2), the "new commandment" (John 13:34), the "new name" (Rev. 2:17), the "new song" (Rev. 5:9), "a new heaven and a new earth" (Rev. 21:1). Indeed, as the New Testament closes, we hear the Lord God proclaiming from the throne, "See, I am making all things new" (Rev. 21:5).

We have a right, then, to expect that the gospel should make a difference. Russian philosopher and theologian Nicholas Berdyaev made this point rather forcefully. "In Christianity," he said, "the central idea is that of transfiguration, not justification. The latter has occupied too prominent a place in Western Christianity." This is not to deny the reality or validity of justification. But Berdyaev's words do emphasize what may too often be obscured in the traditional interpretation of the heart of the gospel.

The important question is how we should characterize the difference and newness that the gospel makes. First, there is what we may describe as a new orientation of the person. If sin can be defined as an attempt to defy the reality that constitutes our world, salvation is the process of coming to terms with it. Put in personal terms, it is the experience of reckoning seriously for the first time with the person and will of God as the determinative factor of our lives. It is living with our faces and not our backs toward God. It is trying to see ourselves in the wholeness of our lives in the light of God. This transfiguration obviously has far-reaching implications, the pursuit of which will give distinctive color to our lives. This change of basic stance, therefore, is fundamental to all the other differences that the gospel does or should make. "If I get the sky right," said the French artist Jean Corot, whose landscape paintings were immensely popular in nineteenth-century Europe, "I get the rest right."

Second, closely related to this change of orientation is the emergence of a new quality of personhood and the beginnings of a new lifestyle. The word *Christian* is so common a term today that we scarcely think of how it came to birth. According to Acts 11:26, it was first applied to the followers of Jesus in Antioch—very likely by Jews or Greeks of the city. Some of the believers were Jews and others were Gentiles. But these terms, with their racial, cultural, and religious connotations, could not describe what was of deepest significance about these people. Here were men and women the quality and character of whose lives could not be explained apart from Christ. They were Christians, that is, Christ's men and Christ's women.

A Christian is one whose very person reflects in some degree the character of Christ. It is God's purpose that we should be "conformed to the image of his Son" (Rom. 8:29). It is Paul's wish for his Galatian converts that Christ be formed in them (Gal. 4:19). It is the work of the Spirit to reproduce the character of Christ in each of us. Paul refers to this as "the fruit of the Spirit" (Gal. 5:22–23). The virtues brought together in this well-known list are the graces of the historical Jesus whose presence as the living Christ is now lived in us by the Spirit.

Christian character, however, must also influence conduct. Our lives must not only bear the imprint of his character but must also express the thrust of his life. If Christ lives at the center of life, he must also shape it at its periphery. To be a Christian is to acknowledge Jesus not only as Savior but also as Lord. There is no aspect of daily conduct that lies outside his legitimate sphere of control; his passion for actualizing the rule of God must be the mainspring of our discipleship.

Third, although the gospel speaks to the individual person, its focus is really on the creation of a new community in the midst of the old. The bonds of this peoplehood are not basically ethnic, cultural, or ideological. This people is a body of which Christ is the head and the Spirit is the vitalizing and uniting bond. It is the community of the reconciled in which the purposes of God for human life are finding fulfillment. But it is not only an exhibit of God's renewing grace and as such a part of the good news of the gospel itself: it is also the instrument by which God continues to create in each generation in every part of the world a people for himself.

If the New Testament letters give us something of the blueprint of the church, the book of Acts provides a series of brief glimpses of the historical reality during the early decades of its history. After reading other materials roughly contemporary with it, one cannot read this document without sensing the freshness of springtime. Heaven has touched earth; life was never again to be the same for those who had been caught up in its blessing.

Fourth, the gospel has brought a new undergirding of hope with regard to the outcome of history. God's purpose to establish his kingdom took a decisive step forward in the Christ-event. In the life, ministry, death, and resurrection of Jesus, a firm pledge was given that the powers of darkness were already doomed: the night might linger for a time, but the dawn was certain. The coming of that day is portrayed in a powerful way in the magnificent vision with which the New Testament closes.

It is this unshakable confidence in the triumph of God's kingdom that is the secret of much in the New Testament that otherwise would be difficult to understand. There is bold

The good news: What difference does it make?

defiance of the forces of sin, joy in the midst of suffering, dedication in the face of great odds, fearlessness in the presence of death—to mention only a few items that come quickly to mind. Our total life as Christians is to be lived out of the future, but it is a future already given to us in principle in what lies behind us. It is a future in which we now participate through the Spirit.

We have been thinking about the difference the gospel is intended to make in human life. Is the brief picture we have drawn from the New Testament a credible one when judged in the light of contemporary Christian experience, whether personal or observable? Has the product, as C. S. Lewis once complained, been over-advertised? Perhaps two comments may be offered in reply. First, the degree of difference that the gospel makes in our experience is dependent on how seriously we take it. The key is in our hand; God will not override our freedom. Second, Christian experience has an open-ended quality: what has been need not determine what may be. We are Christians in the making, and every day is a new opportunity to explore afresh the potentialities of life in Christ in its manifold dimensions. Adventure should be the mood of our pilgrimage until it terminates in God's presence.

Sin, the universal malady

A man stood on a busy street corner in the Chicago Loop one September day in 1972. As people hurried by on their way to lunch or business, the man would slowly raise his right arm. He would point to the person who happened to be nearest him and pronounce in a loud voice the single word, "Guilty!" Then, without changing his solemn expression, he dropped his arm to his side. A few moments later he would repeat his performance, pointing to another person and again saying "Guilty." This strange conduct caught the attention of those passing by. Karl Menninger (who reports this incident in his book *Whatever Became of Sin?*) says that some stopped to stare at the man. Then they looked at one another. But once again their eyes turned to this odd figure. Guilty! Is everyone guilty? Guilty before whom? Guilty of what? How did he know?

This unusual story is a dramatic reminder of Paul's argument in Romans 1:18–3:20, where he, too, points the accusing finger: "There is no one who is righteous, not even one; there is no one who has understanding, there is no one seeks God. All have turned aside, together they have become worthless; there is no one who shows kindness, there is not even one" (Rom. 3:10–12). These lines are quotations from various psalms where the reference is to Israelites. But Paul's intention is to universalize them. No human being in the world is excluded from his charge that "all, both Jews and Greeks, are under the power of sin" (3:9; see also vv. 19–20).

Sin, while not the most important theme in the Bible, is present from beginning to end. It is introduced on the heels of the creation account of Adam and Eve. Although the word *sin* does not actually occur in Genesis 3, the story told there cannot be understood otherwise. It is sin's introduction to human experience. What is more, that primal stone casts its long shadow across the pages that follow until the final chapter of the last book of the New Testament. There we are told that outside the celestial city that is yet to be, there will be "the dogs and sorcerers and fornicators and murderers and idolaters, and everyone who loves and practices falsehood" (Rev. 22:15). Here, as in Genesis 3, sin is not portrayed in the abstract but in personal terms; this view is more or less characteristic of the biblical presentation.

Before turning attention to what the Bible means by sin, it is important to understand the presuppositions on which this concept is based. Four may be identified. First, there is a norm or standard in relation to which conduct can be evaluated. The Bible assumes the existence of God. Furthermore, it maintains that God has made his will known to people through a variety of media, including nature (for example, Rom. 1:19–21), but finding its clearest expression in the Christ-event (John 1:1, 14, 18; Heb. 1:1–3).

Second, sin implies freedom of choice. Sin is not identified with the body as though matter itself were sinful; this was the view of ancient Gnosticism, which made a genuine incarnation impossible (1 John 4:2–3). Neither is sin a predetermined necessity, in which there is no room for decision making. We are like a traveler at a crossroad, not a train on the track. The biblical perspective is well expressed in Deuteronomy 30:19: "I have set before you life and death, blessings and curses. Choose life so that you and your descendants may live."

Third, a corollary of freedom is responsibility. There are options from which we may choose, and we are responsible for the choices that we make. Sin is the failure to use our freedom responsibly under God. The consequences that flow from the misuse of our freedom are therefore not to be understood apart from the framework of moral obligation. Sin is the shadow side of responsibility.

Fourth, basic to and qualifying all the preceding assumptions is the nature of God, from which the concept of sin derives its ultimate character. The category of sin as such is not a uniquely biblical one. What is often forgotten is that the vocabulary for sin in the Bible is not, for the most part, very much different from that used in ancient Egypt, Babylon, or

Greece. What is distinctive is found in the larger context in which that terminology is set, specifically the kind of God with whom we have to do.

What, then, is sin according to the Bible? If we focus on specific texts throughout the Bible, the answer may appear to be quite diverse. In particular situations, a great many different acts or attitudes can be given the label of sin. These range widely from such matters as eating the flesh of an animal that died by itself or was killed by a wild beast (Lev. 22:8–9) to hating both Christ and God (John 15:24). But behind these individual sins is a common denominator that may be said to define sin: it is disobedience to that which is declared to be the will of God.

> According to the Bible, many acts or attitudes can be called sin. But behind individual sins is a common denominator: sin is disobedience to the will of God. But sin is not essentially the breaking of a law; it is the rupture of relationship.

This way of putting the matter, however, should not be understood in an impersonal or legalistic sense. Sin is not essentially the breaking of a law; it is the rupture of personal relationships that are meant to exist between God and people and among people. It is the assertion of human independence in defiance of God's intentions; it is the deification of the creature over against the creator. Sin is portrayed in this way when it is first introduced in biblical literature in Genesis 3, and this understanding remains the core of its conception throughout both Old and New Testaments. The specifics may vary, but the essence does not change.

We will not attempt a systematic survey of the biblical teaching on sin. Instead, a few general observations will be made on the way this theme appears in various parts of the biblical tradition. Let us begin with the Pentateuch (Genesis through Deuteronomy). One comment on the patriarchal narratives must suffice. Even the greatest of those figures, Abraham and Jacob, are not presented as sinless. Abraham was less than completely truthful about his wife (Genesis 20), and Jacob lied to his father to obtain the birthright blessing (27:1–29). Although later Jewish tradition tended to ignore their failures, the biblical account portrays them "warts and all."

The Sinai covenant dominates the Pentateuch from Exodus onward. The covenant lays emphasis on God's prior action of grace in redeeming Israel from Egypt. The stipulations that have to do with Israel's conduct are meant to give shape to their response to that gracious activity. These laws include both moral and ritual directions. They concern relationships both God-ward and among people. Noteworthy is the way Deuteronomy accents the response that is looked for in both of these directions in terms of love (see Deut. 6:4–5). What is required toward the sojourner in Deuteronomy 10:19 surely should not be withheld from the full member of the community, as Leviticus 19:18 makes explicit. Sin, thus, is a failure in love. It is a hardening of the heart (Deut. 15:7; Ps. 95:8). This understanding of sin as a failure to fulfill covenant obligations is illustrated in the historical books. From the Israelite failure at Ai to the fall of Samaria and Jerusalem, the explanation is the same: sin (Josh. 7:11; 2 Kings 17:7–18; 24:19–20). To this running commentary on Israel's historical experience can be added the preaching of the prophets. They, too, see sin either explicitly or implicitly as a breach of covenant responsibilities (Jer. 22:8–9; Ezek. 16:8–34; Hos. 8:1; Amos 3:2).

Although the prophets were building on older foundations, they added their own insights. First, emphasis falls on the moral failures of Israel's life under God. When the ritual sphere is subjected to critique, it is usually because worship is unaccompanied by appropriate ethical conduct (Jeremiah 7; Amos 5:21–24). Second, because God lays claim to the whole of his people's life, their sin is not confined to conduct specifically condemned in the law (Isa. 5:11; Amos 6:4–6). Third, sin is not unique to Israel; the prophets also indict other peoples (Jeremiah 46–50; Amos 1:3–2:3). Fourth, Jeremiah and Ezekiel, while addressing the sinful community in general, are anxious to stress the note of individual responsibility; it cannot be evaded (Jer. 31:29–30; Ezek. 18). Fifth, sin, according to Jeremiah, is deeply and persistently ingrained in the heart of his people (17:1, 9). This claim echoes a note found in Genesis 6:5. The answer to this situation can be found only in a new work of God on the human heart (Jer. 31:33).

Perhaps the most memorable expression in the Old Testament of a personal awareness of the depth and pervasiveness of human sinfulness is in Psalm 51. The psalmist knows not only that his sin is against God but also that it is coextensive with his existence. If ever his heart is to be made clean, God must intervene.

As we turn to the New Testament, we find that Jesus' chief concern was not so much to talk about sin as it was to minister to sinners. Nevertheless there are clear indications in the first three Gospels regarding his understanding of the matter. Sin lives only in deeds but also in the thoughts and intents of the heart (Matt. 5:21–22, 27–28). Jesus saw the evil and corrupt heart as the fountain of all sorts of sins (Mark 7:21–23). Although Jesus did not overlook the sins of the flesh, he was quick to expose those of the spirit; he was particularly critical of the sins of the "good" people of his day (Matthew 23; Luke 18:9–14). If, as seems likely, the parable of the vineyard tenants was told with an autobiographical reference, Jesus regarded his own rejection by his contemporaries as their crowning sin (Mark 12:1–12).

Paul has a great deal to say about sin, particularly in his letter to the Romans. He shares the basic Old Testament framework to understand sin, namely, the refusal to live in obedient responsiveness to God. Certain emphases, however, are noteworthy. Sin can be portrayed as a personified power that holds the sinner in bondage (Rom. 7:8–24). Sin finds its base of operation in the flesh and the opportunity to exert its power in the law; neither, however, is sinful per se. The slavery of sin is vividly described in Romans 7, which is best understood as a description, written from a Christian viewpoint, of those who attempt to keep the law in their own strength. Paul links the universality of sin in the human community in some way to the sin of Adam (5:12). He does not make clear, however, the precise nature of this connection. But it is obvious from what Paul says elsewhere that personal responsibility in the matter of sinning is not lifted from anyone's shoulders (1:18–3:20). The punishment for sin should not be viewed as an arbitrary matter. Given the moral constitution of our world as God has set it up, the practice of sin is self-destructive. This state of affairs is portrayed with unmistakable clarity in Romans 1:18–32: God respects human freedom to sin, but sin by its very nature leads to more sin. The awesome phrase "God gave them up" (1:24, 26, 28) has this meaning.

We must give brief attention to three additional matters of a more general nature. The first is the intriguing question of the origin of sin. Our initial reply might be to cite the account in Genesis 3. At best, however, this text portrays the emergence of sin in the experience of humanity; we are still left with the origin of sin in the universe. If the serpent is representative of the anti-God presence that elsewhere in the Bible is called the devil, how did he come to be? Unless he was created as an evil being, which would be difficult to reconcile with our understanding of God, the answer would seem to lie somewhere within the mysterious depths of free will. The ultimate origin of sin, therefore, is inexplicable, because free will is not determined by anything outside itself.

Second, the term *depravity* frequently has been used in theological discussion to describe the effects of sin on human nature. Sometimes the adjective *total* is added. What should we understand by this terminology? To speak of human nature as depraved is a way of saying that it is corrupted by sin. If the phrase *total depravity* is used, it should not mean that the corruption is total in degree, but only that the whole of human personality (mind, emotions, will) has been affected by sin.

Third, somber as is the biblical portrayal of the human situation under the blighting results of sin, we can be most grateful that it is not the only—nor the final—word. The Quaker George Fox reported a conversation he had with a man in despair over his sin: "I told him that which showed him his sins, and troubled him for them, would show him his salvation; for he that shows a man his sin is the same that takes it away." This is the joyous liberating word of the gospel!

"In wrath remember mercy"

The words in the title come from the prayer of the prophet Habakkuk about the beginning of the sixth century BC. These words of pathos bring together in a terse and moving way two great themes that lie side by side in the whole of biblical literature: God's wrath that issues in judgment and God's mercy that gives birth to salvation. It is not easy to keep both of these themes steadily in focus at the same time. But to emphasize one to the neglect of the other is to distort the biblical message.

Let us begin with judgment. Genesis opens with the beautiful picture of fellowship between God and Adam and Eve in the Garden of Eden. But the story hardly gets under way before the relationship is ruptured, the pair are driven from the garden, and a curse is placed on the serpent and the ground. Henceforth, the human lot will be difficult (Gen. 3:14–24). At the other end of the testament, the story ends with curses being uttered against the contemporaries of Malachi and the threat of an additional curse in the future (Mal. 1:14; 3:9; 4:6).

Scattered between the beginning and the end of the Old Testament record are six different Hebrew words which are used more than four hundred times to describe God's wrath in one form or another. There are, of course, major judgments that punctuate the story, such as the flood (Genesis 6–8), the loss of a generation of people in the Arabian desert (Num. 14:28–29), the fall of Samaria (2 Kings 17:18) and the destruction of Jerusalem (2 Kings 25).

But these incidents are only striking instances of a common theme that is much more pervasive. For example, in the book of Judges, we are repeatedly told that because of Israel's conduct, the Lord was angry and gave Israel into the hands of its enemies (for example, Judg. 2:12, 14, 20; 3:8). The refrain is continued in the books of Samuel and Kings (2 Sam. 24:1; 1 Kings 14:9; 16:2; 2 Kings 13:3; 17:11; 22:13). The prophets, too, are known for their persistent preaching of forthcoming judgment. For example, Amos said God will punish not only the nations surrounding Israel for their sin (Amos 1–2) but also Israel (3:2). The remainder of the book is an almost wearisome repetition of this message.

The prophets who succeeded Amos until the fall of the Southern Kingdom continued to thunder against the sins of both Israel and Judah, threatening certain judgment unless the people repented. And at least some of the prophets who followed the great catastrophe of 587 BC likewise found occasion to speak in similar tones. Thus, sample where we will, we cannot read long in the Old Testament until we encounter in some form the note of divine judgment.

The situation is not radically different in the New Testament. At the beginning of Matthew's Gospel, John the Baptist warns his hearers of the wrath to come from which they can only escape by repentance (Matt. 3:7–10). Near the close of the last book of the New Testament, there is a long dirge over the fall of the great city of Babylon, a code name for Rome. That event is seen as the just judgment of God on Rome because of its sins. Likewise, as in the case of the Old Testament, between the beginning and end of the New the note of God's judgment is frequently heard. It is reflected in the teachings of Jesus, both the nonparabolic (Matt. 5:22–23; 10:15; 11:21–24; Luke 13:1–5) and the parabolic (Mark 12:1–11; Luke 13:6–9;19:11–27).

Paul's letters contain no fewer than twelve references to the wrath of God (for example, Rom. 1:18; 2:5; Eph. 5:6; 1 Thess. 1:10; 2:16) and additional references to divine judgment (Rom. 2:2–16; 14:10; 2 Cor. 5:10; 2 Thess. 1:5). The theme is also present in Hebrews (9:27; 10:28–31), James (2:13), 1 Peter (4:17), 2 Peter (3:7), 1 John (4:17) and Jude (15). Revelation contains a liberal sprinkling of references to God's judgments (15:4; 16:5, 7; 19:2), to his wrath (11:8; 14:10, 19; 15:7; 16:1, 19; 19:15), and to the wrath of the Lamb (6:16). Beyond this specific terminology, however, much of the book from chapters 6 to 18 is given to dramatic descriptions of the outpouring of divine wrath upon the earth. Finally, at the conclusion of chapter 20 is the impressive portrayal of the great white throne judgment which will mark the close of history.

This brief review reveals that the motif of God's judgment is no minor one in the Bible. To take it seriously will shatter any notion that the Bible is a book full of only sweetness and light. Whatever else it is, the Bible is not a sentimental love story. Its pages will not let us forget the sobering fact that judgment is a stark reality with which soon or late we must come to terms. It is a fundamental ingredient of the biblical message. We should not neglect to observe, however, that God's judgments are not portrayed in the Bible as an irrational aspect of his dealings with people. A rationale is provided in the way the Bible outlines the framework within which we live out our lives.

> God's love and wrath are not mutually exclusive concepts but complementary. The fundamental character of God's nature is holy love. But that love reaching out to us is experienced as judgment when we attempt to flee from, reject, or betray it.

What are the elements in this structure that make divine judgment an understandable factor in human experience? The first is the affirmation that God is the creator and Lord of the world. We are God's creatures. Go where we will in God's world, we cannot escape his presence. Ultimately, it is with God that we must reckon. Second, God has a purpose for people that he has disclosed to us. It is his intention that we should live in fellowship with him and with one another as stewards of his world. Third, we have been created with the freedom to fulfill or to reject God's design for us. God respects our freedom and will not force us. Fourth, with freedom comes also the necessity to face its potential consequences. If we choose to align ourselves with the way God has structured reality, we have the promise of well-being. If we choose to defy the cosmic constitution, we can expect difficulty.

God's wrath, then, is not an unpredictable action arbitrarily inflicted on us. It is the consequence of our decision to live life in a way for which we have not been made. We may quarrel with God's order, but if we wish to avoid tragedy, we had better cooperate with it. To try to get out of human existence what God has not put into it can ultimately be no more successful than to attempt to use an automobile that has been admirably designed for land travel to drive through Lake Michigan.

Yet sobering as the note of wrath or judgment is, it is not the sole or major motif of the Bible. This latter is to be found in the love and mercy of God. This theme, no less than that of judgment, frames both Old and New Testaments.

After the sin of Adam and Eve in Genesis 3 comes the divine promise of a future fatal wound to be dealt the serpent (v. 15). In the last chapter of the Old Testament, the substance of that hope is reiterated under different imagery: the prophet anticipates the day when "the sun of righteousness shall rise, with healing in its wings" (Mal. 4:2). Between Genesis 3 and Malachi 4, the love and mercy of God are celebrated again and again. There is the call of Abraham with a view to blessing for all the families of the earth (Gen. 12:1–3). The selection of Israel to be a people for God's own possession was not attributable to its own merit; the "Lord set his heart" on them (Deut. 7:6–8). When Moses on Mount Sinai had a vision of the glory of God, the Lord proclaimed himself as "merciful and gracious, slow to anger, and abounding in steadfast love and faithfulness, keeping steadfast love for the thousandth generation, forgiving iniquity and transgression and sin" (Exod. 34:6). In the innermost sanctuary of Israel's shrine stood the ark with the golden mercy seat upon it. There, at God's gracious bidding, atonement was to be made each year for Israel's sins (Lev. 16).

The prophets, for all of their preaching of judgment, are not oblivious to God's great love. Hosea memorably speaks in the name of God: "How can I give you up, Ephraim? . . . My heart recoils within me, my compassion grows warm and tender. I will not execute my fierce anger" (Hos. 11:8–9). Micah cries: "Who is a God like you, pardoning iniquity and passing over the transgression of the remnant of your possession? . . . You will cast all our sins into the depths of the sea" (Mic. 7:18–19). Isaiah represents God as saying: "Come now, let us argue it out . . . : though your sins are like scarlet, they shall be like snow" (Isa. 1:18). Jeremiah, deeply aware of Judah's inability to keep the Sinai covenant, is equally certain that God in his mercy will establish a new covenant with his people adequate to their needs (Jer. 31:31–34). Ezekiel affirms that God finds no pleasure in the death of the wicked, but instead desires their repentance. "Why will you die, O house of Israel?" (Ezek. 33:11). Finally, Jonah has to learn the hard lesson that God's mercy extends not only to Israel but also to the people of Nineveh (Jon. 4:11).

The book of Psalms repeatedly celebrates the steadfast love and mercy of God. The psalmists' hearts overflow again and again in praise of God's grace. Representative of this awareness is the passage in Psalm 130: "If you, O LORD, should mark iniquities, Lord, who could stand? But there is forgiveness with you, so that you may be revered. . . . O Israel, hope in the LORD! For with the LORD there is steadfast love, and with him is great power to redeem" (vv. 3–4, 7).

The New Testament, no less than the Old, is framed by the mercy of God. The very first chapter announces the forthcoming birth of one who "will save his people from their sins" (Matt. 1:21). The final chapter ends with the gracious invitation: "Let everyone who is thirsty come . . . [and] take the water of life as a gift" (Rev. 22:17). Again, between these two extremities lies a recurring refrain of grace. Jesus defined his mission as calling sinners to repentance (Luke 5:31–32). He hoped that others would see in a shepherd seeking a lost sheep or a father welcoming home a prodigal son a picture of God's love for the lost (Luke 15). He wept over Jerusalem because of its insensitivity to what alone could secure its true well-being (Luke 19:41–42); he prayed for the forgiveness of those who crucified him (Luke 23:34).

Paul never got over the wonder of the grace of God that met him on the Damascus road (Gal. 1:13–16; 1 Tim. 1:12–17). In a world familiar with wrath, people may now be rightly related to God "by his grace as a gift, through the redemption that is in Christ Jesus" (Rom. 3:24). As Paul reflects on the miracle of God's love and what it may yet hold for this world, he is moved to exclaim: "O the depth of the riches and wisdom and knowledge of God! How unsearchable are his judgments and how inscrutable his ways!" (Rom. 11:33). And to the testimony of Paul could be added those of John, Peter, and the authors of Hebrews and Revelation.

"In wrath remember mercy"

How then can these two notes, God's wrath and his love, be related? In the second century AD, Marcion thought it was impossible. He identified the God of wrath with the Old Testament and rejected both. But in light of the evidence we have reviewed, that solution will not do: there is too much love in the Old and too much wrath in the New to commend it. On the contrary, God's love and wrath are not mutually exclusive concepts, but complementary. To be sure, the fundamental character of God's nature is holy love; if that were not so, the story told in the Bible would never have happened. But that love reaching out to us is experienced as judgment or wrath when we attempt to flee from, reject, or betray it. God has not basically changed, but our stance toward God has conditioned the character of the interpersonal relationship. Without this paradox, holy love would be reduced to mere sentimentality. God's love is not to be confused with that!

Biblical perspectives on healing

Health care in the United States and Canada today has developed into a huge business, with billions of dollars and high percentages of national income spent on physical and mental health care, insurance, and medicine. Interest in healing, of course, is not of recent origin: it is as old as the human race itself. Archaeological remains of ancient civilizations give evidence of primitive forms of surgery. It is not surprising, therefore, that the Bible, with its concern for human existence under God, should include materials bearing on the matter of healing.

We may begin by noting some of the elements that shaped the worldview of the Bible within which both illness and healing are set. Four broad features characterize the biblical perspective. First, we find there no greatly developed sense of secondary causes. The world in its various operations is directly related to God's action or to God's permissive will. To be sure, there are hints of a rational understanding of hygiene in the Old Testament, but the dominant view is that God sends or permits illness. Health is a gift of God to be enjoyed as the result of obedience to his will. Conversely, illness is a punishment for disobedience (Exod. 15:26; Deut. 28:15–68). This view had its built-in difficulties—the book of Job is a passionate protest against it! But in spite of its problems, this view remained the dominant one even in New Testament times. Indeed, Judaism worked out an elaborate system of correlation between specific sins and particular illnesses. Doctors and medicines, not unknown in the Jewish community, were for the most part held with certain reserve: God was the great physician from whose hand healing and health were to be sought.

Second, the Bible emphasizes the unitary nature of the human person. While the Bible has no word like our *psychoso-*

matic, the idea is there in rudimentary form. The Greek conception of the person as essential spirit which exists as a prisoner in the body is not Hebraic. The Hebrews thought of a human being as an animated body rather than an incarcerated spirit. It is for this reason that when serious attention was directed to the matter of life after death, it took the form of the resurrection of the body rather than the immortality of the spirit. The wholeness of the person as psychosomatic organism means that in considerations of illness and health, concern for the spirit was not divorced from concern for the body.

This fact helps us understand two things in the New Testament: the attention Jesus gave to the healing of the body—he was not content to address himself only to the mind or spirit of a person—and the close relation between forgiveness and healing. The rabbis said that there was no healing apart from forgiveness. Whether Jesus would have put it that strongly is not clear, but the two are brought into close connection in the case of the paralytic (Mark 2:1–12).

Third, the Bible views illness as part of the imperfection of the present order prior to the end. As already noted, there is a broad connection between sin and illness, and when the demonic came into clear focus in Judaism, certain illnesses were attributed to this source. Although Jesus recognized both personal sin and demonic activity as part of the larger explanation of human suffering, he refused to regard all illness as attributable to immediate personal sin or to direct demonic action (for example, John 9:1–12; note also the absence of any reference to demon causation in many of Jesus' healing miracles).

Fourth, there is an expectation of the final triumph over illness and death. This hope is most vividly expressed in such passages as 1 Corinthians 15 and in the book of Revelation. This goal is to be achieved only in the end time when God's purposes for humanity and the world will reach their consummation. Then, in the graphic imagery of Revelation, "pain will be no more" (21:4) and death itself will be thrown into "the lake of fire" (20:14).

When we turn from these general observations to the ministry of Jesus in the Gospels, it is evident that healing both of body and of spirit had an important place in his mission. The New Testament church believed that in the person and ministry of Jesus, the new order of the end time (the kingdom of God) had already in a limited way broken into history. The new, to be sure, had not fully come; the follower of Jesus is living in the overlap of the old and the new ages, with one foot in the new age and the other in the old. It is in this context that the healing miracles of Jesus and the early church are to be seen. They are signs of the preliminary and partial breaking in of the end time kingdom in the midst of history.

In this connection a word may be said about the role of faith in New Testament healings. Faith is related to many of the healing experiences, but in no discernibly consistent pattern. Sometimes faith is the result of a miracle (John 9:36–38); sometimes it is present prior to the healing (Matt. 9:27–28); at other times it is the faith of friends rather than that of the ill person that is noted (Mark 2:1–12; Luke 7:2–10); then again, no reference at all is made to faith in other healings (Luke 13:11–17; 14:4; 22:51). But when faith is mentioned, it is always directed to the possibility of help from Jesus. It is not a pep talk to one's own psychic condition—as though health could result from a proper mental state.

> We must affirm God's concern for us as total persons, body and spirit. Matters of health should not be excluded from the area of God's interest in us. But God will not become our puppet. Sometimes, as Jesus and Paul knew, God's purpose may best be accomplished through suffering and death.

What, then, are the implications of this biblical material for us today? The following suggestions are offered for consideration. First, a comment about the biblical view of nature: modern science has greatly modified our understanding of the world in which we live by the development of the concept of *laws of nature*. But law in the modern sense is essentially descriptive of the way things are observed to happen in the physical world; it does not guarantee that new data may not sometime be observed that will call for a revision of the law. One should not forget that the scientist's understanding of natural law today has a certain provisional character. Furthermore, one should remember that science as such cannot give ultimate answers regarding the fundamental reality of our universe; these are matters for the philosopher or the theologian. If as Christians we believe that the ultimate reality at the heart of our universe is personality, then law must be defined in relation to will and purpose. Thus, both the constancy and the novelty that are so much a part of our experience of the natural order about us may find a more basic and common point of reference, namely, the will and purpose of God.

Second, while some illnesses may be the direct result of personal sin, certainly not all are to be accounted for in this way. Illness is part of the present imperfect order prior to the perfection of the end time. To expect the healing of all illness now is to look for the end before the end. The often-debated question whether or not healing is in the atonement must be answered in a qualified way. It is there in the sense that the cross and resurrection of Jesus are a pledge of the final abolition of all illness and death. But while that final victory still eludes us, in the providence of God we may and do experience temporary throwbacks of the forces of illness and death that anticipate their ultimate defeat.

Third, we must affirm God's concern for us as total persons. This concern includes the needs of the body as well as the spirit. Matters of health, therefore, should not be excluded from the area of God's interest in us. "The heresy of all heresies is to shut out Christ from any area of life as though he were not relevant to it," said B. F. Westcott. Surely our faith includes warrants for bringing health concerns, whether personal or those of friends, to the Lord in prayer.

Fourth, faith in God should not be pitted against medical science and skill in the area of healing. God stands behind all healing, whether it occurs with medical aid or without. No person can give health to another; at best, one can only provide favorable conditions under which healing may more readily occur. Medical science is a gift from God to us and should not be ignored or despised. Conversely, prayer should not be the last resort to which we turn only when all human help has failed. The relationship between the use of medical aid and reliance on God and openness to all that God has for us should be complementary, not competitive.

Fifth, we have no right to demand healing from God, whether through or apart from medical services. To do so is to lose sight of two biblical emphases. One is the "not yet" character of our present existence referred to earlier: the banishment of all illness and death is still a future hope. The other is the sovereignty of God. God will not become our puppet. God's purpose is to glorify his own great name in and through his dealings with us. Sometimes, as Jesus and Paul knew, that purpose may best be accomplished through suffering and death rather than healing.

Finally, because healing has a place within the framework of the gospel, we should neither distort its importance—by making it the sum and substance of the gospel—nor ignore it—as though the gospel has no relevance for our physical needs. This balance is not always easy to achieve, but we need to seek it constantly in this present imperfect order.

Let us praise God!

An imaginative story has been told about a conversation with Lucifer after he had been cast out of heaven for conspiring against the Almighty. "What have you missed most," he was asked, "since you were banished from the celestial courts?" "The trumpets," said Lucifer, "the trumpets in the morning!" He no longer heard the note of praise, and life was not the same.

Praise is an authentic strain in biblical religion. It is heard again and again in the pages of both the Old Testament and the New. We readily recall the Psalms, many of which begin with the exclamation "Praise the Lord!" or its equivalent—and many of which end with a similar statement. Others contain the element of praise at one point or another in the hymn. Still others are entirely given over to the praise of God.

A notable example is Psalm 148. It issues a call to heaven and earth and all that fills them to offer praise to God. In light of the prominence of the note of praise in these poems, we can understand why the Jews called the Psalms the Book of Praises. But the theme of praise in the Old Testament is by no means confined to this particular book. At one end of the testament is the celebrated song of Moses after the deliverance at the Red Sea (Exodus 15). At the other end is Daniel's prayer of praise (Dan. 2:20–23). Between these two passages and elsewhere are scattered other expressions of praise. We also recall the established system of worship associated with the tabernacle and later with the temple, where worshipers offered individual and corporate praise.

The praise of God was an important part of Jewish piety and worship in intertestamental and New Testament times. The hymns discovered at Qumran bear witness to a spirit of praise in that wilderness community. The liturgy of the Palestinian synagogue in the time of Jesus or shortly thereafter includes a series of benedictions in which the worshiper repeatedly blessed God for God's greatness and goodness. One likely had a form similar to this: "Blessed art thou, O Lord, the most high God. Maker of heaven and earth, our shield and the shield of our fathers! Blessed art thou, O Lord, the shield of Abraham!"

> **Praise is the only proper response to what God has done for us in Christ. Praise is also our duty to ourselves. And praise is our duty to others: praise from the life of one Christian often begets praise in the life of another.**

The New Testament also is a book of praise. The announcement of the birth of Jesus to the shepherds was accompanied by a great outburst of praise (Luke 2:13–14). The people who beheld the miracles of Jesus on occasion gave praise to God (see Luke 19:43). Jesus was disappointed when those who benefited from his ministry did not give praise to God (Luke 17:18). The last act of worship Jesus shared with his disciples before going to Gethsemane was the singing of a hymn (Mark 14:26). After the resurrection and the ascension, the disciples "were continually in the temple blessing God" (Luke 24:53); their life after Pentecost continued to be one of praise (Acts 2:46–47).

One reads with exhilaration the story in Acts of the early church, with an eye to the mood of joy, enthusiasm, and praise that pervades the account. One striking feature of the narrative is the association of worship with suffering (see Acts 4:23–31; 5:41; 16:25), a paradox that can only be understood experientially. The Epistles are full of praise, as doxologies abound in this material (see Gal. 1:5; Rom. 11:36; 16:27; Phil. 4:20; Eph. 3:21; 1 Tim. 1:17; 6:16; 2 Tim. 4:18; Heb. 13:21; 1 Pet. 4:11; 5:11; Jude 25).

The opening chapter of Ephesians is notable for its extended ascription of praise to God (1:3–14). The author begins by blessing God, and what follows is punctuated by the recurring phrase "to the praise of his glory" or "his glorious grace." For the Jewish Christian community to which Hebrews is addressed, praise has taken the place of sacrifice (see Heb. 13:15). This substitution was already known in Judaism in circumstances where animal sacrifice was impossible, but it was a temporary substitution. In the Christian community, however, it became permanent. The strains of praise are heard again in Revelation. The earthly or human situation is portrayed in somber colors, but the eye of the seer looks beyond the human scene to the heavenly choirs and hears their offering of praise to the one whose hands hold the destiny of all things. "Great and amazing are your deeds, Lord God the Almighty! Just and true are your ways, King of the nations! Lord, who will not fear and glorify your name? For you alone are holy" (Rev. 15:3–4). In this concluding book of the New Testament, the Lord is constantly being praised and glorified.

To the testimony of the biblical materials we may add that of the later Christian community. It has been said that in the early centuries of the Christian era, the church was the only thing that came down the road singing. An early Christian summed it up picturesquely when he wrote, "Praising we plow and singing we sail." The Christian centuries are rich in their witness to the role of praise in the life of God's people.

John Wesley died in the year 1791. The day before he died, he wanted to rise from his bed. While his clothes were being brought, he began to sing Isaac Watts's great hymn: "I'll praise my Maker with my breath, and when my voice is lost in death, praise shall employ my nobler powers." He sang it with such spirit and power that his friends were amazed. The next morning he wanted to sing it again, but he was too weak. All he could manage was, "I'll praise, I'll praise."

Some fifty years later, Hanns Lilje, a bishop in the German Lutheran Church, was arrested in 1944 and put in prison because of his opposition to Hitler. In a book about his experiences, *The Valley of the Shadow*, he relates how on one occasion he heard a fellow Christian prisoner in a cell some distance away whistle the tune of Charles Wesley's "Oh, for a thousand tongues to sing my great Redeemer's praise, the glories of my God and King, the triumphs of his grace!" Lilje immediately rushed to the bars of his cell and there vigorously joined his Christian comrade in whistling the tune.

In more recent times, God has been at work renewing his people by a fresh stirring of his Spirit. Where this has happened, an invariable result has been a renewal of praise.

Dorothy Ranaghan, writing about the charismatic movement in Catholic circles in the early 1970s, ventured the opinion that one of the purposes God may have been seeking to accomplish through these new encounters with the Spirit was "to raise up a people of praise." She reported that one of the favorite hymns in these circles has this text: "Praise him in the morning, praise him in the noontime, . . . praise him when the sun goes down." Rodman Williams, writing about the same renewal experience, said, "If there is any one expression that breaks forth again and again it is 'Praise the Lord!' Many of us to be sure had often in the past read this expression in the Psalter, sung it from the hymnbook and used it variously in worship. But now it has become the deeply felt and joyously expressed verbalization of a way of life in which the Lord is constantly being praised and glorified."

Praise then belongs to genuine Christianity. Some years ago, the Scottish preacher James Stewart published a sermon entitled "Our duty of praise." He made the point that praise is not a matter of inclination but of simple duty. He suggested that this duty moves in three directions. First, it is a duty to God, the only proper response to what God has done for us in Christ; to fail to offer praise is to be guilty of gross insensitivity to the goodness of God. Second, it is our duty to ourselves. Praise has mysterious healing powers: "When life grows sore and wounding, and it is difficult to be brave, praise God, . . . and in the very act of praise the wound will begin to heal," said Stewart. Third, praise is our duty to our brothers and sisters. Praise from the life of one Christian often begets praise in the life of another; one song gives birth to another. Stewart recalled what one of Francis Xavier's contemporaries said of this pioneer of modern Catholic missions. If one of Francis's companions was sad, Francis would go and look at him as a way to dispel the sadness. In this way our praise can help another.

But if praise is a duty, it ought not be the product of mere obligation. Such praise lacks the pulse of life. It is formal and cold. True Christian praise must have about it the qualities of spontaneity and gladness. How, then, can this kind of praise be achieved? Turning our attention inward to analyze the state of our feelings and then attempting to conjure up the right one is like trying to lift ourselves up by our own bootstraps. Neither is it adequate to fasten attention on our particular circumstances, for these in themselves may evoke no desire to praise. On the contrary, true praise is most likely to be born out of an appreciative contemplation of God's great mercies to us.

Joseph Addison points us in the right direction, the celebration of God's greatness, power, and grace: "When all thy mercies, O my God, my rising soul surveys, transported with the view, I'm lost in wonder, love and praise." Addison's hymn rightly calls attention to the multitude of God's mercies to us. Praise should have a broad base in the whole of life, but the mercies of God do have a center from which the constellation is to be viewed and understood. That center is not located in the gifts we usually associate with nature or the material aspects of our lives. It is found in the relationship sphere, in God's gift of himself to us in Christ. That gift, contemporized by the Spirit, is the mercy in the light of which all other mercies are seen and experienced for what they truly are. Here then is the taproot of Christian praise.

Sex, marriage, and the Bible

In Marc Connelly's 1930 play, *Green Pastures*, one of the characters says, "Everything nailed down is coming loose." This remark might be spoken with great feeling today—at least for many people over fifty—when it comes to matters of sexual behavior.

Sex has always been an important part of human society, and deviant sexual behavior is not new. Today, however, there seems to be a public preoccupation with and an exploitation of sex in American society that is new. English anthropologist Eric Dingwall has said that "the United States is almost, if not quite, the most sex-obsessed country in the world." The role that sex plays in advertising, on the stage, in films, in periodicals and novels, in entertainment, in business, and in various other aspects of our life gives grounds for such a judgment.

It is not easy to live in a time of rapid change. Landmarks have a way of disappearing almost overnight. Guidelines that once were distinct become blurred. Anchors no longer seem to hold. The familiar landscape has been rearranged, and it is difficult to feel comfortable with the new view. Such developments are unsettling and can be frightening.

How are Christians to find their way in such times? We may, of course, roll with the punches or drift with the tide. We may seek to accommodate our ideas and conduct insofar as possible to what is generally regarded as acceptable in society at large. This course may seem to be the easiest. But to tailor conduct to prevailing judgments is not the Christian answer. "To align the church to the world, in the name of aligning it to reality," says William Barclay, "is the quickest way to suicide for the church."

For Christians, the Bible must function like a compass. True, it is not so easy to use as is the physical compass: the directions frequently are less specific, and the readings are more difficult to get. But the Bible does speak to sexual ethics. We cannot ignore what it has to say if we wish to lay claim to being Christian. What are the major emphases that it provides?

First, as people we are more than animals. Sexuality, therefore, is not to be understood merely in terms of the reproductive instinct that is found in animals. Personhood is not to be defined in terms of sexual drives. On the contrary, sex functions are caught up and transfigured in personal existence. We are creatures with dignity and destiny. We are called to work out a meaningful existence under God. It is in this larger context of what it means to be human that sexuality, in its broad and its more restricted senses, must be understood. While sexual drives are a very real part of life, they are not the whole of it, and their satisfaction is not the chief good in life. Sex finds its true meaning as it is caught up and integrated into the total pattern of life under God in the human community. Sex is neither a god nor a demon but rather an opportunity and a challenge in the quest to achieve a meaningful existence.

Second, sexuality and sex are good. Maleness and femaleness exist by the design of a good creator. Sin may distort and pervert the expression of sexuality, but sexuality is not itself sinful. The body and its functions—including sex—are not to be despised in the interest of spirituality. It should not be forgotten that the Jewish synagogue saw fit to include the Song of Solomon in the canon, and the Christian church followed suit. This book is a vigorous and beautiful celebration of the human body, the mutual love of man and woman, and the delights of physical intimacy.

Third, sexuality is intimately linked to community. The male-female relationship in marriage may be regarded as the archetype of human community. Here the meaning of "being for-the-other" is meant to be experienced in its fullest sense. Sexual differentiation, therefore, has more than mere reproductive significance: it is the structuring of personal existence for mutual belonging—"It is not good that the man should be alone" (Gen. 2:18). He needs another in whose presence he may learn the meaning of his existence and in whose fellowship life may be immeasurably enriched. But sexuality and sex have significance for community in another sense. They are the basis not only for marriage but also for procreation. The perpetuation of the race is tied up with sex. This fact means that our use of sexuality cannot be merely a private concern: it has a public character and is a matter of social interest. The Bible bears witness to the corporate dimensions of human sexuality and sex in the regulations that are found in the teachings and codes of both the Old Testament and the New. In these, certain relationships and conduct are forbidden, and others are enjoined.

> **The sexual act is meant to be the sign and seal of a mutual self-giving in the bonds of lifelong fidelity. In our permissive society, this standard may appear to be rigorous. But to be fully human as God intended has never been easy!**

Fourth, God's intention for marriage is that it should be a permanent union between a man and a woman until it is broken by death. While the fact of divorce is recognized in the Bible, it is ascribed to the hardness of the human heart and is declared to be contrary to the will of God. At the heart of the marriage relationship is a covenant of mutual love and self-giving which is made without reservation and is to be observed with fidelity until the death of the spouse. Intentional temporary marriages have no biblical sanction.

Fifth, marriage from the New Testament point of view is no longer seen merely as an order of creation but in relation to the kingdom of God that has broken into history with the coming of Christ. Jesus spoke of those who have made themselves eunuchs—have renounced marriage—for the sake of the kingdom of God (Matt. 19:12). Paul writes of those who have the charisma of celibacy (1 Cor. 7:7; a charisma is a grace-gift given for the building up of the church). Marriage is thus no longer a duty resting on all, as in Judaism; the urgency, therefore, has been lifted from marriage as a means of procreation. Sterility need not be regarded as a withholding of the divine favor. But if marriage in the New Testament is not a general obligation, neither is celibacy. The decision to marry or to refrain is related in principle to the will of God as expressed in the bestowal or the absence of the gift of celibacy. The first question, therefore, for the Christian is not, Whom shall I marry? but, Should I marry? To ask this question seriously may provide not only a stance from which to resist the pressure of a sex-dominated, marriage-oriented culture, but also a new perspective for understanding those who have voluntarily chosen celibacy as a way of life.

Sixth, the sex act is set firmly in the context of marriage. Both fornication and adultery are condemned as contrary to the will of God. Why coitus should be restricted to the marriage relationship is not given systematic exposition in either the Old or the New Testament. But it is worked at indirectly in several passages.

Two passages of special significance are 1 Corinthians 6:12–20 and Ephesians 5:21–33. In the first passage, Paul is dealing with the Corinthian attitude that saw no wrong in a Christian having sexual relations with a prostitute. Apparently the Corinthians justified their conduct on the basis that bodily drives are meant to be fulfilled. They made no distinction between the satisfaction of the hunger urge and the sex urge: both are of the same type and their fulfillment is alike amoral.

Paul disagrees with this assumption. He makes the point that the fulfillment of the sex urge involves one with another person in a way in which the eating of food does not. That is— to use the terms of Martin Buber—in the sex act you move from an "I-it" type of relationship, such as obtains in the eating of food, to an "I-thou" plane of relationship, a relationship between two people. Paul is now ready to deal with the question of what is wrong with a Christian's having coitus with a prostitute. Such conduct, he says, involves becoming "one body with her" (1 Cor. 6:16), and such a union Paul believes to be inconsistent with the Christian's union with Christ. Why is this so? Obviously, Paul does not mean that there is something wrong with sexual union as such. In that case, marriage would be forbidden to the Christian. Paul, however, makes no such prohibition.

The answer rather is to be found in a distinction between different kinds of "one body" relationship. To understand what makes the difference between the right and the wrong kind, we can get help from Ephesians 5:21–33. Here Paul discusses Christian marriage and illuminates the relationship by using the analogy of Christ's relationship to the church.

Now an analogy does not mean similarity at all points between the two things that are being compared. What then is the point at which the relationship between Christ and the church has special bearing on our understanding of what is wrong in the "one body" relationship that is condemned in 1 Corinthians 6:15–20? The analogy in Ephesians 5:21–33 focuses on Christ's love and self-giving for the welfare of the church. To understand what Paul means requires that we read the Gospels again from beginning to end, where we find the story of a man-for-others par excellence. Jesus' life displays love for others that was faithful to death: concern, sharing, self-giving to the utmost.

This life is the model of the relationship that is to obtain between a man and a woman in marriage, and it is precisely this type of relationship that is lacking in the situation described in 1 Corinthians 6:12–20, a union that involves turning a "thou" into an "it." This union of bodies is only on the physical level. But what the act of coitus is meant to symbolize, as interpreted by the relationship between Christ and the church, is totally lacking. Prostitution is a clear case of the misuse of sex. But the point from the Ephesians passage—which has relevance to all coital acts—is that Christ's utter love and faithful self-giving provides the framework within which coitus is designed to take place. Where true love and genuine commitment are lacking, coitus is emptied of its intended meaning. The sexual act is meant to be both the sign and the seal of a mutual self-giving in the bonds of lifelong fidelity.

In our permissive society, this standard may appear to be rigorous. But to be truly and fully human as God has planned for us has never been an easy matter!

The quest for peace

In 1960 a Norwegian statistician with the aid of a computer set himself the task of counting history's wars. He concluded that in the 5,560 years of recorded human history, there had been 14,531 wars—an average of more than two and a half wars per year. He discovered that of the 180 generations of recorded human experience, only ten had known the absence of war. The twenty-year period after the end of the World War II saw no fewer than forty wars—just below the historical average.

In spite of the technical progress of civilization, we do not seem to be making any real strides toward eliminating war as a method of dealing with national and international problems. This sort of data sparked a *Time* magazine essay several years ago entitled "On War as a Permanent Condition." Perhaps this observation does not come as a surprise to Christians acquainted with the Bible and with Jesus' words to his disciples: "When you hear of wars and rumors of wars, do not be alarmed; this must take place, but the end is still to come. For nation will rise against nation, and kingdom against kingdom. . . . This is but the beginning of the birth pangs" (Mark 13:7–8).

But we find another vision in the Bible. The prophets look forward to a time when nations "shall beat their swords into plowshares, and their spears into pruning hooks; nation shall not lift up sword against nation, neither shall they learn war any more, but they shall all sit under their own vines and under their own fig trees, and no one shall make them afraid" (Mic. 4:3–4; see Isa. 2:4).

How are these two outlooks to be related to each other? What can we hope for in our generation? What responsibility do we have in the quest for peace? Such questions demand that we go back to the Bible to look more carefully at what it has to say about peace.

The Bible contains both history and theology. In it we find a record of what has happened and a vision of what ought to be. From the standpoint of historical record, the Bible can hardly be said to be a book of peace: war and conflict loom large in its pages. But we must not confuse performance with norm. The thrust of the biblical message frequently not only exceeds the performance of even the community of faith; it is sometimes in direct opposition to it.

> **The church is to carry forward the reconciling ministry of Christ in every age and culture by proclaiming the gospel, by Christian service to people in need, by testimony to political powers, and by involvement in the structures of society.**

The word translated as "peace" in the Old Testament basically means "well-being." It is used in a great variety of contexts with various shades of meaning. Well-being may be expressed in bodily health, as in Genesis 43:27, or in the supply of the material needs for physical comfort, as in Judges 19:20. Frequently the word is used in reference to the stability or prosperity of a group or nation. In many passages it points to an amicable relationship between people. The word thus means more than the absence of conflict or, as it was sometimes defined a few decades ago, the state of cold war between two hot wars.

The basic meaning of peace as well-being is qualified in the Old Testament in various ways. Several of these developments may be noted. First, peace is related to covenant. Sometimes it has no particular religious significance as, for example, in Joshua 9, where a treaty of peace is sealed between two human parties by a covenant. But in other passages, it refers to a relationship between God and God's people in which God takes the initiative to establish a covenant of peace. Peace in this sense is rooted in the will of God who makes the covenant, a gracious gift to humans.

Second, the linking of peace to covenant brings another idea into focus in addition to that of grace: peace is not to be enjoyed apart from obedience to the God of the covenant. On this point the true and the false prophets in Israel divided company. For the true prophet, peace was morally and spiritually conditioned; for the false prophet, it is a national prerogative of the people of God. So—at least for the true prophet—peace and righteousness are closely linked. Third, according to the prophets it was precisely because the people of Israel did not render wholehearted obedience that they did not know the well-being or peace that God intended for them. Peace, therefore, came to be thought of as lying beyond the day of judgment, when God would punish the people for their sin; so Jeremiah could write to the exiles in Babylon about the peace God planned for them. As we move toward the end of Old Testament history, peace increasingly is a firm ingredient in the future hopes of Israel.

Fourth, attention may be called finally to the way peace—wholeness or well-being—and vicarious suffering are related in Isaiah 53. No longer does peace simply follow suffering in the experience of one people, but the kings of nations now confess that the servant of the Lord (the Israelite community or its representative) through his sufferings will bring wholeness and well-being to the nations.

The interest in peace is not left behind when we pass from the Old Testament into the New. Indeed in Luke 2:14, the birth of Jesus is announced to the shepherds as an event that offers peace and goodwill to people. As in the Old Testament, the meaning of the word *peace* is essentially positive. Yet it is evident within the pages of the New Testament itself that the birth of Jesus did not bring the cessation of all conflict among humans. On one occasion, Jesus himself said, "Do not think that I have come to bring peace to the earth; I have not come to bring peace, but a sword. For I have come to set a man against his father, and a daughter against her mother" (Matt. 10:34–35a). The book of Acts records the fulfillment of this prediction.

The reason for this state of affairs is not arbitrary but is deeply rooted in the cleavage between the order of grace and sinful human society. Like the contemporaries of Jesus, society at large rejects "the things that make for peace" and consequently lives by the sword. One New Testament writer closely and concisely analyzes the problem: "These conflicts and disputes among you, where do they come from? Do they not come from your cravings that are at war within you? You want something and do not have it; so you commit murder. And you covet something and cannot obtain it; so you engage in disputes and conflicts" (James 4:1–2). War is the attempt of one group to establish its own "well-being" at the expense of the other—and in defiance of the biblical understanding of human well-being and how it is to be realized.

In the New Testament no less than in the Old, peace is no mere political concept. Strife between individuals and war between nations are alike evidence of humanity's fallen state. It is against this background that we must understand the Christ-event and its sequel in the church. Here we find an attempt to deal with human fallenness by establishing a new order in the midst of the old. The great word that characterizes both the work of Christ and the mission of the church in society is *reconciliation*. Right relationship to God has as its corollary the possibility of a new relationship between human beings.

What, then, is the role of the church in relation to the biblical vision of peace in our world? First, the church is called to bear witness to the gospel of peace. This witness includes both an analysis of the religious roots of human fallenness and a proclamation of what God has done to meet this problem. It involves a radical definition of what is meant by peace that goes beyond any conventional secular definition. Second, the church is called not only to proclaim a message but to provide in its life an embodiment of the new order to which it bears witness. In the fellowship of the church, Jew and Gentile (and all their modern equivalents) are no longer to live with a "dividing wall of hostility" between them. In the place of such warring factions is a new being who is no longer known by such names as Jew and Gentile but is called Christian. Because of a common reconciliation to God, both Jew and Gentile and their modern counterparts are now brought into a new relationship to each other. The degree to which this reconciliation is affirmed and realized in experience is the measure of the extent to which the church is really the church.

Third, the church is also to be the agent for making peace in the world. The church is to carry forward the reconciling ministry of Christ in every age and culture. This task may and must be done on various levels: by the proclamation of the gospel; by a ministry of Christian service to people in the wholeness of their need; by testimony to political powers concerning God's will for humanity; and by involvement in the current structures of society, in ways consistent with the end we seek, to lessen tension and to build understanding and cooperation. Because peace in the biblical sense cannot be divorced from its frame of reference and its undergirding ideas, it follows that until these tasks are recognized and these conditions are met, peace in this sense cannot be fully realized. Today such recognition is far from general in human society.

The development of weapons making possible race suicide has not fundamentally changed the nature of the human predicament or the relevance of the biblical message to it. What it has done is underscore afresh the seriousness of the problem and the urgency with which we as Christians must seek to fulfill our mission. In the early years of the twentieth century, Rudyard Kipling visited the town of Medicine Hat in southeast Alberta, Canada. Learning of the large underground natural gas resources in the area, he described the town as one that had "all hell for a basement." What Kipling said of Medicine Hat might today be said of our entire world with an even greater sense of realism. This situation would be frightening indeed if not for the vision granted to the eye of faith—that this world is God's and its ultimate destiny is still in God's hands. It is God's good pleasure that someday—whether soon or late, we do not know—every knee in the universe will bow to Jesus Christ and every tongue confess that he is Lord to the glory of God the Father (see Phil. 2:10–11). In that faith we live and work.

The new Jerusalem

ESSAY
12

G. K. Chesterton once described Jerusalem as "a small town of big things." That is an apt description, whether the reference be to the city of our century or to the city of the first century. Neither could be regarded as large in comparison with other cities of past times or today's world. But we should not confuse size and significance, particularly when the role of a city in religious history is in question.

Of all Palestinian towns and cities, Jerusalem has held a place of primary importance in biblical history. It is mentioned for the first time in connection with the Israelite conquest of Palestine in the thirteenth century BC (Josh. 10:1, 3, 5, 23). It did not come under Israelite control, however, until the time of David; the story of its capture is briefly told in 2 Samuel 5:6–10. From the time of David onward until the end of the monarchy, Jerusalem was the capital first of the united kingdom and then of the southern kingdom (Judah). David also brought the ark to Jerusalem (2 Samuel 6) and thus made it an important religious center.

Its religious role was further strengthened by the construction of the temple under Solomon and the religious reformations highlighting the temple and its worship under the later kings, Hezekiah and Josiah. The fall of Jerusalem in 587 BC marked the end of political independence, except for a brief period under the Maccabean and Hasmonean rulers (164–63 BC), until 1948. Jerusalem, however, had continued importance administratively, although the Roman procurators had their headquarters in Caesarea. With the rebuilding of the temple after the return from exile in Babylon, Jerusalem grew in importance as the religious center of Judaism. This importance was attributable, of course, to the symbolism attached to the temple as the dwelling place of God.

The growing focus of attention on Jerusalem after the Babylonian exile and into the early Christian centuries could be documented in a variety of ways. Of particular interest is the way Israel was spoken of as occupying the center of the earth (Ezek. 38:12). Jerusalem, in turn, was thought of as the heart of that center (in Jewish writings not included in the Old Testament): Enoch's visit to Jerusalem, for example, is described as his going to "the middle of the earth" (1 Enoch 26:1); likewise, in the Sibylline Oracles V 248–250, Jerusalem is declared to be "the city of God at the center of the earth." The focus could be sharpened still more. Mount Zion, on which the temple was built, is said to be "the center of the navel of the earth" in the book of Jubilees 8:19. The thrust of these passages, according to W. D. Davies, is that "Israel . . . is the center of the earth, Jerusalem the center of Israel, Mt. Zion the center of Jerusalem."

Of greater significance for our purpose is the way Jerusalem gradually gathered to itself the hopes of God's people for the future, a theme picked up by the prophet Isaiah in the eighth century BC. In a memorable passage, the prophet foresaw a time when the mountain of the house of the Lord would be established as the highest of the mountains, and all the nations would come to it to be taught the law of the Lord. Under the Lord's rule there would be universal peace (Isa. 2:2–4). Jeremiah later spoke of a day when "Jerusalem shall be called the throne of the LORD, and all the nations shall gather to it, to the presence of the LORD in Jerusalem" (Jer. 3:17).

The fall of Jerusalem to the Babylonians in 587 BC was a traumatic experience, but it did not kill hope for the city's future. Jerusalem would again be restored, according to the prophet Ezekiel. He set out a detailed description of the new temple that was to replace the destroyed one (Ezekiel 40–48). The new Jerusalem would have enlarged boundaries, embracing more than one and one-half square miles (Ezek. 8:30–35). It would be a city of beauty (Isa. 60:13–18; see 54:11–12). The new temple would be a house of prayer for all nations (Isa. 56:7). Gentiles would come from afar to Zion to worship and to bring their tribute (Isa. 60:4–7, 11–14; 66:18–21).

Along with this interest in the fortunes of and the hopes for the earthly city was the concept of a heavenly Jerusalem. A

Jewish writing roughly contemporary with the book of Revelation refers to a heavenly city prepared before creation which was shown to Adam before he sinned and subsequently also to Abraham and to Moses (2 Baruch 4:1–7). The rabbis had great interest in the heavenly Jerusalem. They speculated about its location; one said it was eighteen miles above the earthly city. None of the earlier texts suggest that the heavenly city would descend to earth to replace the earthly one: the celestial city would remain in the heavens, and the future earthly city would be rebuilt by human hands.

> The community that is a gift from God is not without the presence of God. The holy of holies has been replaced by a spacious city in which all God's people are granted free admittance into the divine presence.

In light of the prominence accorded Jerusalem in the materials just surveyed, it is not surprising that the city should become the symbol for the Christian hope of the ultimate triumph of God's purpose at the end of history. The book of Revelation closes with the exalted vision of the new Jerusalem descending out of heaven to earth and becoming the scene for the dwelling of God with God's people (Rev. 21:1–22:5).

A careful reading of these materials will make it clear that the description of the city, although rooted in historical memory, is not simply a transcript of the earlier reality; it is a radical transformation of it. The framework within which the city is seen is the new creation—the new heaven and the new earth. The vision of the city itself represents a flowing together of many images from a variety of sources. The imagery is shaped by the theology that is seeking expression. Unless we recognize this fact, we will find it difficult to put the diverse elements together into a cohesive whole.

The point may be illustrated by noting some specific details in the description. The city, for example, is said to be a cube fifteen hundred miles in length, breadth, and height (Rev. 21:16). These dimensions would cover a ground surface from the Black Sea in the north to the second cataract of the Nile in Egypt in the south, and from the Mediterranean Sea in the west to a point east of the Persian Gulf—an area of 2.25 million square miles! The size of Jerusalem in the first century was somewhat less than one square mile. According to Revelation 21:12, each of the four walls surrounding the city has three gates, making a total of twelve. The Jerusalem of Jesus' day probably had little more than half that number. Both the city and the street are of pure gold (21:18, 21). Even Solomon's Jerusalem, where silver was made to be as stone in the city (1 Kings 10:27), fell far short of this grandeur. Through the middle of the street of the city flows a river, on either side of which is the tree of life (22:1–2). This picture again does not reflect the historical city but introduces, among other things, imagery related to the garden of Eden (Gen. 2:9).

Many other examples could illustrate how the portrayal of the new Jerusalem differs from the historical city of the first or any other century. Not only is the description of the new city significantly different from the old, but the language is metaphorical rather than literal. The author is using symbols out of the familiar world to represent realities that belong to the new order to come. The symbols are windows through which we are allowed to look in on that transcendent order. The windows should not be confused with the reality that lies beyond them.

What then is this magnificent vision attempting to communicate? Although the vision begins with the imagery of a city descending from heaven, the city is described "as a bride adorned for her husband" (21:2). The city indeed is identified as "the bride, the wife of the Lamb" (21:9). Again, although the city is described at great length, it is clearly only the setting for the dwelling of God with God's people (21:3). The author's interest, therefore, is not in a city as such but in a community. The impersonal is a way of portraying the personal.

If the reality to which the symbolism points is a community, how can it be characterized? Five observations can be made. First, the community is not a human achievement; it is a gift from God. This is the meaning of the descent of the city from heaven (21:2, 10). Earlier the book describes a movement "arising out of the sea" (13:1) and "out of the earth" (13:11); what has its origin in this way is described under the imagery of a beast. The beast is able to bring about a certain togetherness among the people of the earth, but genuine and abiding community is a gift from God.

Second, the community that is a gift from God is not without the presence of God in it: "See, the home of God is among mortals. He will dwell with them as their God; they will be his peoples, and God himself will be with them" (21:3). This divine presence is also implied in the fact that the city has no temple. Ezekiel's vision of the restored Jerusalem has an extended description of the new temple (Ezekiel 40–48). The passage concludes: "The name of the city from that time on shall be, The LORD is There" (48:35). Precisely because the Lord is in the new Jerusalem of the end time, no temple is necessary. The converse of God dwelling with his people is the privilege of their access to him. This access is portrayed symbolically in the cubical structure of the city. In the tabernacle and temple the holy of holies (where God was thought to dwell) was of cubical dimensions; access to God's presence was the privilege of only one man on one day out of the year, while the remainder of the community was excluded. Now the holy of holies has been replaced by a spacious city in which all God's people are granted free and full admittance into the divine presence.

Third, the existence of the community is conditioned by Christ. Although the city comes from God, it is "the bride, the wife of the Lamb" (21:9). The Lamb is mentioned no fewer than seven times in Revelation 21:1–22:5. This imagery for Christ suggests his redemptive work. The people of God are not to be defined by race, ethnic culture, or national identity but by their relationship with Christ. They are those whose names are written in "the Lamb's book of life" (21:27). In addition, the wall surrounding the city bears "the twelve names of the twelve apostles of the Lamb" (21:14). The wall that separates the community from the non-community is the apostolic witness to Christ. Response to this testimony is foundational to the life of community (see Eph. 2:20).

Fourth, although the community is characterized by fellowship between God and his people, it is not a democracy. God is not just another member of the community with equal voting privileges. This vision includes three references to the throne of God (21:5; 22:1, 3). If the location of the throne in the first reference is unclear, there is no doubt about its presence in the city in the remaining passage. God is in the midst of his people as king. But associated with God on the throne is the Lamb (22:1, 3). God's sovereignty is not to be understood apart from Christ. What is more, that sovereignty is not of brute power but of grace. From the throne flows "the river of water of life" (22:1) which has as its corollary the invitation: "To the thirsty I will give water as a gift from the spring of the water of life" (21:6).

Finally, the activity of the community is said to be worship (22:3) as the appropriate response to grace. Those who worship God, however, are described as his servants. Whether more than worship in the restricted sense may be involved in their service for him is not clear. If so, these two activities should not be sharply separated; they are only two sides of the same coin. To be truly Christian, worship must issue in service, and service must be rooted in worship.

This then is something of the kind of community at the end of time toward which God is moving throughout the whole of history. This grand vision is meant to be more than a matter of glad hope for the future. It should have some foreshadowing today in the community of God's people. The distinction between then and now cannot be one of kind but only of degree. The recognition of this fact provides us with serious agenda today, tomorrow, and until that great day when we too join that blessed company in the new Jerusalem that is yet to be.

Part 2

Opening the
Old Testament

The creation story in wider perspective

Distinctiveness is frequently highlighted by comparison or contrast. A potato, for example, is more clearly seen for what it is when it is set alongside a tomato. The peculiar character of poetry is more easily grasped when a poem is studied in relation to narrative prose. The New Testament is new because it differs in certain respects from another testament also known to us.

The uniqueness of the Genesis account of creation may be recognized by comparing it with a modern scientific textbook version of beginnings. Such a comparison may be helpful, but it is not the best place to begin, for the Bible is not a modern textbook of science. It is an ancient religious book, and as such it should be compared first of all with other ancient religious texts dealing with creation. When we do so, two results are likely to follow: we will get a new appreciation of how much the biblical account differs from other ancient accounts, and we will see the relevance of the biblical story for a more adequate understanding of the Hebraic-Christian faith.

We are indebted to archaeology for tools to pursue this comparative task. In 1853, archaeologists digging on the site of ancient Nineveh discovered the royal library of Ashurbanipal, the last great king of the Assyrian Empire, who died in 637 BC. A strong political and military figure, he also had unusual cultural interests. His library included tens of thousands of clay tablets, among which were copies of ancient Babylonian materials. They included the Babylonian Epic of Creation, which is generally dated to the early part of the second millennium BC. The poem as preserved consists of about a thousand lines. Only a brief summary can be given here.

The Babylonian epic begins with the remote past when only two divine principles existed, the mystical figures of Apsu and Tiamat. The first of these represents the primordial fresh waters, the second, the salt waters. Apsu and Tiamat become the parents of the gods. The birth of the gods out of the primeval watery chaos leads to conflict, and the young gods annoy their parents until Apsu finally decides to destroy them. One of the children, Ea, learns of the plan and murders his father, Apsu. To avenge the murder of her husband, Tiamat organizes a band of gods under the leadership of her second husband, Kingu, to slay the other gods. These gods become afraid and ask Marduk, the son of Ea, to defend them.

> **The God who stood at the beginning of Israel's history also stood at the beginning of all things and all history. With that firm conviction in mind, Israel could not entertain a creation story such as the Babylonian epic.**

Marduk agrees to do so in exchange for the supreme rank in the assembly of the gods. He is granted it, and he prepares for battle. The account pictures dramatically the battle with Tiamat and her forces. Tiamat attempts to swallow Marduk. But he shoots an arrow into her open mouth and kills her. Her helpers are captured and cast into prison.

After the battle, Marduk returns to the corpse of Tiamat and thinks about what he might do with it. He decides to split it laterally into two equal parts: one half becomes the sky, and the other half, the earth. He also makes the heavenly bodies to control the times and seasons. He announces plans to build a great temple on earth, the temple of Babylon, and assigns the rebel gods the task of building it.

The gods, however, are not to be responsible for the care of the temple. For this purpose, Marduk creates humankind. Kingu, the leader of the rebel gods, is slain. From his blood, Marduk makes humans, who are to be the slaves of the gods. The poem ends with the Babylonian god Marduk being celebrated as king of the gods forever.

Scholars have pointed out certain similarities between this epic and the account in Genesis 1:1–2:3. Both refer to the watery chaos at the beginning of time. Also, the sequence of events in creation is roughly the same: the making of the firmament, the dry land, the heavenly lights, humankind. Finally, dividing Tiamat's body to form the sky and the earth may remotely reflect the establishment of the firmament above and the appearance of the earth beneath in the biblical account.

Much more significant than the similarities, however, are the striking differences. For one, the Babylonian poem is polytheistic, while the biblical account is monotheistic. Next, although at times the gods of the poem seem to be distinguished from nature, they are also personifications of it; in the Genesis story, God is clearly distinct from nature. Then there is the element of violent conflict, which is so prominent in the Babylonian epic: it has no parallel in the Genesis account.

Beyond these specific details is the more fundamental difference in the larger framework within which each account is to be understood. The Babylonian poem was recited annually at the New Year festival in the spring of the year. Every spring, the Tigris and Euphrates rivers flooded the plain, reminding the Babylonians that their ordered world was once again on the edge of primeval chaos. After the flooding came the winds that dried up the water and brought back the dry land once more.

It is natural that humans in such a situation would understand their existence as being caught up and determined by the cyclic interplay of great cosmic powers. The annual recital of the myth of creation, with appropriate ritual performances in the Babylonian temple, gave a sense of contact with and participation in those cosmic realities by which their lives were determined. But note that the Babylonians' framework for understanding their existence was the recurring cycle of nature.

It is otherwise with the biblical account. The creation story is an integral part of a much larger story that fills the pages of our Bible. This story is not at all confined to the repetitious cycle of the seasons. While the story has its setting in the natural order, its framework is not nature but history: it deals with the outworking of a great divine purpose through many years and with a view to a specific goal.

The Bible begins with beginnings, with the creation of the world and human beings. But then it moves without undue delay to what is obviously of primary concern in the pages of the Old Testament, namely, a people called out of Egypt and taken up into covenant relation with God. Thus from one point of view, the creation materials serve as an introduction to the main part of the story. In another sense, however, the main part of the story provides the stance from which the introductory chapter is properly to be understood.

That statement requires some explanation. Israel was not just another political state among others in the Near East. The nation understood its origin to be the result of a miracle of divine grace: Israel existed because God had acted to bring it into being. God was its creator. God was also Israel's king, who ordered their life and in whose hands was their destiny. Israel's existence, therefore, was understood from a religious point of view. More specifically, this religious stance was determined by a unique encounter with God in Israel's own immediate history.

Now it was from this decisive experience at the heart of its very existence as a people that Israel looked out on the world and attempted to understand it. The prophets sought to bring the implications of the covenant character of Israel's life to bear upon the nation's conduct. Future blessing or woe was dependent on response to the covenant. God was not a fickle or capricious deity: God had declared his will in the covenant that lay at the foundations of Israel's history.

The exodus-Sinai complex of events provided not only a basis for shaping the future ongoing life of Israel but also for looking back to beginnings in the past. The God who was active in Israel's history was no god-come-lately on the scene. The God of grace and power who gave Israel birth must also have shaped the stage on which the people's life in covenant relation with him was to be lived out. The God who stood at the beginning of Israel's history also stood at the beginning of all things and all history. With that firm conviction in mind, Israel could not entertain a creation story such as the Babylonian epic. Such a myth was inconsistent with Israel's knowledge of God in its own history.

Thus far we have been dealing with the relation between the creation materials in Genesis and Israel's existence as the covenant people of God. The Genesis account, however, serves not only as a broad background for the more immediate concern of Israel's beginnings: it also provides a point of reference for understanding God's workings in later biblical history. God's creative power in the beginning, for example, is appealed to as an assurance that God will be able to redeem Israel from exile in Babylon (see Isa. 40:12–31; 42:5–9; 49:9–13). Associated also with this new act of redemption, a new beginning for Israel, is the vision of a new heaven and a new earth (Isa. 65:17; 66:2).

But the fresh beginning beyond the exile ultimately proved disappointing. Therefore God acted once again in the coming of Jesus. Paul speaks of Jesus as the "last Adam" (1 Cor. 15:4–49), for in him a new humanity was and is being created in the midst of the old (see Col. 3:10–11; Eph. 2:15; Gal. 3:27–28). Also linked with the final consummation of the new creation is the vision of a new heaven and a new earth (Rev. 21:1; see also 2 Pet. 3:13; Rom. 8:19–25). The biblical story in Revelation ends with a new creation: the end is related to the beginning in Genesis with creation. Each grows in meaning when read in light of the other and, of course, the intervening materials.

The creation of
man and woman

Contemporary issues have a way of freshly focusing our attention on particular biblical texts. Texts read scores of times in the past suddenly demand more careful scrutiny than we have hitherto given them. Traditional interpretations and prejudices arising out of our cultural environment have a way of coloring our reading of Scripture. Too frequently we are oblivious to this fact; it is not until we are forced to reexamine the text with special care that we discover the differences between what a passage actually says and what we thought it was saying.

The discussion in Christian circles of the status and role of women is a case in point. A casual reading of the first three chapters of Genesis is likely to endorse the following more or less traditional understandings: because the man was created first and the woman later, she is therefore inferior in status and subordinate in role to him. Again, because the woman was derived from the man and was made to be a help for him, she is not intended to be his equal. Furthermore, because the woman not only sinned first but induced her husband to sin, she is more gullible and less trustworthy than man. Finally, because God said that the man shall rule over the woman, it is clear that she is assigned a position under man.

But are these readings of the text really accurate? Can they be supported by a detailed, clear-eyed examination of the data? In brief, are these understandings read out of the passage or into it? These questions can be answered only by returning and looking again at the text with eyes as wide open as possible.

Before turning to the male-female theme in these chapters, some general observations on the material as a whole may provide helpful orientation. First, the literary form of these chapters is narrative in character; it is story rather than abstract argument, and the language is pictorial and dramatic. God, for example, is portrayed under a variety of images including potter, gardener, executive, legislator, anesthesiologist, surgeon, and builder. There is "the tree of life" and "the tree of the knowledge of good and evil." The serpent speaks. The cherubim with flaming sword guard the way to the tree of life. These and other images address the imagination and point to profound realities that lie beyond a mere surface meaning of the language. Respect for the literary medium is important for a proper approach to these materials.

Second, the stage on which the action of the narrative is played out includes both heaven and earth. Although the scope is cosmic, the focal point is clearly humankind. This focus is evident from the sheer amount of space (proportionately) that is devoted to Adam and Eve. Even more significant is the presence of two creation accounts and the different ways they are structured. The first account in chapter 1 moves progressively from the chaotic waters of verse 2 to the climax of creative activity in making the first human pair. The second story begins with a brief description of the setting for the creation of humankind and then greatly expands that element. Obviously, the author wishes to draw attention to this aspect of God's creative work. Thus, in chapter 1 the human pair is the pinnacle of a pyramid, while in chapter 2 they are the center of a circle.

Third, the first and second creation accounts are joined together by the statement: "These are the generations of the heavens and the earth when they were created" (Gen. 2:4a). This is the first of eleven occurrences of the formula "This is the list of descendants of . . ." (NRSV) scattered throughout the book. The formula introduces both genealogies proper (5:1; 10:1; 11:10; 25:12; 36:1, 9) and also narrative accounts (2:4; 6:9; 11:27; 25:19; 37:2). The genealogies, furthermore, are of two types. One is a vertical genealogy tracing a particular line of descendants from generation to generation. Thus, in two tables in the book (5:1–32; 11:10–32), the net effect is to tie together Adam and Abraham. The other three tables provide information on various subgroups within a family, such as the descendants of the sons of Noah (10:1–32), Ishmael (25:12–18), and Esau (36:1).

It is important to note the relationship between the vertical type of genealogy and the narrative material introduced by the genealogical formula. The vertical genealogies provide a link between Adam and Jacob and thus establish a framework within which the stories of the patriarchs can be set. Now the particular function of the genealogical formula in Genesis 2:4 is to connect the preceding and more comprehensive creation story with the more restricted one that follows. More specifically, it is the bridge that connects the creation of the world with the human-centered history that opens with the second creation account. That human-centered history includes both the broader human family and the line of more special interest to the author of the book. This line is pursued from Adam to Jacob and his sons by means of both vertical genealogies and narrative episodes.

> **The literary form of these chapters is narrative, and the language is pictorial and dramatic. God is portrayed as gardener, legislator, anesthesiologist, surgeon, and builder. These images address the imagination and point to profound realities.**

We are now ready to look at the materials in the two creation narratives that have to do with the origins of the human family. Genesis 1:26–31 contains six ideas: the divine consultation prior to the creative act; humankind consists of both male and female; both genders reflect the image of God; two obligations are laid equally on each sex—procreation and sovereignty over the lower orders of creation; the provision of food for the human pair without any restriction; the divine evaluation of the creative product, including humankind, is "It was very good."

Two of these items call for additional comment. The first of these is the observation that the word "man" (*adam*) in verse 26 and following is inclusive of both male and female. This inclusion is implied in the use of the plural pronoun "them" in verse 26, which refers to the word "man" occurring earlier in the sentence. The point is made even more explicitly in verse 27 where the creation of "man" is paralleled by the statement "male and female he created them." The term "man," therefore, is used generically to mean humankind. It should be noted also that both male and female share alike in God's single creative act: no priority in appearance is granted to one or the other sex.

The second comment has to do with the way both the male and the female are said to have been created in the image of God. Scholars have had an ongoing debate regarding the precise meaning of the phrase "the image of God." Basic ingredients in this concept would certainly include the personal and relational capacities that characterize human existence. These abilities both link us to God and also separate us from the animal world in ways that are unique among God's creatures. In this regard, however, there is no distinction between male and female; indeed, both maleness and femaleness as such may be essential in some profound and mysterious way to the full embodiment of the divine image.

Let us now turn to the creation account in Genesis 2:4b–25. This story is told in more detail than the one in the first chapter. When compared with that account, this one has certain distinctive features. The following may be noted. Humankind, in the generic sense, is shaped from the dust of the ground and is given life by divine inbreathing. This creature's locale is restricted from the earth generally to a garden, and their assignment is restricted from sovereignty over creation to tilling and keeping the garden. God places a limitation on what food they may eat—the fruit of one tree must not be eaten on pain of death. God recognizes the need for human companionship. When this companionship is not found among the animals, God makes a creature comparable to the one originally shaped from the dust, from a rib drawn from that creature. Sexual polarity now characterizes human existence; male and female come together to form a "one flesh" union in marriage.

Some general comments can now be made on aspects of special interest in this account. First, the twofold constitution of the human creature is made clear in the unique character of the creative act. Like the animals, the human is formed out of the ground. Unlike them, however, God breathed into this being "the breath of life." The human creature, therefore, is related both to the earth and to God. This recognition is important for the proper understanding of a human being. To ignore one or the other of these constituent elements can only result in a distorted view.

Second, does this passage suggest that the female is inferior to the male? Three bits of data are sometimes taken to point in that direction. The phrase "a helper fit for him" is often understood to mean "a suitable assistant." But the language does not imply this inferior status. The word "helper" is, of course, a relational term, yet it does not in itself imply inferiority. In this instance, the context provides the needed help. The Hebrew word translated "fit" points to equality and suggests a counterpart. What is in mind is a creature who would answer to the other as an appropriate other. The animals are "helpers," but they are not "fit" for the one into whose nostrils God has breathed the breath of life (Gen. 2:20).

Also, the making of woman out of a rib from the side of *adam* is sometimes said to suggest her inferior status. This inference too is improper. The rib, like the dust of the ground, is no more than raw material from which a creature is shaped by the creative hand of God. The female is no more subordinate to the male on this account than is *adam* to the ground (*adamah*) from which this original creature was made. The context again is the clue to the significance of the rib. The female is said to be "bone of my bones and flesh of my flesh"— pointing to solidarity and equality.

Finally, "to name" is generally understood to mean that what is named is brought under one's power. Naming thus implies subordination, as when the man names the birds and the animals (Gen. 2:19–20). But the naming formula (to call or to give a name) is not used in relation to the woman until after the fall, when the man called his wife's name Eve (3:20). The statement she "shall be called woman" (2:23) does not correspond to the naming formula. It lacks the word "name," and "woman"—the object of the verb "called"—is a common noun not a proper one. It points to gender and type rather than to personal identity.

As a third general comment, in reviewing the structure of the passage as a whole, we observe a progressive movement of thought in two respects. On the one hand, the creation of woman is the climax of God's creative work in this account, just as the creation of humankind (male and female) is the climactic creative event in the first creation story. On the other hand, there is a three-stage movement in the second account from man in the generic sense as one who is undifferentiated sexually, to sexual polarity in the creation of male and female, to the "one flesh" union of male and female in marriage at the end of the passage.

Fourth, two striking features in this passage set it apart from the general cultural practice of the ancient world. For one, it includes a story about the creation of woman. The literature of the ancient Near East has no known parallel to this aspect of the story. Second, the male would leave his parental home and cleave to his wife (2:24). This pattern was not the practice in Israel, nor was it the case generally in Near Eastern antiquity. Both of these observations support the positive attitude toward womanhood which we have seen taking shape throughout this study.

But the question can still be raised: Is this perspective not actually compromised by the materials in chapter 3? After all, the woman is first in the fall (3:6); the man now gives his wife a name, Eve, thus bringing her under his power (3:20); and the woman is told that her husband shall rule over her (3:16).

The second and third observations can be explained as the result of the fall: the subordination of the woman to the man does not represent the original divine intention as it can be gathered from chapters 1 and 2. More difficult is the first point, namely, the role of woman in the fall. It may be said, however, that the narrative of the fall in itself does not necessarily imply the inferiority of the woman to the man. Indeed, it might read in the reverse: the woman could conceivably be viewed as the strong, alert, sensitive member of the team while the man plays a passive, docile role. The devil might have reasoned that if he could get the woman, he would surely have the man as well! If this interpretation is adopted, this story would then also run counter to the usual stereotype of woman in ancient society.

The Old Testament patriarchs

The light modern archaeological discoveries have thrown upon the patriarchal age (2000–1200 BC) has sufficiently illuminated the background world to enable us to see the biblical figures of Abraham, Isaac, and Jacob as real people who were part of a fascinating, dynamic historical situation. Of course, to date no actual documentation of the existence of Abraham, Isaac, and Jacob has been produced by archaeologists. All we know about them is what is found in the biblical materials themselves.

What sort of a figure was Abraham? He is represented in the Genesis material as a semi-nomad who, having come from Mesopotamia to Palestine, moved about with his household and herds from one place to another, including the Negev, and on one occasion went as far as Egypt. Abraham, then, was not a solitary individual with only his wife and a few close family members and relatives about him. According to Genesis 14:14, he was able to muster 318 trained men from his own ranks who could pursue the captor of Lot. Abraham thus is properly to be regarded as a clan chieftain.

Abraham, however, was not a true nomad who lived in the desert. On the contrary, he moved on the fringes of settled society. Perhaps he was more deeply involved in the life of his world than we have traditionally thought. William F. Albright has put forward the interesting idea that Abraham may actually have been a caravan leader in the commercial donkey caravan business of the day. Albright notes that Shechem, Bethel, Hebron, and Gerar, places that figure significantly in the Abraham stories, were on the main caravan route through Palestine.

The materials available are of course far too meager to enable us to construct a biography in the modern sense of

Abraham or of any of the patriarchs. Rather, these materials provide a kind of introduction or prologue to the events that led to the formation of the nation, namely, the exodus and Sinai experiences. As such they provide not only important background happenings but also basic theological perspectives that help us understand the history of Israel that follows.

It may be helpful to look briefly at the religious background of Abraham and the character of his religious experience. According to Joshua 24:2, Abraham's family in Mesopotamia served pagan gods. We cannot here describe in detail the religious thought and life of these ancestors, but because both Ur and Haran were centers of the moon cult, Abraham's family may have shared in this worship. In any case, during the patriarchal age a highly developed polytheism with thousands of gods existed in Mesopotamia.

In this religious system, the world was viewed as a cosmic state whose operations were under the direction of an assembly of the gods. The gods were arranged in a hierarchical order. Each city-state had its own chief deity who was also a member of the divine assembly. The people of the city-state were the slaves of the deity, providing daily for his well-being so that he could live in a manner befitting a god. The king of the city-state, or in some cases of a number of city-states, was the executive agent of the god whom he represented. Families also had their own special gods who could intercede with the higher gods in behalf of their protégés.

For these Mesopotamians an intimate link existed between the gods and humans and nature. They believed the annual cycle of the seasons and the fertility of nature depended on the activity of the gods: the annual mating of the god and the goddess in the spring of the year brought about the renewal of vegetation.

We do not know to what extent Abraham and his family before him may have shared such religious beliefs or what was the precise pattern of their piety. What is clear from the biblical record is that at some point Abraham broke with his religious tradition and his homeland and moved westward around the Fertile Crescent to Palestine. This he did in response to the call of God.

How Abraham thought of the "new" God who had spoken to him is difficult to say, because the record is not concerned with the detailed structure of Abraham's theology. One thing, however, is clear: the God of the patriarchs was a personal and clan God and not a deity tied to a geographical area or to a given temple. He accompanied the patriarchs on their travels and is identified to the successive patriarchs as the God of their fathers.

> The patriarchal stories are set against the background of creation and humanity's failure to fulfill the divine intentions for our life. God undertakes a fresh act of grace, calling a man, a family, and a people through whom God intends to bring blessing to all.

The materials in Genesis 12–50 are largely various stories about each of the patriarchs: chapters 12–25 have to do with the family of Abraham; chapters 26–36 with the family of Isaac; and chapters 37–50 with the family of Jacob, and in particular with his son Joseph. We must now inquire about what the materials mean. Of what significance are the patriarchs in the faith of Israel? How do the patriarchs fare in Judaism and in the early church?

Three principal themes run through the Genesis patriarchal stories. The first is that of election. God is represented as taking the initiative in dealing with these people. He chose them before they chose him: God spoke first, he confronted them. God was the prior actor and remains sovereign in the whole of this remarkable story. The ground of God's choice of Abraham is not disclosed. It is hidden in the mystery of God's own free and gracious will. It is the expression of God's purpose to gather a people for himself. It should be noted that while election has to do in the first place with an individual and a family, it is nevertheless with a view to bringing blessing ultimately to all the families of the earth.

The second theme is that of covenant. The word itself does not occur in connection with the call of Abraham in Genesis 12:1–3; we must turn rather to the remarkable story found in Genesis 15. The content of the covenant has to do with the promise of posterity and land. The form of the covenant is unique. Unlike the covenant at Sinai (Exodus 20), here only the role and responsibility of God are noted. No human obligations are added: God pledges to fulfill his word, and

Abraham stands in the role of the passive recipient of the promise.

The covenant is reaffirmed to Abraham in Genesis 17, which also says that God will establish his covenant with Isaac (vv. 19, 21). The substance of the covenant promise to Abraham is repeated in Genesis 22:15–18, is reaffirmed to Isaac in Genesis 26:3–5, and to Jacob in Genesis 28:13–15. The reader thus is not allowed to forget that God has bound himself in solemn promise to the patriarchs. For the fulfillment of the promise one must pass beyond Genesis to the books that follow, namely, Exodus through Joshua.

God's providence is the third theme. The God who called is also the God who is active in working out his purposes in and through the lives of those whom he summoned. This activity is most dramatically illustrated in the experiences of Jacob and Joseph. Jacob is hardly above reproach in his conduct, and Joseph is the victim of his brothers' hatred. But God is able to subsume human failures under the larger outworking of his purpose. Call and covenant imply destiny. No longer does life move in the endless, repetitive cycle of Mesopotamian or Canaanite thought.

The patriarchal stories, then, are deeply significant when seen in light of what precedes and what follows these materials. They are set, for instance, against the background of the story of creation and of humanity's failure to fulfill the divine intentions for our life. God undertakes to deal with this problem in a fresh act of grace. He calls a man, a family, and a people through whom God intends to bring blessing to the entire human race. Furthermore, the patriarchal stories serve as both the historical and the theological prelude to the beginnings of Israel's national history in the exodus-Sinai cluster of events.

There are occasional references to the patriarchs beyond the first five books in the Old Testament. But it is in later Judaism that these people, especially Abraham, are celebrated as national and religious heroes. Many legends and miracle stories are attached to Abraham's name (for example, Job 11:18–22). Descent from him is one of the glories of Israel. He becomes the example of perfect obedience. He is said to have kept the whole law before it was given on Mount Sinai. As a reward for his obedience, he is taken into covenant with God. Abraham's righteousness becomes a treasury of merit for all his descendants.

It is against this false glorification of Abraham and the perversion of the covenant that Paul fights vigorously in Romans 4 and Galatians 3. Whereas some Jewish thinkers were inclined to understand the great text of Genesis 15:6 as teaching that God recognized Abraham as righteous because of his obedience, in Romans 4 Paul argues for another interpretation. He begins not with the idea of faith, but rather with the word "reckon," and with the aid of Psalm 32:1–2, says that Genesis 15:6 excludes the conception of justification on the basis of meritorious works. Justification is not so much the adding up of assets as the refusal to reckon liabilities; that is, it is a matter of forgiveness.

Paul further points out that Genesis 15:6 was spoken prior to Abraham's circumcision in order that he might be the father of believing Gentiles, as well as of those Jews who "follow the example of the faith that our ancestor . . . Abraham had before he was circumcised" (Rom. 4:12). The logic of this argument is that being a child in Abraham's family is not a matter of blood but faith (see Gal. 3:6–9). The ultimate significance of the patriarchal materials is thus seen to be a gospel that is good news for all, Jews as well as Gentiles.

The conquest and the problem of violence

Probably no other parcel of real estate has been the focus of such intense interest by so many people in the course of human history as Palestine. It is holy land to three great religious traditions: Judaism, Christianity, and Islam. It is the primary theater of action for the biblical story; with the call of Abraham early in the first book of the Bible, attention begins to center on it (Genesis 12). The New Testament closes with a vision using imagery drawn from its most important city, Jerusalem (Revelation 21–22).

If Palestine first appears in Old Testament literature as a land promised to Abraham and his descendants, its ultimate possession by the Israelites was not easily achieved. This is the significance of the term *conquest*, which is usually associated with the occupation of the land. Whatever may have been the divine plan for the fulfillment of the promise to Abraham, Palestine did not become the home for Israel apart from much blood, sweat, and tears. Furthermore, the tale raises difficult questions for the morally sensitive.

Before these issues can be properly understood, some general orientation is necessary. Let us begin with a brief description of the situation in Palestine just prior to the Israelite conquest, that is, in the thirteenth century BC. Politically, it lay within the sphere of Egyptian sovereignty. Toward the latter part of the century, Egyptian influences in Palestine began to wane, because of pressure from several sources. One was the imperial ambitions of the Hittites of Asia Minor to extend their kingdom into Palestine. But even more important was the impact of peoples from southern Europe who began to press into the lands surrounding the eastern end of the Mediterranean Sea. They came in successive waves over an extended period of time. One of these tribes was the Philistines, who were later to give the name Palestine to the land that earlier was called Canaan. If the main phase of the Israelite conquest took place in the latter part of the thirteenth century, it corresponded with a period when Egypt was occupied with other major concerns that were destined to exhaust her vitality.

Within Palestine itself, the political situation was a veritable hodgepodge of small city-states. This political pattern was fostered by the broken terrain of the country, which was unsuitable to the establishment of a strong centralized government as in Egypt or Mesopotamia. A city-state consisted of a fortified city with surrounding satellite cities and villages, the whole of which was ruled by a petty king. Because the economy was mainly agriculturally oriented, these city-states were concentrated largely on the coastal plain, the Jordan Valley, and the Plain of Esdraelon running from Mount Carmel to the Jordan Valley. The hill country was more sparsely populated and was less adapted to defense with chariots and other heavy military weaponry. The number of city-states nearly doubled during the fourteenth and thirteenth centuries BC. The result was a weakening of their strength. With the decline of Egyptian power and involvement in Palestinian affairs, the city-states were left to fend for themselves against external aggression.

The ultimate possession of Palestine by the Israelites was not easily achieved. The term *conquest* is usually associated with the occupation of the land. The tale raises difficult questions for the morally sensitive.

The population of Palestine was composite. The terms *Canaanite* and *Amorite* are normally used to describe the inhabitants of the land: both words designate predominantly Semitic peoples, a racial stock from which Israel also came. Non-Semitic elements such as the Hittites and Hurrians were also represented among the population, but these were minority strands.

Economically and culturally, the Canaanites were more advanced than the invading Israelites. They had built cities, some of which were strongly fortified. They knew how to construct drainage systems and provide secure water supplies. Some of their houses were of ample size and well constructed. The Canaanites were a trading people, having business con-

The conquest and the problem of violence

tacts with Egypt, Mesopotamia, and southeastern Europe. They exported timber and were proficient in the textile arts and in the purple-dye industry. The economy, however, was based on agriculture.

Literacy apparently was widespread. The most significant cultural achievement was in the realm of writing: the Canaanites developed a linear alphabet. It was passed on from them to the Greeks and thus became the foundation for our western method of writing. As we now know through archaeological discoveries in the last century, the Canaanites produced a considerable body of literature, which provides contemporary students with primary materials for understanding the people into whose land the Israelites came.

Canaanite religion was essentially a fertility cult with a male and female pantheon. Important figures in the cult were the god Baal and various female consorts, such as Asherah and Astarte (or Ashtoreth), about whom we hear in the Old Testament. Cultic practice included ritual prostitution, which was believed to insure fertility among humans, animals, and in vegetation. The Israelites were strictly enjoined to have no part in this religion.

We must now turn to the conquest itself. Several accounts have come down to us. Let us give attention first to the fullest record, which is found in the first twelve chapters of the book of Joshua. According to these materials, the Israelites, under the direction of Joshua, undertook three major campaigns. After crossing the Jordan—a story told in great detail—the Israelites encamped at Gilgal, northeast of Jericho. From there they laid siege to the walled city of Jericho, which fell to them in a dramatic victory after seven days (Joshua 6). From Jericho they advanced to the city of Ai, where ultimate victory was preceded by defeat (Joshua 7–8). It may be noted that Israel undertook this first campaign after a spy mission sent out from a base east of the Jordan.

Having established a foothold in the center of the land, the Israelites then moved southward through the hill country. The Gibeonites tricked the Israelites into making a covenant with them to preserve four of the Gibeonite cities (Joshua 9). When a coalition of five kings decided to take punitive action against the Gibeonites for making peace with the Israelites, the Gibeonites appealed to Joshua for help against them. In a surprise attack, Israel defeated the coalition army and slew the kings (Joshua 10). This victory was followed by others in the southern hill country, the lowlands, and the Negeb (10:40–43).

The third campaign was carried out in the northern hill country, where Joshua met a coalition of kings under the leadership of Jabin, the king of Hazor, a city north of the Sea of Galilee (Joshua 11). The story of the conquest as a whole concludes with a listing of all the kings Joshua defeated, a total of thirty-one (Joshua 12). All in all, this military record is impressive.

In addition to the narrative found in Joshua 1–12, a much briefer report is given in Judges 1, which serves as an introduction to the period of the judges. This account differs in several ways from the one in Joshua. First, the activity of individual tribes is singled out, whereas in Joshua the people as a whole appear to act under the leadership of Joshua. Second, Joshua's role as a military leader is not mentioned—it is referred to only after his death (Judg. 2:23)—while in the book of Joshua his leadership is consistently prominent. Third, in Judges there is a frank admission that Israel was unable to conquer the Canaanites in many places. This note does not occur in Joshua 1–12, although it is found in several later passages (15:63; 15:10; 17:12, 18).

Modern scholars have suggested that the Israelite conquest may have been aided by cooperation from disgruntled Canaanites and by Hebrews already settled in Palestine before the invasion under Joshua. The case of Rahab might offer some support to the first proposal at least (Joshua 2; 6:22–25; see also Judg. 1:22–26).

A reading of the conquest narratives leaves no doubt that the occupation of Palestine was a costly enterprise in terms of human life and suffering. It was brutal and bloody. The populations of entire cities were put to the sword. Repeatedly the Israelites "struck them down until no one was left who survived or escaped" (Josh. 8:22; see also 10:28, 35, 37, 39, 40; 11:11, 14). The slaughter was indiscriminate.

Difficult as this observation is, the problem is compounded by what appears to have been a divine sanction of Israel's conduct. The Lord is represented as having given over to Israel city after city for total destruction (Josh. 6:2; 8:1, 8, 18; 10:12, 19, 30, 32; 11:6, 8). We note that "it was the LORD's doing to harden their hearts so that they would come against Israel in battle, in order that they might be utterly destroyed, and might receive no mercy, but be exterminated, just as the LORD commanded Moses" (11:20).

We confront an obvious moral problem here. What response can we make to it? The following are some representative approaches that have been taken. First, and perhaps the most radical, is the total rejection of the Old Testament as irreconcilable with the moral stance of the New. In the second century AD, Marcion took this position. He regarded the God of the Old Testament as a wrathful deity wholly different from the Father of Jesus Christ. The Old Testament had no place in his Bible.

Next is the liberal evolutionary view, which holds that these materials belong to the primitive stage in human moral development. In the maturation process, progress toward more acceptable, humane conduct could be expected. The primitive, if necessary in the development process, should not be glorified or normalized.

Other Christians invoke the principle of progressive revelation: God is said to have accommodated to the limitations of God's people in that historical situation. God's will expressed in the framework of the old covenant was then superseded by the mandates of the new, and what was permitted before is now forbidden.

Still others hold that God never sanctioned violence and bloodshed. Israel's perception of God's will was distorted by the cultural conditioning of the historical environment. The revelatory process had a human reflex factor in it that resulted in a product that was something less than God's real intention for Israel.

Our survey of various approaches cannot be pursued further. Some suggestions made by Millard Lind in his book *Yahweh Is a Warrior* may help us as we conclude our reflections.

First, the conquest stories should be set in a larger context if they are to be properly understood. Attention may be called to three elements that help shape that context. The first is the song of Moses celebrating the deliverance that God wrought for God's people at the Red Sea (Exod. 15:1–18). God took the initiative and acted in the form of a nature miracle. There was no human fighting. This event provides a basic perspective for understanding God's intention for his people with regard to warfare. Human participation, so characteristic of warfare among Israel's neighbors, is absent; God was Israel's king and defender. In the second place, this absence of human participation is further underscored in the covenant concluded at Sinai. In contrast to contemporary treaties between king and vassals, Israel was not obliged to come to the aid of the king militarily if attacked. Military action was not a stipulation in Israel's covenant: God would defend God's people (Exod. 23:20–33). Third, the fall of Jericho is the first event in the narrative of the conquest after crossing the Jordan. It is told in detail (Josh. 5:13–6:27) and appears to be symbolic of the total conquest. Again, God's action in miracle is at the heart of the narrative. The element of human participation, while present, is of the nature of a mop-up exercise (Josh. 6:21).

Second, Lind points out various ways these accounts downgrade the human role in warfare. As noted earlier, the Lord is said repeatedly to have delivered the Canaanites into Israel's hand. It is also significant that Israel rejected the conventional symbols of military warfare in refusing to appropriate the captured horses and chariots of the enemy (Josh. 11:6). And Joshua had no ongoing military successors: leadership was not assigned to a military caste in early Israel.

Third, the destruction that befell the Canaanites is viewed as a divine punishment for their wickedness (Deut. 9:4–5). This view does not prove Israel's righteousness, nor does it lift responsibility from them for what they did. But it does locate the conquest in the larger outworking of God's governance of the world. Sin does matter to God.

Fourth, the general thrust of the Old Testament is not finally toward violence and bloodshed but toward peace. There is, for example, the vision of a coming day when the peoples of earth "shall beat their swords into plowshares, and their spears into pruning hooks; nation shall not lift up sword against nation, neither shall they learn war any more" (Mic. 4:3; see also Isa. 11:6–10; Zech. 9:9–10).

Finally, when we have done our best to understand the conquest materials, a measure of difficulty will likely remain to trouble us. But the path we are called to walk as Christians is the one marked out for us by Jesus of Nazareth—not the one Israel traveled as it conquered Palestine more than a thousand years earlier.

The prophetic concern for justice

"It is a great mistake," William Temple once said, "to suppose that God is only, or even chiefly, concerned with religion." By *religion*, of course, he meant such things as going to church, reading the Bible, praying, and similar activities. It is not that these are unimportant—but God's attention is hardly restricted to them, or even focused primarily on them. The Hebrew prophets underline this truth with almost monotonous repetition: God will not tolerate the sundering of religion and ethics, faith and morality, worship and discipleship. To do so is to destroy the integrity of both.

It was precisely this sort of divorce that constantly plagued the Israelite community under the monarchy, and it was the eighth-century BC prophets—Amos, Isaiah, and Micah—who brought the problem into focus. It was not a new phenomenon in their day, but certain historical developments in that century served especially to highlight it. Under Jeroboam II's rule from 786–746 BC, the northern kingdom (Israel) reached the zenith of its political power and economic prosperity, but the material wealth was not evenly distributed. A few were rich and many were poor—some desperately so. This situation was the result of two factors, one political, the other religious.

The development of the monarchy resulted in a certain reorganization of the social and financial structure of society. A centralized state institution replaced the old tribal unit with its relatively simple structure, introducing a social stratification unknown before in Hebrew life. The support of the monarchy also imposed a new financial burden on the people. While under Jeroboam II Israel saw both military success and commercial expansion, the resultant profits from booty and trade were not evenly distributed but were garnered by a comparatively small group. Thus social and economic cleavages tended to split the earlier more or less homogeneous structure of Israelite life.

Parallel with these political developments in Israel was the tendency to distort religion. Although the blood purge of Jehu attempted to exterminate the house of Ahab, which gave overt support to the Phoenician Baal cult (see 2 Kings 9), this strategy did not succeed in putting an end to Canaanite religious influence in Israel. It is evident from the eighth-century prophets that while religious shrines were thronged with people, the worship was thoroughly mixed with local elements. This integration of Canaanite rites and theology with the ancestral faith so weakened the latter that it was unable to offer any effective resistance to the secularizing forces at work in Israelite society. As the prophets saw it, the northern kingdom was pursuing a course that—unless radically altered—would surely result in judgment.

The contemporary situation in the southern kingdom (Judah) was not as critical as in the North. Neither the social deterioration nor the religious apostasy had gone quite as far in Judah as in Israel. But as Isaiah and Micah made clear, Judah was by no means free of the disease that had so deeply infected her sister state. Both these prophets accused the wealthy landholders of unscrupulous and oppressive dealings with the poor. Bribery had corrupted the administration of justice, so the poor had no means of redressing their grievances. The religious leaders, the official prophets and priests, instead of criticizing such conduct were themselves not above reproach; they were more interested in a good living than in a truly spiritual ministry to their people.

Now we will be unable to understand the prophetic critique of Hebrew society in the eighth century BC, whether in the northern or the southern kingdom, unless we see these figures as reformers. The prophets were not innovators who were pioneering new paths of social and religious development. No, they were people who were recalling their contemporaries to ancient standards that had been forsaken. God's people, they charged, were being caught up in Canaanite habits of thought and ways of life. Their unique heritage, shaped by the exodus and Sinai experiences, was no longer shaping the present as it should. Unless the present trends were checked and reformation undertaken, all would be lost.

What was the ideal to which they must make a return? Let us note two dimensions of the prophets' concern for social justice.

First, the prophets emphasized the equality of all people under God. This conviction has its roots in the exodus experience, in which God moved to free a people who could not liberate themselves. It was not by human effort but by divine action that Israel came to birth as a people. This divine grace allows no room for the kind of stratification that assigns superiority to one person over another.

"It is a great mistake," William Temple once said, "to suppose that God is only, or even chiefly, concerned with religion." The Hebrew prophets underline this truth with almost monotonous repetition: God will not tolerate the sundering of religion and ethics, faith and morality, worship and discipleship.

This basic equality is recognized in the absence of class legislation—apart from the slave—in the covenant code (Exodus 21–23). This is a unique feature of early Israelite law as compared with other ancient law. The Babylonian Code of Hammurabi, for example, is tailored to social caste and professional status. But in Israel all are subject to the same code. Furthermore, when Israel subsequently came to have a king, he, too, was expected to be subject to the same basic law as were his subjects (see Deut. 17:14–20). This conception is unparalleled in the ancient world, where the king was the lawgiver and hence not subject to the law.

A second feature of the covenant code that the prophets emphasized is its prominent concern for the welfare of the underdog: the stranger, the widow, the orphan. Whether alien or native-born, such people must not be oppressed; indeed, God champions their rights (see Exod. 22:21–23). Likewise, one must not require interest from a poor neighbor. If one takes a neighbor's garment as a pledge, it must be returned before sundown to give needed protection during the night (see Exod. 22:25–27). Even the live property of an enemy is protected from mistreatment by laws demanding the treatment that one would normally give one's own oxen (see Exod. 23:4–5).

The prophetic concern for justice

The Deuteronomic code is clear in its demand for justice: "Justice, and only justice, you shall pursue, so that you may live and occupy the land that the LORD your God is giving you" (Deut. 16:20). Justice must be administered impartially to "the small and the great alike" (Deut. 1:16–17). Here, too, the welfare of the poor is carefully safeguarded. One expression of this concern is the law mandating the remission of debts every sabbatical year, which would enable the economically unfortunate to get a fresh start.

Not only did Israel have legislation to provide the guidelines for justice, they also had the machinery necessary for its administration. The earliest arrangement was the local village court of the elders. The elders were people of status in the community who were heads of families and leading citizens. They were called together when a local matter involving community decision arose. The place of assembly was at the gate of the town.

We find a description of such a court in action in the book of Ruth (4:1–12). Boaz wished to buy the property Naomi was selling and to marry Ruth according to the Hebrew practice of preserving a family line and its inheritance in Israel. But Boaz was not the closest relative of Elimelech, and this relative had, if he chose, the privilege of buying the property and marrying Ruth. To dispose of this matter, Boaz sat at the town gate. He stopped the nearer kinsman on his way out of the town. Then Boaz chose ten elders from the town, and he then presented the matter for discussion and decision. When the matter was resolved, the court disbanded and each again went about his business.

This communal, ad hoc arrangement was not the only way official decisions were made or justice was dispensed. Under the monarchy we hear of the appointment of judges by the king in various cities of his realm (see 2 Chron. 19:5–6). We also learn of a Jerusalem court composed not only of elders but also of priests and Levites; this court heard not only local cases but cases referred to it from outlying towns (see 2 Chron. 19:8–11). After the establishment of the monarchy, the king also could dispense justice (see 2 Samuel 14–15). The priests, too, as teachers of the law, would naturally function in making legal decisions. In the case of an especially difficult matter, they might also inquire of the Lord for a divine oracle.

We find references to the administration of justice in both the northern kingdom and the southern kingdom in the eighth-century BC prophets—Amos in Israel and Micah in Judah. Amos refers to the communal village court that met at the gate of the town and criticizes it for a lack of justice (Amos 5:12, 15). Micah's reference is less explicitly to the popular court at the village gate, although this assembly may well be in his mind (Mic. 3:1–3, 9–12).

Now we can understand how injustice may have been done in these village courts, especially in the prosperous days of the eighth century. As already noted, a stratified society had developed, with wealthy merchants, estate owners, and nobles at the top. The vested interests of these prominent people in the towns and cities may have made them prone to give partial judgments in the legal assembly. Where professional judges were appointed (see 2 Chron. 19:5; Deut. 16:18–20), perhaps the rich sought to bribe them. The same practice may have been at work in the popular village court (see Mic. 3:11). Some have suggested that the judicial reforms that established a high court in Jerusalem to which difficult cases could be referred (see 2 Chron. 19:8–11; Deut. 17:8–9) may have been in part at least an attempt to transcend the weakness of the local legal assembly.

Such measures, however, were not the prophetic answer to the problem. On this matter—as in other areas of conduct—the prophets sought to confront men and women with the ancient faith of their forebears and to impress on them its implications for practical living. The key to the problem was essentially a religious one: life in all of its aspects must be lived in the light of God's intention for human life. We have returned to the covenant and its stipulation. "He has told you, O mortal, what is good," said Micah; "and what does the LORD require of you but to do justice, and to love kindness, and to walk humbly with your God?" (6:8).

The Servant of the Lord: Vision and sequel

ESSAY
18

A major watershed occurs in the structure of the book of Isaiah between chapters 39 and 40. Chapters 36–39 deal with events during the reign of King Hezekiah in Judah (715–687 bc). Assyria was a world power and would continue as such until 612 bc. Politically—despite threatening clouds over the kingdom of Judah—Jerusalem, the Davidic monarchy, and the temple remained intact.

The situation presupposed in chapter 40 and beyond is somewhat different. These chapters make no further reference to Davidic kings reigning in Jerusalem. The temple has been destroyed, but the hope of its rebuilding is entertained (44:28; 66:1). The people are in exile in Babylon, from which they are about to be delivered (43:14; 48:20; see also 40:1–5). The Persian king Cyrus will soon overthrow Babylon (45:1; 46:11)—an event that took place in 539 BC. Jerusalem will again be rebuilt (44:26–28). Joy and gladness will once more be found in Zion, for the Lord "will comfort all her waste places" (51:3).

The fall of Jerusalem proved to be a difficult experience for the people of Judah, for it marked the end of political independence as the Judean state passed out of existence. While that catastrophe was a blow to national pride, even more serious were the theological problems it posed. Why did it happen? What was its meaning? Was God unable to defend them? Had the Lord deliberately cast off his people? Was there a future for them as the people of God? If so, what role did God intend for them among the nations?

It is to people struggling with these questions of faith that the chapters in the latter part of the book of Isaiah are addressed. In this context we find one of the most profound interpretations of Israel's faith and mission in the whole of the

Old Testament. It will not be possible to explore the full range of theological understandings found in these materials, so we will focus on the way chapters 40–55 portray the mission of God's people.

A prominent term in this portion of the book is *servant*. It occurs no fewer than twenty times in these chapters, in contrast to only four instances elsewhere in the book. Only one of these twenty occurrences has no religious association: the servant in view is clearly in God's service. God is heard speaking to and about God's servant. The servant also speaks about himself in relation both to God and to his own people.

> While the fall of Jerusalem was a blow to national pride, even more serious were the theological problems it posed. Why did it happen? What did it mean? Was there a future for Israel as God's people? To people struggling with these questions of faith the latter part of Isaiah is addressed.

While references to the servant are scattered across chapters 40–55, Old Testament scholars generally identify four passages where the servant figure is steadily and distinctly in focus. These passages, often called Servant Poems or Servant Songs, are 42:1–4; 49:1–6; 50:4–9; and 52:13–53:12. In this discussion, we are primarily concerned with these passages. Let us first note some of the major features of the servant concept, then briefly explore what happened to this understanding in later history.

First, can we bring the figure of the servant into sharper focus? It is not easy to do so because of the complexity of the data. The servant seems to be identified with the nation as a whole in 49:3: "You are my servant, Israel." This identification is in keeping with various references to the servant outside these poems (see 41:8; 44:1, 21; 45:4) and is the probable meaning in the first poem (42:1–4). But there are passages both inside and outside the poems where the servant is something less than the entire nation. This fact becomes clear when we note that the servant's mission, at least in part, is directed to Israel (49:5–6; see 42:6–7). The reference in view may thus be to an individual or to a spiritual remnant within the nation, through whom God would accomplish his purposes, because the nation as a whole was unfit for this task. Finally, in the longest and most notable of the poems the thought seems clearly to narrow to a personal figure who becomes the servant in a preeminent sense (52:13–53:12).

How can we understand these various uses of *servant* within the poems? The usual explanation refers to the way Hebrew thought could fluctuate between the group and the individual, so that the community might be represented as an individual or by a member of the group. Conversely, an individual could be regarded as representing or incorporating the group. In the case of these poems, the servant figure functions in both a corporate and an individual sense. The imagery is fluid, and the various meanings are not unrelated but rather flow into each other.

Second, the servant is said to have a twofold mission. There is a mission to Israel. The Lord formed his servant "in the womb . . ., to bring Jacob back to him, and that Israel might be gathered to him" (49:5). This reference might be to restoration from exile. But surely more is intended than a mere physical ministry. Israel is to be helped to become the people God meant them to be. Perhaps something of the renewal of life set out in the vision of 2:2–5 is anticipated.

The servant is also commissioned to be "a light to the nations, that [God's] salvation may reach to the end of the earth" (49:6). Elsewhere this image is understood to mean the bringing of justice to the nations through the sharing of God's law with them (42:1, 4). The nations will share in the knowledge of God through the servant's ministry. The way the two aspects of the servant's work are to be related is not clearly indicated. But surely if Israel would indeed become God's true people, they will then be the medium of God's light to the surrounding nations; this appears to be the divine plan as sketched in 2:2–5.

Third, how is the servant to carry out his mission? Nowhere in the poems is it said that the servant will employ the conventional instruments of brute force so often used to achieve large-scale objectives. On the contrary, two modes are highlighted that on the surface would not seem to offer much hope of success. But God's ways are not the ways of humans (55:8–9): his methods are in keeping with his goals.

What, then, are the ways the mission is to be carried forward? There is, first of all, the spoken word. God has given the servant "the tongue of a teacher, that [he] may know how to sustain the weary with a word" (50:4). Under the blessing of God, the apparently fragile word mysteriously becomes a source of inner strength to people in difficult situations. When necessary, the servant's word can also be "like a sharp sword" and "a polished arrow" (49:2), doing battle with all that stands in opposition to God's will.

Behind the spoken word, however, is the servant himself. What he is and does is an important part of his mission. The fourth poem (52:13–53:12) makes this is especially clear. It portrays the servant as utterly vulnerable to rejection, suffering, and even death. What he is called to experience is not merely a consequence of his ministry but is actually the means of fulfilling it. The sufferings have a vicarious character and, in the providence of God, also redemptive power. Out of them flow miraculously the blessings of healing, wholeness, and well-being for the many desperately in need of these gifts. This insight is one of the most profound that is found in the poems, indeed in the Old Testament.

Fourth, the personal qualities of the servant should not be overlooked. Three in particular are noteworthy. He exemplifies an attitude of openness and responsiveness to God. "Morning by morning," says the servant, "he wakens—wakens my ear to listen as those who are taught" (50:4). Not only does the servant receive a commission from the Lord originally, but he is daily dependent on the Lord for direction in its fulfillment. The general thrust of the call is clear, but the details that are to give final shape to it are not. These have to be discerned at each step of the way.

The servant's relation to others is marked by a high degree of sensitivity. Absent are arrogance, flamboyance, and boastfulness. There are no highhanded, coercive techniques. Rather, the servant pursues his mission quietly and gently, taking care not to break a bruised reed or quench a dimly burning wick (42:3). There is persistence in his dedication: he will not be satisfied short of fulfilling his mission (42:4). Even suffering will not deter him from that intention.

The servant's lack of anxious self-concern is rooted in a willingness to commit himself and his mission into the hands of God. He is responsible for fidelity to the task given him but not for its ultimate outcome. "I have set my face like flint," he says, "and I know that I shall not be put to shame" (50:7). Laboring in that confidence, he can face even death without complaint or self-vindication.

Fifth, if God, who called the servant, also upholds him, we may ask how God does so. The answer is not difficult to discover: God has put his Spirit upon him (42:1). Reference to the Spirit is a way of affirming God's presence in the world in power, carrying forward God's purposes toward fulfillment. This unseen but effective resource is constantly available to undergird the servant in the whole of his life and ministry. It is the secret to the figure and the pattern of ministry here portrayed.

Such, then, are some of the rich facets of the complex servant concept found in these four poems. In its general outlines and basic spirit, it represented both a future ideal and a present calling. What happened to this vision in the period beyond the exile? Did the servant model remain a vital challenge, inspiring and shaping the ongoing life of the people of God prior to the coming of Jesus?

Available evidence indicates that Judaism made little use of it. It is possible that the description of the coming king in Zechariah 9:9 may show some slight influence from the servant ideal, although this is far from certain. Some scholars have pointed to what appear to them to be echoes of this conception in a few noncanonical Jewish writings, but the evidence is debatable. Judaism during the postexilic period was not without its hopes for the future, and these expectations took a variety of forms. But a suffering Messiah did not commend itself as a viable option. Indeed, it is not likely that the suffering servant of Isaiah 53 was ever interpreted messianically in pre-Christian Judaism.

But the vision that long lay dormant like seed under frozen soil was not completely lost. It was destined to spring to life again and to bear its richest fruit in Jesus. According to the New Testament Gospels, Jesus did not apply the title "servant" to himself. Indeed, these accounts include only one explicit quotation from the servant poems on his lips: Isaiah 53:12 in Luke 22:37. Allusions have been seen in such sayings as Mark 10:45 and 14:24, and there are also the clear predictions in his ministry of his forthcoming passion (Mark 8:31; 9:31; 10:33–34)—but without quoting from Isaiah 53. Apparently, however, he did see his arrest as the fulfillment of scripture (Mark 14:49). It is quite possible as well that the heavenly voice at his baptism may be an echo of Isaiah 42:1 at the beginning of his ministry (Mark 1:11).

If Jesus made only limited explicit use of the servant poems, early Christians clearly did interpret him in light of this tradition. His healing ministry is seen to be the fulfillment of Isaiah 42:1–4 (Matt. 12:18–21). The title "servant" applied to him in Acts 3:14, 26, likely reflects influence from these materials. Philip was able to preach the gospel to the Ethiopian eunuch from Isaiah 53 (Acts 8:26–39). In the latter part of the first century, other Christians continued to draw on this great passage to expound the meaning of Jesus' death.

The appropriateness of the servant motif in understanding Jesus and his mission is beyond question. What is not so clear, however, is why there are not more direct quotations from the Servant Songs on the lips of Jesus and in the letters of the New Testament.

Jonah: What is the point?

To the person on the street, Jonah is likely the most widely known of all the Old Testament prophets. Unfortunately, however, this book is known for the wrong reason: Jonah is linked inseparably with a fish story. What occupies no more than three of the forty-eight verses of the book has stolen the limelight. The sideshow has swallowed the main show!

The brief book that bears this prophet's name is one of the great books of the Old Testament. Who its author was we do not know. Unlike the other prophetic books, it is not a collection of sermons but rather a story about a prophet. A passing reference is made to a prophet named Jonah in 2 Kings 14:25; he is identified as coming from a Galilean town located not far from Nazareth. He lived during the reign of Jeroboam II (786–746 BC) in the northern kingdom. Apparently the prophet predicted the territorial expansion of the king's dominion, which the text reports subsequently happened. The origin of the book of Jonah, however, is generally regarded as dating from a later period.

The story is a moving tale told with artistic skill. Readers encounter high drama as they follow the fortunes of the prophet from his original commission, through his disobedience and punishment, to his reluctant obedience and final chiding by God. In the composition of this literary gem, the author effectively uses elements of suspense, emotional ups and downs, economy of expression, vivid description, and lively character portrayal.

But what is the point of the story? To whom was it addressed? Why was it written? When did it make its appearance? These questions are intriguing but more or less difficult to answer. The book lacks the preface so characteristic of modern publications, in which information of this kind is usually given, so the data the book itself provides has been variously interpreted.

An early Jewish interpretation gave Jonah a good press. As a prophet, he knew that the people of Nineveh would repent and that their conduct would put stiff-necked Israel to shame. So Jonah refused to go to Nineveh. Instead he boarded a ship, not to flee from the presence of God but to drown himself in the sea for the sake of Israel. His death, it was said, would result in meritorious benefit to his people.

A contemporary Jewish scholar, Elias Bickerman, offers another point of view in *Four Strange Books of the Bible*. He sees the book as confronting two opposite theological positions. One is held by prophets such as Jeremiah, Ezekiel, Joel, and Malachi. For them the prophetic word is a conditional word: if the announcement of coming judgment is met with repentance, then God will change his mind. God's action is tailored to human response. The other position is that attributed to the figure of Jonah: the word of God, once uttered, is certain to be fulfilled. There can be no change.

> The narrow, selfish sympathies of the prophet Jonah stand out vividly against the divine compassion that yearns for the well-being of Nineveh. Seen from this perspective, the book is an invitation to share in God's great concern for the total human family. It is a summons to mission that we today, no less than Israel in Jonah's day, need to hear.

Bickerman suggests that the book transcends both of these views. He focuses attention on the phrase "concerned for" (4:10–11). This expression, he says, has no "mental association with forgiveness or repentance. It indicates a sovereign and arbitrary action." The book is thus a story about the sovereignty of God. If God once in his sovereign action spared Nineveh, will God not also save Jerusalem by sovereign decision? The final question with which the book ends is thus an encouragement to hope.

Josephus, the first century AD Jewish historian, has a less complicated understanding of the book than either of the preceding views, achieved by omitting most of the materials in chapter 3 and the whole of chapter 4. Jonah, according to Josephus, was commissioned by God to announce to Nineveh that its dominion over the nations was about to end. For some reason—which Josephus does not explain—Jonah was afraid to carry out his mission and decided to run away. After he was delivered from the large fish on the shores of the Black Sea, he prayed to God and was granted pardon. He then went to Nineveh as God had directed him. In Josephus's version, no reference is made to the penitence of the people of Nineveh or to Jonah's subsequent experience.

Turning from Jewish to Christian understandings of the book, we encounter a similar diversity of opinion. T. F. Glasson has called attention to the fact that only two of all the books of the Bible end with a question: one is Jonah, the other is Nahum. Curiously enough, both are concerned with the fate of Assyria and the divine attitude toward it. But the points of view are different. Nahum stresses the justice of God and rejoices in the approaching doom of Assyria. Jonah, on the contrary, under-scores the mercy of God: it "seems almost designed to rebuke the cruel temper of the earlier prophecy." The final question of Jonah is thus regarded as perhaps a conscious attempt "to refute the implication of Nahum's final question."

A widely held modern view is that the book was written to protest a nationalistic outlook that developed in the Jewish community after the exile in Babylon. That such an attitude came to exist in Judaism is generally admitted. John Bright, in *A History of Israel*, reconstructs the situation as follows. From the beginning of their existence the people of Israel believed themselves to be chosen by God to be his particular people. It was God's purpose someday to establish fully his rule in the whole earth. In pre-exilic Israel, this purpose was understood to mean the submission of the nations to God (for example, Ps. 2:10–11; 72:8–19), although how this submission was to be brought about was not given serious or systematic attention.

The fall of Jerusalem in 587 BC and the experience of exile in Babylon put the problem of Israel's role in the purpose of God and the nation's relationship to other nations on Israel's agenda in a fresh and urgent way. One answer given to this question was that Israel, as the elect people of God chastened and purified by suffering, now had a missionary task to fulfill. It was to be "a light to the nations" (Isa. 42:6–7; 49:6). The Gentiles, too, were to be included among the people of God.

After the exile, however, the restored community found itself surrounded in Judea by people who practiced other religions. In an effort to avoid assimilation, Nehemiah and Ezra took steps to build a "wall" around the small community struggling for its life. They demanded thoroughgoing obedience to the law as the mark of the people of God. This requirement, while it might exclude Jews who were unwilling to conform, did not bar non-Israelites from joining the community. The door was open to Gentiles who were ready to meet the conditions of membership.

The concentration of attention on legal obedience, although nobly conceived, had some unfortunate results. Separation from Gentiles became a dominant note in the literature of Judaism; even Samaritans were held in scornful contempt. Along with this attitude of withdrawal, a strong sense of national pride developed. The post-exilic Jewish community gloried in its possession of the law and its privileged status as the people of God. Its language, it was claimed, was that used by God at creation, and its holy city, Jerusalem, was the center of the earth.

Bright's opinion is that the book of Jonah was written sometime in the fourth century BC to combat this narrow, exclusivistic attitude. The figure of Jonah is thus a representative of a smug separation unwilling to see Gentiles included in the embrace of God's care.

Another way to understand the message of Jonah is to regard it as directed against Israel's chronic problem of disobedience to the word of the Lord. The response of Israel to the prophetic word was one of repeated rejection. The call to penitence and renewed obedience was like the seed in one of Jesus' parables that fell by the wayside: it did not penetrate the hard surface and brought forth no fruit. In contrast to the people of Israel, the Ninevites took the prophetic word seriously and repented. The story, thus, is intended to be an object lesson to Israel: it is a call to imitate outsiders' readiness to hear the summons to radical repentance in the face of threatened judgment.

This interpretation would not presuppose a post-exilic date for the book. It would fit well as a complement to the preaching of the great pre-exilic prophets from the eighth century BC onward. These prophets not only spoke of impending judgment but found the indifference and impenitence of God's people hard to understand. There is some evidence for a collection of at least most of the prophetic books in some form by about 500 BC, so Jonah may have been written in the crisis preceding the fall of Jerusalem.

Finally, we call attention to the view of Gerhard von Rad in the second volume of his *Old Testament Theology*, who would put the book in the period sometime after the return from exile. Although the story does no credit to the prophet Jonah, it should not be taken as a final appraisal of all prophecy in Israel. Von Rad finds the significance of the book in the way it turns attention away from the prophetic office as such to God, to whom alone honor is due. Its message is similar to that uttered by the last of the prophets, John the Baptist: "He must increase, but I must decrease" (John 3:30).

In the light of this review, what then shall we say about the book? It may not be possible at this point to recover with certainty the book's precise historical setting. But the story carries fair meaning in itself. Like most drawn-out stories, it can potentially convey more than one meaning; there may well be primary and secondary levels of meaning. What these are will depend on where and to what extent accent is placed on various elements in the story.

One constant feature throughout the story is the reluctance of the prophet to fulfill his mission, which stands in stark contrast to the graphic description of the ready response of the Ninevites. Even if no explicit contrast is drawn between their acceptance of the prophetic word and Israel's rejection of it, this point might be implied—especially if the historical setting is pre-exilic. The same, of course, might also hold for some later period. Interestingly enough, Jesus makes this point in Luke 11:29–31.

The climax of the story, however, surely comes in the dialogue between God and the prophet over the plant in chapter 4. The thrust of this interchange is the wideness of God's mercy. The point is driven home by striking contrast: the narrow, selfish sympathies of the prophet stand out vividly when seen against the divine compassion that yearns for the well-being of Nineveh. Seen from this perspective, the book is an invitation to share in God's great concern for the total human family. It is a summons to mission that we today, no less than Israel in Jonah's day, need to hear.

Reflections on the book of Esther

As the Judean state drew to its close soon after 600 BC, Jews on several occasions were deported to Babylonia. Some of these people or their descendants were later to return to their homeland, but many did not go back. They remained in the lower Tigris-Euphrates valley and in the lands to the east. What happened to them in the next several centuries is largely unknown, limited to a few scattered references. About the beginning of the Christian era, they once again come into view as strong, well-organized communities.

One such brief glimpse into their experience is provided by the book of Esther. The story is set in the Persian court at Susa, some 250 miles east of Babylon, during the reign of Ahasuerus (Esther 1:1). This man is usually identified with the Persian king Xerxes I, who reigned from 486 to 465 BC. Esther, whose Hebrew name was Hadassah, was an orphan who had been adopted by her cousin Mordecai. Through a series of unusual circumstances, Esther rose from obscurity as an expatriate to become queen of the empire. She could appropriately be called "the Cinderella of the Bible."

A major, if not the dominant, interest of the author of this document was to provide an explanation for the Jewish feast of Purim. This festival has no authorization in the Pentateuch and is not mentioned elsewhere in the Old Testament. But it became and remains a popular festival in Judaism. (Today in this festival, the Esther scroll is read, charity is distributed, food gifts are exchanged, and a festive meal is shared.)

The book exists in more than one form. The one familiar to us is the canonical one in the versions normally used in Protestant circles, based on the Hebrew text of the Old Testament. The other is an expanded version, which is found in the Catholic canon represented, for example, in The Jerusalem

Bible. It derives from the Septuagint, the Greek version of the Old Testament produced in the third century BC. The additional material in this version of Esther, consisting of more than one hundred verses, supplements the shorter text at various points with letters, prayers, some background, and interpretive materials. These serve the purpose of filling in gaps in the original Hebrew version. They also serve, as we shall see, to give a somewhat different cast to the book as a whole. These fragments can also be read in the Old Testament Apocrypha under the title Additions to Esther. (The NRSV edition of the Apocrypha indicates the points at which these various passages should be inserted into the canonical text.)

> The plot of the book of Esther involves elements of firm resistance, mounting suspense, spiteful intrigue, decisive action, calculated risk, and radical reversal of roles—all of which are skillfully interwoven to sustain the reader's interest. The leading figures are clearly portrayed but without any serious attempt to explore their inner selves or their motivations.

Historically, attitudes toward the book of Esther have varied considerably both in Jewish and in Christian circles. Although evidence from the end the first century AD indicates that the book was accepted into the Jewish canon, not all rabbis were happy about its inclusion. It is the only Old Testament book not presently represented in the discoveries at Qumran, and the earliest Christian list of Old Testament books (about AD 170) omits it. Martin Luther was quite hostile to the book and wished it did not exist. Its place in the Christian canon, however, has been firm since the latter half of the fourth century.

But many questions about the character and significance of the book are still debated. Certain features in the book pose difficult historical questions, leading some students to regard it as a historical novel based on an actual happening. But at other points the materials do find support from nonbiblical sources. Commenting on this matter, J. M. Myers has written: "The more one reads the book, takes into consideration the names and references to Persian court life, and studies it with the archeological and linguistic aids that have come to hand, the more [one] must be impressed with its reflection of the period from which it purports to come."

We do know something of the Persian king Xerxes I, both from the Greek historian Herodotus, who was his younger contemporary, and also from archaeological discoveries in modern Iran. According to Herodotus, Xerxes was an imposing personality, although somewhat temperamental and rather easily influenced by those around him. He was less than astute as a military strategist. His roving eye for beautiful women led to a tragic domestic affair that cost the life of his brother-in-law and also, after brutal torture, his sister-in-law, whom he had tried unsuccessfully to seduce. He himself was finally assassinated in his bedroom in a plot instigated by family members.

Xerxes was an avid builder remembered chiefly for the magnificent palace and related buildings he constructed at Persepolis, one of the three royal capitals of the empire. The extensive ruins of this city are still impressive. Less tangible evidence remains today of the once stately, although less elaborate, royal buildings at Susa, his winter capital. A clay tablet found at Susa preserves his father's account of the construction of his own palace there. He drew on skills and materials from lands far and near: cedar was brought from Lebanon, stone from southern Russia, gold from western Turkey, silver and copper from Egypt, ivory from Ethiopia and India. The brick makers were Babylonians, the stonecutters were Greek, and the goldsmiths were Medes and Egyptians. The brief description of the architectural details and lavish adornment of the palace given in Esther 1:4–7 is in keeping with the impression derived from archaeological sources.

The other characters who appear in the book of Esther are unknown in the ancient secular sources. Herodotus does refer to Xerxes' queen, but her name is neither Vashti nor Esther. The name *Mordecai* occurs in a Persian document for a finance officer in the court of Xerxes I at Susa; that this was the Mordecai of the book of Esther, however, cannot be proved.

From a literary point of view, the book has been described as worthy to be ranked among the masterpieces of literature. The story is certainly characterized by high drama. The plot involves elements of firm resistance, mounting suspense, spiteful intrigue, decisive action, calculated risk, and radical reversal of roles—all of which are skillfully interwoven to sustain the reader's interest. The leading figures are clearly portrayed but without any serious attempt to explore their inner selves or their motivations. The king acts impulsively but decisively. Esther is a charming woman who knows how to use her feminine graces to good advantage, but she can also be ruthless in the hour of her victory. Haman is a proud, power-hungry schemer who is fatally trapped in his own plans to eliminate a rival. Mordecai is Esther's mentor, emerging from the shadow of the gallows to become second to the king.

One of the curious features of the book is that while the king of Persia is mentioned 190 times, the name of God is completely absent from the Hebrew version. This lack is true of only one other book in the Bible, The Song of Songs, where the omission is understandable, because it is a series of lyrics given to the celebration of the joys of human friendship and of sexual love. But the case is otherwise with Esther, where the fate of the Jewish people in Persia is at stake in a tense bit of history. In such a crisis one would expect some reference to God, particularly because two Jews play leading roles in the most critical moments of the story.

Because God is not mentioned, perhaps we should not be surprised that prayer is also absent from the document—although at least a passing reference to such a resource in a time of great danger would certainly have been appropriate. Neither is there any mention of the Mosaic covenant, so basic to Judaism; again, the critical character of the circumstances would seem to have made such a reference natural. Indeed, the only religious activity that is specifically mentioned is fasting (Esther 4:16; see also 9:31), but this practice receives little emphasis in the legal materials of the Old Testament.

The additions made to the Greek version of the book seem to indicate that these omissions became an embarrassment to the Jewish community at some point. This version makes more than fifty explicit references to God. Furthermore, not only does it repeatedly mention prayer offered to God, but the text of two extended prayers is given—one by Mordecai and the other by Esther. Although it does not explicitly mention the covenant, it refers repeatedly to the laws by which the Jewish people sought to order their lives. Esther is careful to point out that as queen, she has been faithful to Jewish dietary laws. She and her people are in bitter slavery, but God knows that she as wife to a pagan king loathes sexual relations with him. As queen she is required to wear a royal crown, but she does so reluctantly and only when appearing in public. Says she, "I abhor it like a filthy rag." Her attitude toward her role and duties as wife of Xerxes is summed up in her prayer to God: "Your servant has had no joy since the day that I was brought here until now, except in you, O Lord God of Abraham."

Mordecai acts out of religious impulse in his refusal to bow to the powerful Haman. Speaking to God, he says: "You know all things; you know, O Lord, that it was not in insolence or pride or for any love of glory that I did this, and refused to bow down to this proud Haman, for I would have been willing to kiss the soles of his feet to save Israel! But I did this so that I might not set the human glory above the glory of God, and I will not bow down to anyone but to you, who are my Lord."

Various reasons for the absence of explicit religious references in the canonical (Hebrew) text have been proposed, but none is entirely satisfactory. Several things, however, can be said about their presence in the added materials. First, perhaps those who were responsible for these additions thought they were only making explicit what was implicit in the shorter version. It is difficult to account for the actions of both Mordecai and Esther as portrayed there on purely secular grounds. Esther 3:8 recognizes a certain distinctiveness on the part of the Jewish people: "Their laws are different from those of every other people, and they do not keep the king's laws." This verse seems to reflect the basic religious orientation that traditionally was characteristic of ancient Judaism.

Second, even if this suggestion is valid, something more needs to be said. The additions made to the canonical text have the effect of altering the emphasis in the story. Whereas in the shorter Hebrew version Mordecai and Esther are the dominant actors on the stage, in the longer Greek version attention is shifted to God. The human actors are still there, but the spotlight clearly is now focused on God and God's activity. Thus at the end of the book, Mordecai, reflecting on what has happened, is represented as saying: "These things have come from God. The Lord has saved his people; the Lord has rescued us from all these evils; God has done great signs and wonders, wonders that have never happened among the nations."

One of the difficulties many Jews and Christians have with the book of Esther is the vindictive spirit both Mordecai and Esther display. After the plot of Haman is disclosed for what it is and thwarted, Esther and Mordecai virtually become Haman in reverse. When the king gives them the opportunity, they promptly arrange for the slaughter of thousands of their enemies. To pass from Isaiah 53 to Esther is to fall, as it were, "from heaven to earth." The gulf between Esther and Jesus on this matter is equally great.

This observation does not mean, however, that we should ignore the book as though it has no contribution to make to us. It is, after all, a part of the Bible, and the church has long since accepted it. But what should we make of it? First, we should allow this book to retain its particular character. We must not fail to hear its witness to the dark passions of the human heart, even within the community of God's people. We can find here an eloquent testimony to the truth that Israel's election was not attributable to some intrinsic merit but to the sovereign grace of God (see Deut. 7:6–8).

Second, the book vividly documents "the scandal of particularity." The Jews are seen as a people apart from others in the empire. Because they refused to be assimilated, Haman said that it was "not appropriate for the king to tolerate them" (Esther 3:8).

Third, we are reminded again of the mysterious survival of the Jews as a people in the face of determined attempts to destroy them. Seen from the standpoint of the New Testament, their preservation was that salvation might go forth from them to all the peoples of the world.

Fourth, bringing God's purpose through the Jewish people to fruition in Christ provides a perspective from which the earlier parts of the story can now be read with greater discernment. This perspective includes elements of both affirmation and criticism, continuity and discontinuity. The book of Esther, as part of that larger story, must be read in this light.

Part 3
Opening the New Testament

Putting the New Testament together

Can you imagine a church that never saw or even heard about the New Testament? That, to us, is incredible. The church and the New Testament are like Siamese twins. Even on mission fields where the New Testament has not yet been translated into the language of the people, its existence is known. What mission workers share is derived from its pages.

But this link was not always the case. The church began and actually spread over the whole of the Roman Empire without possessing the New Testament. In fact, the church did not have the New Testament as we now know it for several centuries after Pentecost. The books that now compose it were written at intervals over many decades and only gradually were brought together to make up our present collection. The first list of such writings to correspond exactly with the New Testament as we now know it was made in AD 367 in Alexandria, Egypt.

Why was the New Testament so long in the making? Several reasons may be suggested. First, the early church did not feel an urgency to write a Bible. It already had one, the Old Testament, which it had inherited from the Jewish synagogue. The Hebrew scriptures were the Bible of Jesus, his disciples, and the early Christians. The church, therefore, was not without guidance with regard to God's will and purposes for humanity; indeed, the Old Testament was foundational for the faith of the early Christians as it was for Judaism. To be sure, the early church came to read it somewhat differently in the light of Jesus than did the non-Christian Jews. But it was not abandoned.

Second, Jesus gave himself to a ministry of oral teaching and preaching. So far as we know, he wrote no books. The early Christians also felt called to a ministry of the spoken word,

which was largely a matter of showing how Jesus was a fulfillment of God's purpose found in the Old Testament. They had
good news to share, and the principal medium in the earliest
days was the living word. Third, how soon writing came to play
a significant role in Christian circles we do not know; the
earliest preserved writings are some of Paul's letters which
belong to AD 45–50. By the time Luke
wrote his Gospel there had been many
attempts to record the ministry of Jesus
(see Luke 1:1), but all of these except
Mark's are lost to us.

> The New Testament came
> into existence as the result
> of the church's gradual
> recognition that certain
> books were useful in
> nourishing the faith and life
> of the church. Official action,
> when it finally occurred,
> approved what was already
> recognized to be true. We
> could say that the New
> Testament took shape from
> the bottom up rather than
> from the top down.

Fourth, when Christians began to
write about their faith, it was not with the
conscious motive of producing materials
that would be a part of their Bible. They
wrote as members of the Christian community who knew that they possessed the
Spirit of God. In writing, they wanted to
meet various pressing needs in the life of
the church. Sometimes they stated a
purpose for writing (see Luke 1:1–4; John
20:30–31), but usually we must infer it
from the document itself.

Fifth, the fact that in due time the Christian church did add
another body of material (the New Testament) to their first
Bible (the Old Testament) can only be explained by reference
to the significance they found in the person and ministry of
Jesus. The synagogue, which of course saw Jesus in a different
light from that of the church, produced no New Testament.
Judaism did go on to write a considerable amount of material
(including the Talmud) in the early centuries of the Christian
era. But these writings are of a quite different character from
those in our New Testament and were never officially made
part of the Jewish Bible.

The story of the making of the New Testament is a long and
complex one. We can make only a few observations and
comments, beginning with the process itself. The procedure
was less formal than is commonly supposed: the New Testament did not come into existence as the result of the work of a

committee appointed to create it. On the contrary, the development was a matter of a gradual recognition on the part of the church that certain books were, in fact, useful in nourishing the faith and life of the church. Official action, when it finally occurred, was more of the nature of approval of what was already recognized to be true than the initiation of something new. We could say that the New Testament took shape from the bottom up rather than from the top down.

The process was gradual, and it did not proceed uniformly in all parts of the church. In the fourth century AD, for example, the churches in Syria seem to have recognized only seventeen books, while the church in Ethiopia was using thirty-four books. Or take the matter of particular books such as Hebrews and Revelation: in the third and early fourth centuries, the churches in the eastern Roman Empire accepted Hebrews and rejected Revelation, while the churches in the West accepted Revelation and rejected Hebrews.

Although the first list of books to agree completely with our present New Testament did not appear until AD 367, there was general agreement in the church at large on the majority of the present twenty-seven by the end of the second century. The remaining disagreements focused on one or more of the books from Hebrews to Revelation. Evidence indicates that for a century or two after AD 367 some variation of opinion continued to exist on a few of these books.

The need for some clarification with regard to the relative significance of individual writings within the ever-growing mass of existing Christian literature may have been underscored by various developments during the first several centuries. We may call attention to the influential figure of Marcion, who was expelled from the church in AD 144 for heretical teaching. But his influence lived on for a long time as a powerful challenge to the church both in the East and the West. He made his own collection of authoritative writings, rejecting the Old Testament and editing what he accepted from among Christian writings. If Marcion's bible could not be accepted, then what should be?

When the church came to make its selection of authoritative documents, what criteria did it use? Unfortunately, no clear discussion of this matter is available to us. Perhaps the guidelines were more implicit and intuitive than explicit and rational, and the church used no set of consciously formulated principles. Nevertheless, certain things can be said.

First, it is clear that to some extent the matter of apostolic authorship, or at least association with an apostle, was regarded as important for establishing the authority of a given writing. For example, the church in the East accepted Hebrews because it was believed to be from the pen of Paul. The church in the West, on the contrary, did not regard it as Pauline and rejected it. The association of a book with an apostle gave it an advantage over others for which no such claim was made or recognized. But what is the meaning of this criterion? Professor John Knox has argued that its significance can be expressed in the word *proximity*. The apostles stood in a close relationship to Jesus and the events at the basis of the Christian faith; their testimony, therefore, is more authoritative than that of a person more removed in time and space from such an association.

Doubtless this claim contains a measure of truth. Since Reformation times, a doctrine of special inspiration is usually associated with the authorship of books accepted into the canon. It is a curious fact that while such a claim was developed by Judaism in relation to the establishment of the Old Testament canon at the end of the first century AD, the church made no comparable claim for the various lists of New Testament books it drew up in the early centuries. The reason may well be that they regarded all Christians as having the Holy Spirit. The problem, therefore, was not the extent of inspiration—as in the case of the Jewish community, where inspiration was widely believed to have ceased with Ezra; consequently, books appearing after his time could not claim to be inspired. The issue in the early church was rather the standard of inspiration. To suggest as much does not remove the matter of inspiration from a discussion of the canon, but it does change somewhat the perspective from which it is viewed.

Second, if apostolic authorship was a factor in the acceptance of a book as authoritative by the church, it was not the only criterion. Many writings appeared in the second and third centuries which laid claim to apostolic authorship but which were rejected by the church for inclusion in the canon. The reason they were rejected was because their contents did not ring true to the living faith of the church transmitted in the Christian community from the earliest days of the church. In the end, this test was decisive.

What is the significance of the canon for the church today? Why should the present twenty-seven books, no more and no less, compose our New Testament? If God is still active in the world, should not new documents occasionally be added to or perhaps be substituted for those presently there? Christians frequently raise these questions.

Several things may be said in reply. First, the canon was closed long ago by the church, and it is not likely that it will be opened again unless some new documents would come to light that could be established as authentically apostolic. Even if that should happen, it is not probable that the heart of the gospel would be affected. Second, the present New Testament materials play an indispensable role in the life of the church as the primary documents of the Christian faith. Classical Christian writings from later periods cannot perform this function, because they in turn depend on the New Testament for their significance. Finally, although the New Testament canon embraces twenty-seven books, most Christians actually operate with "a canon within the canon." That is, the Gospel of Mark or Paul's letter to the Romans plays a more central role than does Jude or 2 Peter. Although some books may be more marginal than others, each in its own way makes an important contribution to a full and adequate understanding of the Christian faith.

What is a gospel?

Imagine a non-Christian librarian in Rome about AD 70 holding in his hands for the first time a copy of the Gospel of Mark. What would he make of it? Would he regard it as worth cataloging? If so, how would he classify it? Would it belong to the section on history, biography, religious drama, or some other standard category? Would he, perhaps, be completely baffled and conclude that it fitted in none of the existing slots? If so, what sort of a niche would the librarian create for it?

It is difficult for us to recapture the sense of surprise that must have attended such a person's first encounter with such a document. We have trouble imagining it, both because of our long distance from AD 70 and because of our long familiarity with the Gospels. For all its possible similarities with writings already at hand, a gospel was a novel piece. Indeed, it is the one new literary form that the Christian community created and contributed to the ancient world.

Just how new it was we will need to explore. But before we do so, let us give some attention to the word *gospel* as a title for a book. We do not know what title originally stood over any of the first four books of our New Testament. It is not likely that the word *gospel* was a part of such constructions, except perhaps in the case of Mark. Scholars disagree about whether Mark 1:1 was intended as a title for the entire book or as a caption only for the account of John the Baptist's ministry.

Probably the earliest clear use of the term *gospel* as a designation for written records of Jesus' life comes from the pen of Justin Martyr in the middle of the second century AD. He refers to the memoirs that the apostles composed and says that they are called gospels. Although he offers no specific details, likely Justin knew and referred to our present four New Testament Gospels. By the last quarter of the second century, there are explicit references to four gospels, as well as to the fourfold gospel, which securely tie the word to our present documents.

What then is a gospel? We can arrive at the answer to this question only by an examination of the documents that came to bear this designation. As we shall see, a considerable number of writings in the early centuries of the church were known as gospels, but only four were finally included in the New Testament. We may take these four as the basis for arriving at some understanding of what a gospel is. To be sure, even these differ more or less among themselves. But in spite of their differences, they have more in common with one another than they do generally with the noncanonical gospels.

How then should we broadly characterize our New Testament Gospels? First, they are documents about Jesus of Nazareth. Many other people appear in their pages, but he is the central figure. Second, they are brief documents. Perhaps the closest ancient parallel is *The Life of Apollonius of Tyana* by Philostratus, written in the early part of the third century AD. This account, however, is thirty-five times the length of the Gospel of Mark. Third, the language and style are popular, direct, and fresh. They are free from the pompousness, emptiness, and hollowness of much of the contemporary literature. Amos N. Wilder notes that the speech of the Gospel represents "a purification of language."

Fourth, the Gospels are essentially story documents. They are not biographies in either the ancient or the modern sense of the word. They contain biographical information, but the authors' purpose did not seem to be to write a full life-story of Jesus. Mark and John, for example, have no interest at all in the ancestry, birth, childhood, and education of Jesus, while some of these elements are present in Matthew and Luke. The evangelists display no great concern for matters of chronology, geographical setting, the physical characteristics of the main character, and other features that normally belong to biography. Fifth, within the story framework of the Gospels there are sayings, short stories, dialogues, parables, miracle stories, genealogies, and poems. Not all of these elements are found in all of the Gospels, and they also vary in both the quantities and the arrangements of the materials that do occur in each. For example, Mark has a minimum of sayings material; Matthew has grouped the sayings into five panels; Luke has largely concentrated the teaching of Jesus in the framework of the Galilee-to-Jerusalem journey; John lacks the interest in the parables shown by the other three.

Sixth, although the Gospels do not all report the beginnings of Jesus' life, all exhibit considerable interest in his arrest, trial, crucifixion, and resurrection. The Gospels are more than manuals of Jesus' teachings or reminiscences of what he did during his ministry: they also report what happened to him. The story ends in a tale that combines elements of cruelty, compassion, dedication, death, disappointment, surprise, mystery, life, fear, and joy—all in a restrained but powerful way. Seventh, each of the Gospels is anonymous. Tradition has assigned them to particular authors, but the accounts themselves are nameless. The tradition they enshrine is the common property of the church rather than the possession of any individual.

> The testimony of eyewitnesses to Jesus' life and ministry was important for Christian faith—because the faith of the church depended not on timeless ideas but on what was once said and done by a historical figure. This witness needed to be preserved against both unconscious and deliberate distortions.

Other observations could easily be added to this list if a detailed or individual characterization of the four Gospels were attempted. Perhaps, however, enough has been said to mark out in a general way some of the more obvious common features of these documents. It should be clear that they are not ordinary biographies, manuals of ethics, theological tracts, or religious dramas. But in order to understand more clearly what they are, something must be said about how and why they were written.

We must not forget that the Gospels were the product of a living, witnessing, growing Christian community. Our oldest Gospel was not written until about thirty-five or forty years after the church began. If this dating is correct, the church had already spread not only throughout Palestine and Syria, but also westward throughout Asia Minor and southeastern Europe. It may also have penetrated Egypt and the lands to the east of Palestine. In any case, the great contributions of Peter and Paul had been made. The church was no longer a solely Jewish community but probably numbered more Gentiles than Jews in its ranks. The rapid and far-flung expansion of the Christian movement meant encounter with many new situations. The church faced new problems and challenges, both internally and externally—all without any of our present Gospels. The vital faith and remarkable missionary enthusiasm of the church was nourished by a fund of living oral tradition about the life and ministry, death and resurrection of Jesus. This tradition consisted of the memories of those who knew him, especially the apostles.

Why then were the Gospels written? Specific factors eventually made the reduction of the oral tradition to written form desirable. One of these was the gradual disappearance of the eyewitnesses to Jesus' life and ministry. Their witness was important for Christian faith because the faith of the church depended not on timeless ideas but on what was once said and done by a historical figure. This witness needed to be preserved against both unconscious and deliberate distortions. That preservation could best be done in written form. Again there was the matter of translating from one language into another. The native tongue of Jesus and his disciples was a Semitic one, Aramaic. Beyond Palestine, Greek was the common language. The hazards of translation are well known; these are multiplied if the translation process is restricted to an oral medium. Written Greek documents would be highly useful and desirable. Moreover, the functional requirements of Christian worship, the instruction of converts, the communication and defense of the faith—to mention only a few aspects of the ongoing life of the church—could be met more easily and adequately if the tradition were in written form. Such pragmatic considerations must be given due recognition.

These and other factors eventually led to the appearance of our Gospels. What is important to remember, however, is that the present unique form of these documents is shaped partly by the character of the oral tradition available to the evangelists and partly by the needs of the respective situations in which they did their work.

We have been dealing thus far with the Gospels in our New Testament. But as already noted, these were not the only gospels to be written in the first several centuries. A considerable number of additional ones are known to us—some in fragments, others in their entirety. (These are conveniently available in *New Testament Apocrypha*, vol. 1, edited by Wilhelm Schneemelcher and others.) How is it that these gospels did not get into the New Testament canon?

Several reasons may be offered. Compared with those that did get in, these books are incomplete. Some of them deal with the infancy period of Jesus' life; others deal with the passion and resurrection; still others, such as the *Gospel of Thomas*, are concerned only with the teaching of Jesus. None of them approximate the coverage of our present Gospels. Moreover, the contents of these books differ more or less in character from our New Testament Gospels. In the infancy gospels, the boy Jesus performs spectacular miracles that confound his playmates. The passion gospels contain imaginative constructions of Jesus' descent into hell or what happened at the resurrection.

Although these books claimed to be written by apostles or disciples of Jesus, they were not taken up into the canon because their message did not ring true to the living faith of the church. This faith, born out of and shaped by the witness of the apostles to Jesus, found an echo of authenticity in the four Gospels now included in our New Testament that is not found in the other gospels. We might say that these writings excluded themselves by virtue of what they were. To understand fully the significance of this point, these writings need only be read alongside the church's four Gospels.

The origin of Christmas

In the modern church calendar, Christmas is a very important day. In many ways it seems to get more attention than Good Friday or Easter. It is the occasion for programs and festivities that often require weeks of preparation. To be sure, much of the celebration may be only remotely connected with the remembrance of Jesus' birth. But the total effect is to highlight in our consciousness the prominent place of Christmas in the yearly cycle of our lives.

Of course, everyone from the small child to the oldest adult knows the calendar date of Christmas. We may be troubled by the fact that chronological tables put the birth of Jesus in 4 BC or somewhat earlier and wonder why this is so. The answer to this question, however, is not difficult: the medieval monk Dionysius Exiguus, who in the sixth century drew up a calendar that proposed to reckon time from the year of Jesus' birth, made a mistake in his calculations.

The case is otherwise, however, with December 25. There is, of course, no immediate evidence to raise a question about its accuracy. The only data readily at hand that might do so is Luke's reference to shepherds tending their sheep when the news of Jesus' birth was made known to them (Luke 2:8). Palestinian shepherds were not abroad with their flocks in late December, for the rainy season normally begins in late October or November and continues until April. The weather in late December in the hill country can be cold, with frost at night being common. If Jesus was born on December 25, the weather must have been unusually mild.

It is when we begin to inquire about the history of the celebration of December 25 as the birthday of Jesus that we come upon some surprising information. We may begin by noting that one branch of the Christian church, the Armenian, has never observed this date. These Christians celebrate Jesus' birth on January 6. Otherwise, today the practice of all the major branches of the church is uniform.

Moving backward in time, this uniformity of practice around December 25 goes back to about the sixth century, and prior to that a diversity of dates seems to have been observed.

> By celebrating the birth of Jesus on December 25, the date of the chief festival of the Roman cult of sun-worship, early Christians meant to witness to their faith that it was not the sun god but the Son of God who is the true light that enlightens the world and banishes the darkness of sin from human life.

What is even more surprising is that the December 25 tradition fades out completely in the early part of the fourth century. There is no definite evidence that the birth of Jesus was celebrated on December 25 until around AD 336, although the actual practice may be somewhat older. Not only is there considerable variation of opinion about the date of Jesus' birth when we go back beyond the fourth century, but there is also no evidence that Christians were even really concerned about determining a date until the latter part of the second century.

The New Testament literature indicates no interest either in establishing the date or in its celebration. Clement of Alexandria, writing in the latter part of the second century, is the first writer in the church to give evidence of such interest. His own date for the birth of Jesus is November 18, but he notes that some others prefer May 20. Other sources mention still other dates, such as March 28, April 2, and April 19. Most of the dates proposed belong to the spring of the year—as can be seen from this listing; there seems to have been a preference for spring dates.

We have already noted that the church of Armenia throughout its history has preferred January 6 to any other date. Indeed, this date was widely observed in the ancient church prior to the adoption of December 25. How did the church come to select this day? The choice was not the result of clear historical memory but of other considerations. In an essay on the origin of Christmas in his book *The Early Church*, Oscar Cullmann has set these out. What follows is much indebted to his discussion.

In the earliest period, the church's attention concentrated on Good Friday and Easter as the great festivals of the Christian faith. Indeed, early Christians highlighted the importance of the resurrection not only by the annual Easter celebration but also by the shift of the weekly day of worship from Saturday to Sunday. Every Lord's Day was a reminder of Christ's victory of life over death. Christians may even have had a certain aversion to the celebration of birthdays because of the Roman custom of celebrating the emperor's birthday. At any rate, in the third century Origen objected to the custom as being pagan.

The church attached significance to the day of death, not of birth. The uniqueness of Jesus and his work for Christian faith made it inevitable, however, that in time some attention would be given to his entrance into the world. When theological reflection turned to this matter, two positions developed. The one was to become the orthodox view; the other would be rejected as heretical.

To understand the development of the Christmas festival, we need to begin with the heretical speculations that took shape in Egypt in the second century. During this period Christians there made various attempts to combine Christianity with other modes of thought. Some of these systems attached significance to the baptism of Jesus as the point at which whatever uniqueness was assigned to him had its beginning. One such teacher was Basilides of Alexandria, who was influential during the reign of Hadrian (AD 117–138). His followers celebrated the baptism of Jesus on January 6. The festival was called Epiphany from the Greek word for "appearing." The reference, however, was not to the birth of Jesus but to the beginning of what was really important about him.

Why did these people celebrate the baptism of Jesus on January 6? This date is not derived from the New Testament, which is silent on this matter. It may have been chosen in conscious opposition to a celebration held in Alexandria on the night of January 5 and the morning of January 6 in honor of the birth of the god Aeon from the virgin goddess Kore. The participants stayed awake all night making music with songs and flutes to the goddess in the temple of Kore. At the crowing of the cock, they descended by torchlight into a subterranean shrine and brought out a wooden image of the newborn god, which they then carried about in procession accompanied with music. When the procession finished, they returned the image again to the crypt of the temple.

Participants believed that on the night of January 5 and 6, the waters of the Nile possessed special miraculous power. This belief might lend additional appropriateness to the celebration of Jesus' baptism on this date. Over against the other celebrations of the day, the followers of Basilides memorialized that moment when Jesus, having been baptized in the waters of the Jordan, was addressed from heaven with the words, "You are my Son, the Beloved" (Luke 3:22). For them it was on this occasion that the human Jesus was equipped for his special function in the world.

Thus far we have been dealing with the Basilideans and their observance of January 6 as the occasion of Jesus' baptism, which for them was of highest significance. How did this date become the occasion for the widespread celebration of the birth of Jesus in orthodox Christian circles? The answer is that orthodox Christians took it over from the followers of Basilides, even though his teaching was condemned as heretical. But orthodox Christians were not content to make the baptism of Jesus the beginning point of the truly significant Jesus, as did their opponents. They took their cue from the nativity stories in the Gospels of Matthew and Luke and went back to his birth. For them, his birth was the point of origin of what was important about him. Thus, while taking over the original baptismal festival from the heretics, they now added to it the celebration of the birth of Jesus. At any rate, the festival of the Epiphany had this significance as it was observed in the Christian church in Egypt, Palestine, and elsewhere at the beginning of the fourth century. Available liturgical materials used in the celebration of this feast at that time bear testimony to this fact.

If the birth of Jesus was celebrated along with his baptism on January 6, how did it happen that the birth festival was separated from the baptismal celebration and moved to December 25? Many scholars believe that the separation likely took place in Rome during the fourth century, although this practice was not followed in Egypt and Palestine until later. There is evidence that probably as early as AD 336 the Roman church celebrated the birth of Jesus on December 25. How much earlier they may have done so is not clear, nor are the details of the separation available to us.

Apparently, however, both theological and practical considerations were involved. From a theological point of view, the Council of Nicaea in AD 325 spelled out the meaning of orthodox thinking about the person of Christ. It insisted on the deity of Jesus from his birth and condemned those who did not subscribe to this view. Obviously, this conviction excluded an understanding of Jesus that regarded him as a mere man or that attached the beginning of whatever special significance he may have had to the moment of his baptism. It no longer, therefore, seemed theologically appropriate to celebrate both the birth of Jesus and also his baptism in one festival. Because there was no reason to change the date of the baptismal observance, the birth celebration was moved to another time.

But why did they choose December 25 as an appropriate date? A practical consideration seems to have been influential in the decision. In the early centuries of the Christian era, a cult of sun-worship was widespread in the Roman world. Its chief festival fell on December 25. Because Christ is repeatedly represented in the New Testament under the symbol of light, and the church came to regard the prophecy of Malachi 4:2 ("the sun of righteousness shall rise, with healing in its wings") as fulfilled in Christ, what more appropriate date could be found for the celebration of his birth than December 25?

By this Christian festival these early Christians meant to witness to their faith that it was not the sun god but the Son of God who is the true light that enlightens the world and banishes the darkness of sin from human life. As Ambrose in the fourth century put it: "Christ is our new sun!" We, no more than the ancient church, know the exact day on which Jesus was born. But if their faith is ours and inspires our celebration of December 25, then it can indeed be a meaningful Christian festival.

The Gospel according to Luke

New Testament scholar F. C. Grant attempts to express a general reaction among Christians to the Gospel of Luke. "If we had to choose between them—God forbid!—there is little question which of the gospels many would prefer to keep and let the others pass into oblivion." Grant does not hesitate to suggest the reason for his own personal love for this Gospel: "It is Luke who brings us closest, of all the gospel writers, to the Jesus of history who is also the Lord of the church's faith." This book is great, according to Grant, because of the full, rich, and moving portrait of Jesus that it offers.

The uniqueness of this Gospel among the four New Testament Gospels can best be seen when it is compared with the others. For our purpose we may lay it alongside Mark and note a few of the more obvious differences. Some years ago, Roger Lloyd wrote a book entitled *The Private Letters of Luke.* They are bits of imaginary correspondence between Luke and other people known to us from the New Testament. One letter is addressed to Mark, after Luke first came into possession of a copy of Mark's Gospel.

Lloyd has Luke make two observations on the Gospel of Mark. One observation concerns the limited amount of material dealing with Jesus' teachings: Mark does not adequately "show people what [Jesus'] teaching was about the way Christians should behave and what their moral values ought to be. I know that he was not merely a teacher of ethics but he did teach ethics among other things."

The second comment in Luke's imaginary letter to Mark has to do with a certain lack of balance in the passion-resurrection narrative of Mark's Gospel. Mark has given a rather full account of the arrest, trial, and death of Jesus. But the resurrection narrative is brief. "The practical result of this fault of balance is that your story of the Passion of the Lord gives the impression of an event utterly grim, black and hopeless." This deficiency Luke also would remedy with an expanded resurrection narrative.

Turning from the end of the Gospel to the beginning, Luke has prefaced his account of John the Baptist's preparatory ministry with a lengthy, rich infancy narrative which serves in various ways to provide perspective on the story that follows. Luke's account of the Galilean ministry of Jesus is considerably shorter (about eighty-five verses) than that of Mark; this shortening has been achieved largely by Luke's omission of the materials found in Mark 6:45–8:26. Luke, however, has a much longer Galilee-to-Jerusalem travel section than Mark, who confines the journey to one chapter (10), while Luke devotes almost ten chapters to it. In this section of the book is concentrated much of the unique and memorable teaching material of the Gospel of Luke.

If Mark and Luke display formal differences of amount and arrangement of materials, they also differ in outlook and emphases. First, there is a broadness of vision in the scope of Jesus' ministry that has led some to describe Luke as "the universal gospel." At the beginning of the book the salvation which God has prepared in Jesus is said to be "a light for revelation to the Gentiles" as well as "for glory to . . . Israel" (2:32). The Gospel closes with a message of forgiveness for "all nations" (24:47). Between these two points this wide outlook is accented in a variety of ways.

In the second place, Luke has been called "the gospel of the underdog." In its pages one finds a genuine interest in the poor, the outcast, and the disinherited of earth. The dangers of wealth are repeatedly stressed; Jesus is seen to be the friend of the publicans and sinners.

Third, Luke is the gospel of joy and praise. At the beginning of the book Jesus' birth is announced as "good news of a great joy" (2:10). The last glimpse we get of the disciples is that of a band filled with "great joy" and "continually . . . blessing God" (24:52–53). But that is not all: "What a trumpet-note of joy, courage and triumph sounds through the whole Lukan history from the first to the last pages" (Adolf von Harnack).

Luke's Gospel was not the first to be written. He indicates that others before him had undertaken to draw up accounts of the life of Jesus (see Luke 1:1). Why then did Luke attempt to do the same? For information we are dependent on Luke's own words and on the general character of the document. According to his prologue, the book is dedicated to one called "most excellent Theophilus." A common opinion is that Theophilus belonged to the Roman aristocracy and was a man who had had some information about the Christian movement. It was Luke's intention to furnish a trustworthy account of the beginnings of this movement for him and for those whom he represented.

Helpful as this general statement is, it leaves many questions unanswered. Can the situation that Luke faced and what he hoped to accomplish be given more specific shape and content? At what points was there need for possible correction of or addition to the information about Jesus previously available? Did some particular problem need attention? If so, what was it, and how could it best be handled?

Such questions, insofar as they can be answered at all, must be dealt with on the basis of material in the book, first, in comparison with the other Gospels and, second, in relation to all that we know about the status of the Christian movement in relation to the broader political, cultural, and religious scene at the time when the Luke's Gospel was written. All attempts at such interpretations and reconstruction will necessarily fall short of demonstrable proof, as is evident from the variety of proposals that biblical scholars in our time have made. Let us note a few of these proposals.

A first interpretive approach is that Luke wished to vindicate the Christian movement in Roman eyes because of the suspicion under which it had fallen as the result of recent events in Rome and in Palestine. In AD 64, Nero charged the Roman Christians with setting fire to the city and severely persecuted them as enemies of the state. Two years later, the

> As the companion of Paul in his missionary work, Luke shared the concern to bring men and women to understand and embrace the gospel. Not the least important element in the pursuit of this passion was just the hope of telling the story of what happened in the ministry of Jesus.

great Jewish rebellion against Rome broke out in Palestine—
where the Christian movement had its origin under one who
had himself been crucified by Roman authorities, supposedly
as a political subversive. Was the Christian movement a threat
to the peace and well-being of the Roman Empire?

Those who believe that Luke is speaking to this question
point out that he goes out of his way to allay such fears. There
are four passages in the trial of Jesus where Luke alone, of the
first three Gospel writers, clearly indicates Pilate's belief in
Jesus' innocence of a capital crime against the state (see Luke
23:4, 14, 16, 22; compare to parallels in Matthew and Mark).
Likewise in Acts (which he also authored), Luke is at pains to
show that no political charge against the apostles is sustained
when it has been investigated by Roman officials (see Acts
16:39; 17:7–9; 18:14–17; 19:36–41; 23:28–29; 24:5; 25:25;
26:32; 28:30–31). Indeed, a Roman proconsul, Sergius Paulus,
instead of opposing the Christian faith, became an adherent of
it (Acts 13:12).

A second school of interpreters think Luke intended to
speak to the problem occasioned by some Jews' rejection of the
Christian gospel. Could Gentiles confidently accept a religion
that had been rejected by some of the very people among
whom it had arisen? Luke-Acts in its own way is a commentary
on the problem dealt with by Paul in Romans 9–11. Luke's
answer, within the Jewish hermeneutical debate, is that Jesus
fulfills the Jewish hope. In his view, the Old Testament fore-
shadows the inclusion of the Gentiles in the purposes of God as
well as the struggle that inclusion would entail for many Jews.
But, despite the struggle, Luke and Acts both clearly demonstrate that the opening of the door of faith to Gentiles was
under the guidance of the Spirit of God.

A third line of approach sees Luke's purpose in his two-
volume work as an attempt to show the relationship between
the Jesus of history and the Christian church. By following his
Gospel with Acts, Luke has built a bridge between these two
periods in a way the other evangelists have not. The Gospel of
Luke ends with the account of the resurrection and ascension
of Jesus. But this is not really the end of the story; it is only the
end of the beginning. This continuation is made clear in the

way Acts begins by returning to the resurrection and ascension as the prologue to the ongoing story of God's action through Jesus in history.

A fourth perspective is to understand Luke's purpose against the first-century background of questions about the nature of Christ or the delay of the return of Christ. Some were attracted to the spiritual Christ but had no real interest in the historical Jesus; Luke is said to be concerned to show that the spiritual Christ is none other than the Jesus of history. The tie between the two both in the Gospel and in Acts is provided by the disciples who witnessed Jesus' pre-passion ministry—and who then bear testimony that the risen Christ is indeed the Jesus they had known in Galilee and who had been crucified in Jerusalem.

A final way of viewing the purpose of Luke-Acts is to see it in relation to the plan of salvation. The plan consists of two parts: what Jesus began to do during the days of his earthly ministry (the Gospel), and what he now continues to do in the world (Acts). The continuing story of his activity in the world (Acts) is a way of confirming the truth of the beginning of the story (the Gospel) to those who were not personally eyewitnesses of that part of salvation history.

From this brief report of some modern ways of understanding the purpose of Luke in his Gospel, it is evident that the evidence can be read in various ways. Without denying that Luke may have had one or more such specific objectives in mind as he wrote, perhaps we should not attempt to define his purpose in a too-sharp or too-exclusive manner. It is an amazing fact that his story has been useful in meeting a great variety of needs both in the internal life and in the missionary outreach of the church from the first century to the present. Surely as the companion of Paul in his missionary work, Luke shared the concern to bring men and women to understand and embrace the gospel. Not the least important element in the pursuit of this passion was just the hope of telling the plain story of what happened in the ministry of Jesus.

The message of the Fourth Gospel

"No man could in a lifetime write all I now see; how can I put it into one book?" So said Henry Ward Beecher in 1886 about *The Life of Jesus Christ*, on which he was then working. This feeling must also be familiar to anyone who, having lingered long over the pages of the Fourth Gospel, attempts to summarize its message in a brief essay.

Fortunately, however, the key ideas of this Gospel are not many. Instead of spreading his interest widely, the author has chosen to focus on a few themes that are developed throughout the Gospel. To these themes he makes a return again and again, from various points of view and in different contexts.

We observe many striking differences between the Fourth Gospel and the Synoptics (Matthew, Mark, Luke), but we would be wrong to suggest a basic cleavage in message. John does not offer another gospel in the sense of a different gospel: there is only one gospel in the whole of the New Testament—indeed, in the Bible. Nevertheless, new vistas open on the gospel from the pages of this book. What is more or less implicit in the Synoptics is here, on occasion, made explicit. New dimensions of the gospel are explored, some new vocabulary is employed, and distinctive emphases emerge. The Gospel of John enables us to see a bit more of the multicolored richness of the Christ-event.

How then shall we characterize the message of the Fourth Gospel? All the major themes of the book are introduced in the prologue (John 1:1–18). The remainder of the Gospel may be viewed as an expanded commentary on the prologue. Another way of stating the relationship would be to regard the prologue as a summary of the book.

Four themes in the prologue may be singled out for notice. The first of these is *the Word*. These words introduce the main subject of the book. The term, of course, has a precise meaning: it points not to an idea but to a person. The heart of the gospel is not a thought but an event, the advent of a presence. In consequence, the message of the book is essentially a story rather than a discussion.

Now, interestingly enough, "the Word" as a title for Jesus appears only in the prologue. In the remainder of the Fourth Gospel, Jesus speaks the word; he is the one also to whom the written Word (the Old Testament) bears witness. But in the prologue Jesus *is* the Word. The term here is likely a bridge-word employed to make contact with the mind of the reader. In the larger world at the end of the first century, the Greek term *logos* ("word") was common in religious and philosophical circles. People were talking about the *logos*. The word was in the air. John latches on to this interest: "Let me tell you," he says, "what the *logos* is. It is none other than he whom we have come to know in history as Jesus of Nazareth!" But after this identification has been made, the title is dropped. The subject has been introduced. The stage is now set for the story that follows in the book itself.

> John does not offer another gospel in the sense of a different gospel: there is only one gospel in the whole of the New Testament—indeed, in the Bible. Nevertheless, new vistas open on the gospel from the pages of this book.

The second great theme of the prologue is that of *witness*. If Jesus is the central character of the story, his person and role must be understood. The spotlight focuses on him from many quarters, and he is seen in a variety of ways. Who are the witnesses that bear testimony to him? Among them are John the Baptist (1:6–7, 15, 19–27, 29, 35–36; 3:28–30; 5:33–35; 10:41), the Father (5:37; 8:18; 12:28–29), the Old Testament Scriptures (5:39), Jesus' works (5:36; 10:25, 37–38), and the Holy Spirit (15:26; 16:13–14). Not least among the witnesses are the disciples and those touched in one way or another by his ministry. What a great company it is! Virtually every page of the Fourth Gospel offers one or more of such testimonies.

And what testimony is borne to Jesus? No simple answer is adequate, for the witness is wide in scope and rich in content. Broadly speaking, it falls into two types: the witness concerning his person, and the witness relative to his function. In regard to the first, it is clear that Jesus was truly human, "the Word became flesh." So authentically human was Jesus that he grew weary in travel (4:6), shed tears of grief over the death of a friend (11:35), and lived daily in dependence on his Father (5:19, 8:28–29, 12:49).

Equally clear, however, is another dimension of his person. He is more than "bone of our bone and flesh of our flesh"; Jesus is the Son of God in a unique sense. The Word that became flesh was the Word that shared in the Godhead (1:1). Jesus could say, "The Father and I are one" (10:30) or, "He who has seen me has seen the Father" (14:9). "He had come from God" to tarry for a short time among humanity and then "was going to God" (13:3). His role is variously described: the light of the world (8:12), the revealer of the unseen God (1:18), the giver of life (10:10), "the Lamb of God, who takes away the sin of the world" (1:29), the judge of humanity (5:22), the way to God (14:6), the resurrection and the life (11:25)—to mention only a few of the many ways in which his function is portrayed.

But Jesus' mission in the world was not without qualification; the witness borne to him did not become automatically effective. With this observation we come to the third great theme of the Fourth Gospel: *human response*. The response is twofold: acceptance and rejection, or faith and unbelief. "He came to what was his own, and his own people did not accept him. But to all who received him, who believed in his name, he gave power to become children of God" (1:11–12). This twofold response can be traced throughout the book.

The presence of Jesus confronts men and women with the crisis of decision. They must make up their minds about him. The person of Jesus in the Fourth Gospel undergoes no development (as in the Synoptics); the portrait remains constant from beginning to end. What development there is in this Gospel occurs in the lives of those who come into contact with Jesus. It is conditioned on their response to Jesus. Some go on to faith and life; others prefer the darkness of unbelief that leads to death.

The purpose for which Jesus came was not "to condemn the world, but in order that the world might be saved through him" (3:17). But throughout the Fourth Gospel we see many who are not being saved. Why is this so? Some passages in the book seem to speak in terms of predestination (see 6:37, 44, 64–65; 10:26; 12:39–40). These passages, however, are balanced by many others that invite men and women to faith (see 4:1–26; 6:28–29, 35, 40; 7:37; 8:12; 9:35–37; 10:27–28; 11:25–26; 12:25–26). Indeed, people are responsible for their unbelief (see 5:40). They prefer the darkness to the light (3:19); they love the praise of others more than the glory that comes from God (5:44; 12:43). Taken as a whole, the Fourth Gospel comes down on the side of freedom and responsibility. Indeed, the book would never have been written had the author not held this view of our relationship to the mission of Jesus (see 20:30–31).

The response that the Fourth Gospel hopes to elicit is described by the verb *believe*. Interestingly, the word *faith* does not occur in the entire book. The verb *believe* throws emphasis on the dynamic character of the relationship between the individual and Christ; the relationship cannot be reduced to a static entity that can be kept as a treasure in a chest. As is the case with all personal relationships, it is spiritual in character, and it exists only as our surrender to Christ is daily reaffirmed.

Our response to Christ is decisive for our destiny: "Whoever believes in the Son has eternal life; whoever disobeys the Son will not see life, but must endure God's wrath" (3:36). God "has given all judgment to the Son" (5:22), and "the hour is coming when all who are in their graves will hear his voice and will come out—those who have done good, to the resurrection of life, and those who have done evil, to the resurrection of condemnation" (5:28–29). But that final judgment will not be arbitrary: it will simply be a confirmation of the judgment that we are now passing on ourselves in our response to the light that has come into the world in Christ.

This judgment helps explain the note of urgency so prominent in the book: "The light is with you for a little longer. Walk while you have the light, so that the darkness may not overtake you. . . . While you have the light, believe in the light, so that you may become children of light" (12:35–36). Response in the present moment, rather than in the past or the future, is of critical importance in shaping destiny. Is it the face or the back that is now turned toward Christ?

It is God's intention and the author's hope that the response will be one of faith. The Fourth Gospel was written for that purpose: if and when this response is made, what then? Here we come to the fourth great theme of the book, one that may be expressed in the word *experience*. "From his fullness have we all received, grace upon grace" (1:16): this experience is comprehensively described by the term *life*, which is one of the characteristic words of the Fourth Gospel. Jesus came that men and women "may have life, and have it abundantly" (10:10). To inspire belief in Jesus as the Christ, the Son of God, is the immediate purpose of the book. The ultimate purpose, however, is that through faith in Jesus men and women "may have life in his name" (20:31).

The life of which the Fourth Gospel speaks and to which it points is called "eternal life." It has its source in God, it is the life for which we have been made, and it is life in fellowship with God. As such it is a present reality, but it is not bounded by time or space. Death cannot touch it. It was in the presence of death that Jesus said, "I am the resurrection and the life. Those who believe in me, even though they die, will live, and everyone who lives and believes in me shall never die" (11:25). Here is life with length, breadth, and depth beyond all that we can imagine! It is to this great gift that the Fourth Gospel invites us.

Messiahship in a new key

One of the most momentous days for Jesus and for his disciples came near the close of his ministry. The setting was north of Galilee in the district of Caesarea Philippi. The disciples had been exposed to Jesus, his teachings, and his deeds, over a prolonged period of time. What did they think of him? Did their perceptions correspond with his self-understanding and intentions? Jesus wanted to know, so he put to them the question: "Who do you say that I am?" (Mark 8:29).

Peter, as always, was ready with an answer: "You are the Messiah." Jesus did not reject the title; neither did he probe Peter's meaning. But he did forbid public proclamation of what Peter had just said. More importantly, Jesus proceeded to unveil a frightening future for himself—one of rejection, suffering, and death. For this Peter was not prepared. His response was forthright and firm: "God forbid it, Lord! This must never happen to you" (Matt. 16:22). Jesus' reply must have startled Peter even more: "Get behind me, Satan! For you are setting your mind not on divine things but on human things" (Mark 8:33).

Peter's reaction to Jesus' announcement of impending suffering and death is understandable, for it was in keeping with his view of messiahship. To be sure, the messianic beliefs of first-century Judaism varied considerably. But the dominant conception among the rank and file of Palestinian Jews was of a political, national, even military leader. The messiah would be a second David who would again bring freedom from foreign oppression and usher in an era of material and spiritual well-being in a restored national state. Power, triumph, freedom, plenty, glory—these were essential ingredients in popular messianic hopes. Peter's expectations were probably no exception.

Jesus did not share Peter's dream. Does this mean that he refused to think of himself and his mission as in any sense messianic? That would be putting it too strongly. Various elements in the gospel tradition, to say nothing of the clear conviction of the early church, suggest that Jesus had some kind of messianic awareness and status. It is equally clear, however, that Jesus did not buy into the conventional mentality. He was uncomfortable with the prevailing model. In his hand, messiahship was to become a new creation. The reconstruction would be spelled out in the totality of what he was and did. Peter and his fellow disciples would have to learn to think about messiahship in a new key.

What then is the shape and style of Jesus' messiahship? We may begin with the matter of terminology. Returning to Jesus' response to Peter's confession, we note a change of titles for Jesus. Whereas Peter called Jesus "the Messiah," Jesus response referred to himself as "the Son of Man." This change may not at first appear significant, yet it is a part of a larger pattern: others may refer to Jesus as the Messiah, but his own favorite self-designation is the phrase, *the Son of Man*.

The source and meaning of this title have been matters of endless debate. Most likely, Jesus drew it from the vision found in the Aramaic version of Daniel 7:1–14, where the scene is one of judgment meted out on the beast who has "a mouth speaking arrogantly." The judge is described as "an Ancient One" (v. 9). To this venerable figure came another, "like a Son of Man" riding on "the clouds of heaven" (v. 13). To him the judge gave "dominion and glory and kingship . . . that shall not pass away, and . . . shall never be destroyed" (v. 14).

The vision is followed by an interpretation in Daniel 7:15–28. The Ancient of Days represents God; the king who speaks "words against the Most High" is not expressly named but is usually thought to be Antiochus Epiphanes (175–164 BC), whose oppression and persecution of the Jews precipitated the Maccabean revolt in 168 BC. The "one like a Son of Man" to whom a kingdom is given in the vision is now identified as "the holy ones of the Most High" (vv. 18, 22, 27). The "one like a Son of Man" thus appears in the vision as an individual figure, but in the interpretation is given a corporate reference.

The imagery is intended to point to the humanness of the one to whom God gives dominion; that humanness contrasts with the representation of world rulers as beasts. Note that the Son of Man symbolism is set in a context of suffering followed by vindication and dominion. The transition from oppression to triumph is not attributable to the initiative of the "one like a Son of Man" but is the gift of the Most High. The movement from the singular to the collective reference is probably not without significance when the phrase is picked up and used by Jesus.

When we turn to the New Testament, the phrase as a title for Jesus occurs almost without exception on his own lips. It appears once in Acts on the lips of the dying Stephen (7:56; see also Rev. 1:13; 14:14). Apparently it was not a current title for Jesus in the early church. Furthermore, in the Gospels the title is ascribed to Jesus in sayings that have to do with his pre-passion ministry (Mark 2:10, 28; Luke 7:34; 9:58; 19:10); his suffering, death, and resurrection (Mark 8:31; 10:45; 14:21, 41); and his future exaltation, return, and judging activity (Mark 8:38; 13:26; 14:62; Luke 18:8; Matt. 19:28).

> No Palestinian Jew of the first century would have regarded one who suffered a death of the kind Jesus endured to be a suitable candidate for a messianic role. The Messiah was expected to vanquish his enemies; he was not expected to be done in by them. It was for this reason that Peter at Caesarea Philippi could not tolerate Jesus' announcement of his passion.

Why did Jesus employ this title for himself, and what did he mean by it? The phrase does not have a messianic meaning in Daniel 7:13. In the first century or later, in certain circles of Judaism, the title apparently designated a heavenly redeemer figure, but it was not a common messianic title in the conventional sense (see John 12:34). Why Jesus chose to use it for himself we can only guess; no explanation is given in the Gospels. The phrase as found in Daniel symbolizes the suffering-vindicated people of God. Their destiny was now to be played out par excellence in his vocation and suffering.

If Jesus derived his favorite self-designation from Daniel 7:13, he was not solely dependent on this passage for the understanding of his messianic mission. Although he avoided the public use of the title *Messiah*, messianic texts were not foreign to his consciousness. Of special interest is the heavenly voice on the occasion of his baptism: "You are my Son, the Beloved; with you I am well pleased" (Mark 1:11). Many scholars believe that the first part of this utterance echoes the line in Psalm 2:7 in which the LORD addresses the Israelite king on the occasion of his enthronement: "You are my son." This psalm was interpreted messianically in Judaism. If this reconstruction is correct, then a messianic vocation was affirmed for Jesus at the inauguration of his ministry.

But this observation must be qualified by another. The second part of the heavenly utterance—"with you I am well pleased"—is widely believed to reflect God's address to the servant of the LORD in Isaiah 42:1–4 as the one "in whom my soul delights." Isaiah 42:1–4 is the first of four servant poems in Isaiah 40–55 that constitute a high-water mark in Old Testament theology. (The other servant passages are Isaiah 49:1–6; 50:4–9; and 52:13–53:12.) The servant seems to be a fluid image, sometimes representing the whole of Israel (49:3) but more often distinguished from the larger community and having a mission both to it and also to the Gentile world. The well-known fourth poem (52:13–53:12) is characterized by its vivid description of the vicarious redemptive sufferings of the servant.

Whether Jesus already anticipated suffering and death as the outcome of his mission when he stood on the threshold of his career is impossible to determine. But it is clear is that by the time his Galilean ministry was drawing to a close, that conviction had crystallized. And when it did, the image of the suffering servant in Isaiah was probably in the background of Jesus' thought.

There is only one explicit quotation from Isaiah 53 on the lips of Jesus in the first three Gospels. It is in Luke 22:37. In the discussion after the Last Supper, he quoted Isaiah 53:12: "For I tell you, this scripture must be fulfilled in me, 'And he was counted among the lawless'; and indeed what is written about me is being fulfilled." Beyond this direct link, an allusion to the fourth servant poem may perhaps be intended in the cup-saying at the Last Supper (Mark 14:24). There the imagery of covenant ratification, drawn from Exodus 24:8, is qualified by the phrase "of many" (see Isa. 53:12). A clearer allusion is likely to be found in the saying in Mark 10:45: "For the Son of Man came not to be served but to serve, and to give his life a ransom for many." This saying reflects the thought of Isaiah 53:10.

The New Testament church seems to have understood Jesus' ministry and death as a form of the servant in Isaiah. Matthew saw Jesus' ministry as the fulfillment of Isaiah 42:1–4 (Matt. 12:15–21). The reference to Jesus as God's servant in Acts 3:13, if not in 4:27, may have this background. Philip was able to speak to the Ethiopian eunuch about Jesus from Isaiah 53:7–8 (Acts 8:26–35). The passage in 1 Peter 2:23–25 clearly recalls Isaiah 53:5–6. It is possible, of course, that the church may have initiated this interpretation of Jesus' ministry. But more likely the roots of this association go back to Jesus' own self-understanding.

The impact of the servant image on Jesus should not be seen only in the limited data provided by the one direct quotation and the several allusions already noted. The general spirit and character of his ministry, issuing as it did in death followed by vindication, parallels the description of the servant. Jesus, like the servant, was endowed with the Spirit (Isa. 42:1); carried on his ministry without noisy fanfare (42:2); was gentle with the bruised and the weak (42:3); had an obedient ear (50:4–5); and was dedicated to the establishment of justice in the earth (52:1, 4), to bring Jacob back to the Lord (49:5), and to be a light to the Gentiles (49:6). In the pursuit of his mission, Jesus, like the servant, would suffer opposition, abuse, and eventual death (50:6–7; 53:3–5). But death was to issue in blessing for the undeserving (53:4–6). As he faced suffering, he believed that God would vindicate him (50:8); God would be truly glorified in him (49:3).

One could present extensive documentation of the servant pattern in the gospel tradition of the ministry, passion, and vindication of Jesus. To be sure, the fulfillment outran the model, but in any case, it did not contradict it. The story stands in contradiction to the conventional model of Jewish messiahship. At no point is this more clearly seen than in the voluntary vicarious suffering and death of Jesus on a Roman cross as one supposedly under the curse of both humanity and God. No Palestinian Jew of the first century would have regarded one who suffered a death of the kind Jesus endured to be a suitable candidate for a messianic role. The Messiah was expected to vanquish his enemies; he was not expected to be done in by them. It was for this reason that Peter at Caesarea Philippi could not tolerate Jesus' announcement of his passion.

But the cross was only the climax of a life and ministry that at many points were at variance with popular messianic expectations. Only a few features can be noted. First, Jesus' insistence on love for the enemy, although not unknown in Judaism, was not a feature of the messianic portrait. Second, the threat of the exclusion of some Jews from the coming kingdom and the inclusion of some Gentiles was not a plank in popular messianism (for example, Luke 4:16–30; Matt. 8:11). Likewise, the gift of the kingdom to the outcasts of Jewish society was an offense to the pious (for example, Luke 15). Finally, Jesus' lack of interest in "the land question," with its political implications, would not have been seen as character-istically messianic. For these and other reasons it is not surpris-ing that when the disciples reported what their contemporaries were saying about Jesus, they included no mention of the possibility that he was the Messiah (Mark 8:28).

According to the Gospel of John, when Pilate put the question to Jesus: "Are you the King of the Jews?" Jesus replied, "My kingdom is not from this world" (18:33, 36). Jesus did not mean to deny his kingship, nor did he mean that his reign has nothing to with this world. He meant to affirm that it was not the usual type. It was messianism in a new key, strange to Rome and Judea alike.

If the foregoing account of Jesus' messiahship is an accurate statement, we must not overlook its implications for defining the character of discipleship. Having spoken at Caesarea Philippi to what messiahship meant for him, Jesus immediately added a word about the pattern of discipleship for those who would follow him (Mark 8:34–38). The pattern is cut out of the same piece of cloth. That lesson was hard for the disciples to learn. It remains equally difficult for us!

Jesus as a miracle worker

If we could read the Gospel of Mark with fresh eyes, we might conclude that Jesus was essentially a miracle worker. The story of his public ministry is scarcely begun when we hear of Jesus in a Capernaum synagogue. The worshipers on that day were "astounded at his teaching," but no detail is given. What is spread out for the reader is the account of a miracle. Present in the assembly was "a man with an unclean spirit." Jesus promptly undertook to set him free from his bondage. The result was that all in the synagogue were amazed at what they saw. Then comes the summary remark: "At once his fame began to spread throughout the surrounding region of Galilee" (Mark 1:28).

Jesus' spreading fame was fueled by a series of additional miracles which take up the remainder of the first chapter. Peter's mother-in-law was cured of a fever (1:29–31). At sundown, when the Sabbath had ended, in a mass healing service "he cured many who were sick with various diseases, and cast out many demons" (1:32–34). Then the Gospel writer describes a tour of Galilean synagogues which included the casting out of demons (1:35–39). This section is followed by a detailed account of the healing of a leper (1:40–44). The chapter concludes with a summary statement portraying immense popularity: "Jesus could no longer go into a town openly, but stayed out in the country; and people came to him from every quarter" (1:45).

But chapter one is only the beginning of a miracle-studded story that spans the whole of Jesus' ministry until his final entry into Jerusalem. By some counts, no fewer than 209 of Mark's 661 verses (31 percent) deal with miracles. Matthew and Luke reproduce most of the miracles reported in Mark; each includes additional accounts and references. The Gospel of John describes eight miracles—but notes that Jesus performed many others that are not recorded there (John 20:30).

Impressive as this data is, it would be wrong to conclude that Jesus was primarily a miracle-worker. Two considerations prompt restraint. First, even in the Gospel of Mark it is evident that Jesus was widely recognized as a teacher. Mark begins his account of the Galilean ministry with a general descriptive statement that focuses on Jesus' preaching ministry rather than his miracles (Mark 1:14–15). No fewer than twelve times in the Gospel, Jesus is addressed as teacher. There are even more references to his teaching and preaching and, of course, excerpts of the same. His teachings are more fully represented in the Gospels of Matthew and Luke than in Mark.

Second, we find evidence that Jesus did not wish to be known basically as a miracle-worker. On various occasions he refused to produce miracles on demand from his audience (Mark 8:11–12; Luke 4:16–30; 23:8–9). This refusal was in keeping with a basic decision he made in the wilderness before beginning his public ministry (Matt. 4:1–11). Thus, while miracles did have an important place in his mission, they were neither the whole of it nor necessarily the dominant feature.

Let us turn from these general impressions and considerations to look more carefully at the miracle tradition in the Gospels. The miracles may be classified using the following four categories: physical healings, exorcisms, resuscitations, and nature miracles. The first two groups constitute the bulk of those reported in detail and those referred to more generally. There are three resuscitations and six or more nature miracles. It may be of interest to note that the first three groups are also represented in the life of the early church; only the fourth type is absent from Acts of the Apostles.

Miracle stories, however, are not confined to the ministry of Jesus or to the early church. They are found more broadly in the literature of the Old Testament in Judaism, and in the ancient world more generally. It is important, therefore, to ask if any distinctive features characterize the Gospel miracles. Several considerations are in order.

The first is a matter of terminology. The New Testament Gospels normally avoid the usual way the cultures of the day designated miracles, as astonishing or creating wonder. The first three Gospels regularly describe Jesus' miracles as "mighty works" (Mark 6:2, 5), using a Greek term from which the English words *dynamo* and *dynamite* are derived. It is a word associated with God in the Old and New Testaments; indeed, it can be a paraphrase for God (Mark 14:62). The miracles are concrete expressions of the power of God at work in Jesus. In the Gospel of John the miracles are called "signs." The deeds themselves do not exhaust their significance: they point to a reality "beyond." Both terms are meant to distinguish the miracles of Jesus from the mere wonders or prodigies of the ancient world.

> The most distinctive feature of Jesus' miracles is the context in which they were done. They were miracles of the kingdom. They are not to be seen as sharply separated from "the gospel of the kingdom" that Jesus proclaimed. In one sense, they bore authenticating witness to that message. They were "enacted parables" of the kingdom.

Second, the Gospel miracle stories are not characterized by the elements of magic and incantation so common in the healings and exorcisms of antiquity. Jesus used no herbs or medicines. Three times he employed spittle, the significance of which is difficult to determine. Touching or the laying on of hands is also mentioned in some healings. Prominent in the physical healings and especially in the exorcisms is the spoken word—simple and direct, but full of power. The unadorned word of Jesus, like the word of the Lord in the Old Testament, was charged with God's power to do his bidding (see Isa. 55:10–11). His contemporaries recognized this power in his words (see Luke 7:6–8).

In the third place, Jesus did not do miracles that hurt or punished people. He did nothing comparable to Elijah's calling down fire from heaven to consume more than a hundred men representing the king of Samaria (2 Kings 1:1–12). Indeed, when James and John suggested to Jesus that he deal with the inhospitable Samaritans in that manner, he rebuked them (Luke 9:51–55). The only exception to a positive use of miraculous power is the cursing of the fig tree (Mark 11:12–14). Whatever we make of that incident, it did not harm people.

Fourth, Jesus did not perform miracles to serve his own needs or for personal advantage. When he was hungry in the

Jesus as a miracle worker

wilderness, he rejected the temptations to satisfy his hunger by turning stones into bread (Matt. 4:2–3) and to enlist a following by performing a demonstration miracle (Matt. 4:5–7). Likewise, at the end of his ministry he refused to avail himself of miraculous protection from heaven to avoid arrest by the authorities (Matt. 26:53). The renunciation of personal gain stands in contrast to the spirit that motivated the magician Simon (Acts 8:9–24) and many others like him in the ancient world.

The most distinctive feature of Jesus' miracles is the context in which they were done. They were miracles of the kingdom. They are not to be seen as sharply separated from "the gospel of the kingdom" that Jesus proclaimed (Matt. 4:23). In one sense, they bore authenticating witness to that message (see Luke 5:18–26). They were "enacted parables" of the kingdom. In another and more profound sense, they were the gospel manifested in deed. The gospel was not only word, but word and deed.

That his miracles were signs and fragmentary embodiments of the kingdom may be seen clearly in Jesus' interpretation of the meaning of his exorcisms. In response to the criticism that he was in league with the prince of demons, Jesus pointed out the absurdity of the idea of Satan casting out Satan, and then he drew a more logical conclusion. "If it is by the finger of God that I cast out the demons, then the kingdom of God has come to you" (Luke 11:20). Similarly, in the exorcisms that his disciples performed, Jesus "watched Satan fall from heaven like a flash of lightning" (Luke 10:18). In the liberation of the demon-oppressed and possessed, the rule of God was being realized in the midst of history.

We should also view in this light the miracles of physical healing and the resuscitations. They were signs of the order yet to be, in which illness and death shall have no place (Rev. 21:3–4). But they were also preliminary, partial, and temporary glimpses of that future order already in the present age; the coming kingdom in its fullness was already casting its shafts of light backward into the shadows of the time before the end.

It is possible also to understand the significance of at least some of the nature miracles in a similar way. The stilling of the storm (Mark 4:35–41), for example, can be viewed against the background of imagery associated in the Old Testament with both creation and redemption. In Genesis 1:1–2, God in creating the world brings order out of the primeval chaotic waters. God then redeems Israel from the hand of the Egyptians at the Red Sea by crushing the symbolic figure, the dragon Rahab, who was the personification in ancient Near Eastern thought of primeval chaos (Isa. 51:9–10). In the full and final redemption at the end of time portrayed in Revelation, both the dragon and the sea disappear from view (Rev. 20:2, 10; 21:1). If read in this larger theological framework, Jesus' stilling of the storm carries overtones of meaning that can deepen our understanding of his person and his work.

Whether these meanings should be seen in these miracles may be a matter of scholarly dispute. It is clear, however, that in the theology of the early church, Christ was seen to be significant for the whole of God's creation. He was related to both the beginning and the end of the cosmos and also to the period between (see Col. 1:15–20; Heb. 1:1–2).

Finally, corresponding to the intimate link between the miracles and the kingdom that Jesus proclaimed is another distinctive feature, the role of faith in relation to the miracles. Nearly two-thirds of the references to faith in the first three Gospels occur in relation to miracles. It does not follow that faith is always in evidence when a miracle occurs; indeed, in many passages no mention is made of it. In about an equal number, however, it is either explicitly referred to or clearly implied. In no passage is faith explicitly said to be the direct result of a miracle, although in a few it may well be implied. In one passage, miracles are offered as an overt invitation to faith (Luke 7:18–23). The situation is different in the Fourth Gospel: the expressed purpose of the book is to offer signs (miracles) so that readers will come to faith (John 20:30–31).

Two observations may be made on the relation of faith to miracle in the gospel tradition. First, when we compare these accounts with Jewish and Hellenistic miracle material, we observe that the faith motif is unique to the Gospels. In a study of twenty-one representative miracle stories in rabbinic literature, L. J. McGinley pointed out that "faith is never demanded from the patient." Likewise, after examining Hellenistic miracle stories, Norman Perrin says that nothing comparable to the New Testament statement "Your faith has saved you" is to be found in this material. The miracles of the Gospels are thus set in a religious framework that highlights the relational factor pointing to faith.

Second, where faith was not present prior to a miracle, could a miracle precipitate it? As already noted, the author of the Gospel of John expressed this hope, and there is some evidence in that Gospel—and by implication also in the other three—that Jesus' miracles could and did inspire belief. But that outcome was by no means certain. Indeed, in the majority of cases it apparently did not happen (see Matt. 11:20–24; John 12:37). Where the disposition to believe was lacking, the miracles could be explained in ways compatible with unbelief (see Luke 11:15).

In conclusion, brief attention must be given to the question that haunts many modern readers of the Gospel miracle-stories: Did they really happen? We have been so thoroughly conditioned by modern scientific and philosophical thought that the word, if used at all, is often written "miracles." We may allow that the healing miracles can perhaps be explained, but the nature miracles as straightforward accounts are suspect. What can we say in reply?

Although our knowledge of the physical universe is much greater than that available to people of the first century, it is far from comprehensive. Reality may well be much more complex than we presently suspect. It is sobering to remember that only recently have we become aware that matter and energy are in a dynamic relationship to each other. There are depths in the realm of mind and spirit that we have only begun to explore.

Let us remember as well that those who were closest to Jesus during his ministry were repeatedly made aware that they did not fully understand him. The resurrection helped them put meaning into those earlier perplexities. Yet mystery still remained for them—as it does for us. If the Christ of the resurrection is not someone wholly other than the Jesus of history, who are we to affirm too dogmatically what were then the limits of his powers?

The revolutionary Jesus

Have you ever stood on a footbridge looking over the guardrail at the smooth surface of the water below? If so, you probably saw a reflection of your own face in the water: you provided the image for what you saw. What happens in such a situation also happens in many other settings. It is likely to happen when we read the New Testament Gospels looking for the face of Jesus.

The evidence of this phenomenon is the great variety of ways Jesus has been perceived by different readers of the same New Testament documents. In *Jesus Now*, Malachi Martin reviews some of the ways the figure of Jesus has been distorted at the hands of those who wished to enlist him for their cause. There is "Jesus Caesar," "Jesus the Monk," "Jesus the Protestant," "Jesus the Liberationist," "Jesus Black," "Jesus Femina," and "Jesus Gay"—to mention only a few of the interpretations he surveys.

If this diversity is disturbing, it is also to some extent understandable, for the historical circumstances from which we look at Jesus have a way of conditioning what we see in him. The spirit of the age; our social, cultural, economic, and religious background; our personal experience; our interests; our fears and hopes—these and similar factors tend to put blinders on us, shutting out some of the light that we would otherwise see. Conversely, these same elements may help us see more clearly what in other times and circumstances was not so evident.

What then can we do about our situation? To be aware of the problem is a helpful first step in dealing with it. We must look again and again at all the evidence before us in the New Testament Gospels, forcing our eyes as wide open as possible to see what is there. We need to reflect on what we bring as interpreters to the text that may determine what we see. We must discuss with others, asking what they see from their perspective. Their reading may alert us to things that otherwise escape us. We need to pray for illumination, asking God to help us see as truly and clearly as we ought to see.

Let us return to the figure of Jesus. One of the popular contemporary ways of interpreting him is as a revolutionary. It is often said that we are living in revolutionary times, and in recent years a growing mass of literature dealing with revolution and a theology of revolution has appeared. It is only natural that attempts should be made to link Jesus in some way with the political, social, and economic ferment of our times. No one who has given serious attention to the Gospels would likely deny that Jesus was a revolutionary in some sense. The important question is, what kind of a revolutionary was he? At what points and in what manner did he take issue with his contemporaries?

Some have tried to associate Jesus with the Zealot movement in first-century Judaism. Jewish nationalism was alive in Palestine under the Roman occupation. It was nourished from two sources, one practical and the other theological. The practical concern was that the Romans imposed a program of taxation on subject peoples. This system did not take into account the fact that the Jews already had a tax program of their own which was prescribed by the law and therefore was binding on them. The result was a combined taxation burden that has been estimated at between 30 and 40 percent of the income. Understandably, this matter was a source of irritation in the Jewish community.

The other source for resistance to Rome was a theological conviction. God was king of his people, and that kingship excluded the recognition of any other sovereignty. To call Caesar "king" or "lord" and to submit to his claims on them and their land as God's property might be interpreted as a compromise of the first commandment. Resistance to Rome could be seen, therefore, as a logical necessity arising out of genuine piety.

As a matter of fact, Jewish response to Rome took various forms. The Sadducees, the temple-centered party of wealth and power, although not in love with the Romans, were not ready to tolerate acts of resistance. Such conduct might threaten the status quo and jeopardize their position. The Pharisees were more interested in religious matters than in politics. They saw the Roman occupation as a judgment on the nation for disobedience to the law. God would overthrow their rule and restore the kingdom to Israel when the people offered true obedience to the law. This obedience became the primary interest of the Pharisees.

> **Jesus was not a revolutionary in the sense of advocating violent action against Rome, but he was a revolutionary in his own way. He was critical of the existing parties in the name of the new order that God intended to establish among people. He died as a radical in the company of other radicals (of another sort).**

The ardent nationalists took another line. They were not willing to wait for God to bring in the kingdom through their obedience to the law. Instead they called for active armed resistance to the Romans as the way God would accomplish his purpose. In consequence, they were ready to use violence and ultimately led the nation into the tragic war that culminated in the fall of Jerusalem in AD 70. These people are usually referred to as the Zealots.

Was Jesus a revolutionary in this militant nationalistic sense? In *Jesus and the Zealots*, S. G. F. Brandon has argued that Jesus, although not a card-carrying Zealot, was actively sympathetic with the movement and worked in his own way for the freedom of the Jews from Roman control. There is some evidence, of course, that might be taken to point in this direction. The title Pilate placed over Jesus on the cross, "The King of the Jews" (Mark 15:26), would indicate that Jesus was crucified as a political threat to Caesar. Among his disciples, Jesus had one who is identified as a Zealot (Luke 6:15). Jesus spoke to his disciples before his arrest about buying a sword (Luke 22:36). The disciples apparently expected Jesus to restore the kingdom to Israel, implying an end to Roman rule (Luke 24:19, 21; Acts 1:6).

The weight of Gospel evidence, however, is against interpreting Jesus as a sympathetic associate of the militant Jewish nationalists. Brandon, to support his view, is forced to resort to dealing radically with the present Gospel text. He does not satisfactorily explain why the church, when it got going, made Jesus an active supporter of the doctrine of love for the enemy. This principle would represent a complete reversal of what Brandon supposes was his actual attitude during his ministry.

If Jesus was not a revolutionary in the sense of advocating or employing violent action against Rome, he was, nonetheless, a revolutionary in his own way. The theme of his ministry was the announcement that the kingdom (or rule) of God was at hand and a call for radical repentance in order to enter it (Mark 1:15). He fitted into none of the existing parties: he was critical of them in the name of the new order that God intended to establish among people. The righteousness that he demanded went beyond that of the most religious people of the day (Matt. 5:20). So revolutionary was his perception of and dedication to the will of God that, when the chips were down, even his own disciples forsook him. He died as a radical in the company of other radicals (of another sort).

The description of the revolutionary Jesus thus far has been a very general one. We can be more specific. Let us note some particulars. First, Jesus' attitude toward the enemy, whether within the nation or outside it, was not the conventional one. The ardent nationalists hated the tax collectors because they worked with the enemy and thus were traitors to their people. But Jesus welcomed tax collectors into his company and ate with them (Luke 15:1). Indeed, he said they might enter the kingdom before some Pharisees (Luke 18:9–14). Again, Jesus refused to adopt his people's typical attitude of scorn toward Samaritans. He not only ministered to them (John 4:1–42) but used one to illustrate what it means to be a neighbor (Luke 10:29–37). Then, too, the Roman soldier, who might at any time compel an unwilling Jew to carry his pack for a mile, is not to be hated or cursed but loved and prayed for (Matt. 5:41, 43–44).

Second, Jesus dared to criticize some respected religious institutions and practices in Judaism. He saw the law, as it was interpreted by some rabbis, as distorting the original purpose of God (Matt. 5:21–48). He boldly cleansed the temple of practices that had become a front for greed and selfishness

(Mark 11:15–18). He defied some Sabbath prohibitions, because they no longer served human welfare (Mark 2:23–3:6). He ignored some ritualistic practices, because they too often obscured rather than dealt with the deeper realities of the heart (Mark 7:1–23).

Third, Jesus took a radical stand against the persistent desire for personal power and status over others. True greatness, he said, does not consist in lording it over others but in service to them (Mark 10:35–45). This redefinition of greatness was not only an ideal that he taught but was also given concrete embodiment in the totality of his ministry. It was powerfully symbolized in his washing of the disciples' feet (John 13:1–17). And it was brought to supreme expression in his voluntary death as "a ransom for many" (Mark 10:45).

Jesus and discipleship

Visitors to the outer court of the temple in the time of Jesus likely would have seen one or more rabbis with students gathered about them. There the more important Jewish teachers of the day conducted their schools for those who desired more advanced instruction than was offered in the synagogue. They met in the shelter of the colonnades along the outer walls or wherever appropriate space was available.

The subject matter for study was, of course, the scriptures—their proper understanding and their application to life. In the post-exilic period, a body of oral tradition having to do with the meaning and practical relevance of the biblical texts gradually took shape. It was the task of rabbinic teachers to transmit to their pupils this growing mass of interpretive material. Students were expected to memorize what they were taught, with memory taking the place of the modern notebook. Much repetition was therefore necessary before students could be trusted to transmit faithfully to others what they had been taught.

Jesus, too, was a teacher who had disciples from whom he chose a small group for special training. As might be expected, there were many similarities between Jesus' school and those of other Jewish teachers. But there were also certain important differences.

First, Jesus was not a typical rabbi. He had never studied under a recognized teacher, nor had he mastered the history of rabbinic interpretation on this and that text. His authority to teach, therefore, was questioned by many of his contemporaries (John 7:15).

Second, although Jesus was known and addressed as a teacher, he resembled in many ways the figure of a prophet. He taught "as one having authority and not as the scribes" (Mark

1:22). He had a charismatic quality that was lacking in the conventional teacher. Each of the Gospels prefaces Jesus' public ministry as a teacher with the account of his receiving the Spirit. We are expected to view his person and his ministry of word and deed through this window.

Third, the category of teacher-prophet is not finally adequate to characterize Jesus. He knew himself as one called to a unique role in the fulfillment of God's purposes for God's people. Jesus believed that the end-time kingdom of God was breaking into history in and through his ministry. He came not only to interpret the will of God expressed in the scriptures but also to actualize it. The notes of crisis, urgency, and fulfillment that mark the teaching of Jesus were not typical of the average Jewish rabbi of that day.

> **Discipleship is not so much a pattern to be followed woodenly as it is a relational reality that gives birth to a certain style of life. There is no New Testament Greek word for *discipleship*. Instead of using an abstract term—a static concept—the Gospels speak of following Jesus.**

Fourth, Jesus' relationship to his disciples was different from that of other teachers. Jesus did not call people to be students in the sense of devoting themselves to a life of study. Rather, he wanted to enlist them in his movement. The word *disciple* has a broader meaning than *pupil*: perhaps *apprentice* would be a better term. Jesus called people to follow him so that they in turn might "fish for people" (Mark 1:17). Then, too, one never hoped to graduate from the rank of Jesus' disciple to become a teacher in one's own right (Matt. 23:8–10). It is true that in the apostolic church teachers did arise, but they never really moved into Jesus' role. They remained subordinate to him. They were still disciples— although this name seems to have dropped out of common usage quite early in Christian circles.

Furthermore, the claims that Jesus made on his disciples seem to go beyond those made by the ordinary rabbi. To be sure, the student owed his teacher respect and service: pupils would follow their teacher at an appropriate distance; they were expected to act as servants supplying the needs of their teacher; they were to do most of the things that slaves would ordinarily do for their master. But the claims of Jesus on the

Jesus and discipleship

devotion and loyalty of his disciples were absolute. "Disciple-ship," says F. Hahn, "means to be totally bound to Jesus' person and His mission." It means to deny self (Mark 8:34), to allow no ties of family (Luke 14:26) or of possessions (Mark 10:17–31) to come ahead of him. Such total allegiance to Jesus is not seen as a substitute for loyalty to God; it is rather an expression of such loyalty. The claims that Jesus made on his disciples can only be understood as arising out of his own sense of unique personhood and role.

Let us turn from these observations regarding the nature of the relationship between Jesus and his disciples to look more carefully at the pattern of discipleship. What is its specific character? How is it expressed? What are its distinctive features? What does it mean to profess discipleship? Before identifying certain specific features that appear in the Gospels, a few general comments are in order.

To begin, discipleship is rooted in grace. The initiative in entering into a disciple relationship with Jesus lies with him rather than with the prospective disciple. Jesus seeks out and calls individuals to become his disciples; he does not wait passively for them to seek him out. In this respect Jesus differs from the typical rabbi, and discipleship correspondingly receives a different slant.

Furthermore, discipleship begins with the call to repen-tance in light of the good news that the reign of God is break-ing into human experience in and through the person and work of Jesus. Repentance is one of the notes in Mark's summary of Jesus' ministry (Mark 1:14–15). Its meaning is illustrated repeatedly in the pages of all four Gospels. It involves a break with an outlook that refuses to see in Jesus the authentic and decisive agent of God for achieving God's purpose to create community between God and humanity and among people. It means a radical reorientation of life around Jesus.

Then, too, the pattern of discipleship is derived from Jesus' own life and ministry. He does not point people to a way of life that he is not prepared to follow. The reign of God to which he calls people to respond is already being actualized in his own life. He is the Word made flesh (John 1:14); he is "the way, and the truth, and the life" (John 14:6) of the kingdom. What it means to respond to God and to others as members of the new order is given discernible shape and form in Jesus' ministry.

Finally, discipleship at heart is not so much a pattern to be woodenly followed as it is a relational reality that gives birth to a certain type or style of life. There is no New Testament Greek word for *discipleship*. Instead of using an abstract term—which might suggest a static concept—the Gospels speak of following Jesus. This language implies action. Just as the Israelites who followed the pillar of fire at night in the wilderness had to move when it moved in order to stay in the light, so also disciples can only stay in Jesus' light as they follow him (John 8:12). Following Jesus is a dynamic quality that resists any attempt to reduce the pattern to a timeless stereotype, rigid formalization, or legalistic prescription.

If discipleship has a certain open-ended character, it is not, however, without clear guidelines. It is life with a particular tone and marked by a certain style. What are some of the features that give it color? First, if discipleship begins in grace, it is also a way of life that continues to be marked by a lively sense of grace. The prayer that Jesus taught his disciples to pray includes the petition for forgiveness that implies awareness of failures (Luke 11:4). The parable of the workers in the vineyard (Matt. 20:1–16) powerfully undercuts the sense of merit. Jesus' final meal with his close followers, which later became a rite celebrated among the disciples, points also to grace as the presupposition of discipleship from first to last.

Second, although it has its individual dimensions, discipleship involves life in community. Interpersonal relationships within the community must not be marked by a struggle for position and power over others. Greatness, on the contrary, lives in the service of others in the spirit of the great servant (Mark 10:35–45; John. 13:1–17). There is no place for the depreciation of others (Matt. 18:10). Broken relationships are to be worked at by an unlimited willingness to forgive (Matt. 18:21–22) and by taking the initiative in seeking to restore an erring brother or sister through penitence to full fellowship in the community (Matt. 18:15–18).

Third, the obligation to deal redemptively with broken relationships between disciples must also determine the way disciples relate to enemies who mistreat and persecute them. The law of retaliation is to be replaced by a positive outreach of love (Matt. 5:38–48). God's way of dealing with moral evil at the cross is meant to shape the way disciples continue to deal with it (1 Pet. 2:18–24).

Fourth, disciples are called to share in Jesus' concern for the poor and the outcasts of society. This point is made indirectly but tellingly in the parables of Luke 15 (the lost sheep, the lost coin, and the lost son). It finds expression also in Jesus' advice to the host at a dinner party (Luke 14:12–14) and in the parable of the rich man and Lazarus (Luke 16:19–31).

Fifth, a corollary of a concern for the poor is a loose attachment to material possessions. Disciples are not to lay up treasures for themselves on earth or to focus undue attention on matters of food and clothes (Matt. 6:19–33). They are warned against covetousness and thinking that life consists in things—a point vividly underscored by the parable of the rich fool (Luke 12:12–21).

Finally, discipleship lives only in a faith obedience response to Jesus. This is made clear in the story at the close of the Sermon on the Mount (Matt. 7:24–27). Physical proximity to Jesus is not enough. Disciples are known by their sharing in the mission of Jesus (Luke 9:49–50). Even family ties are not enough, for Jesus' true family members are those who do the will of God (Mark 3:31–35). It is possible to profess Jesus as Lord, but if that profession is not translated into living and doing God's will, our discipleship is meaningless (Matt. 6:21–23).

Jesus, the teacher among teachers

Jesus was known during his ministry by various names and titles. With many of these we are familiar: Son of Man, prophet, Lord, Christ, son of David, son of Joseph, son of Mary, Son of God. Surely one of the most common titles, however, was *teacher*. The words *teacher* and *rabbi* are applied to him more than fifty times in the New Testament Gospels. To these figures can be added many references to Jesus' teaching in synagogues, in towns and villages, in houses, in the street, by the seaside, in the temple, and in the out-of-doors more generally. What is more, the Gospels contain many teachings of Jesus. The conclusion is thus put beyond dispute: Jesus was widely known among his contemporaries as a teacher. Indeed, at the end of his ministry one charge brought against him before Pilate was: "He stirs up the people by teaching throughout all Judea, from Galilee . . . even to this place" (Luke 23:5).

That Jesus, as a religious leader, should have functioned in a teaching role should not be surprising. Judaism was historically and religiously oriented. It was shaped by a heritage of religious and ethical traditions that was regarded as essential to its self-understanding and future well-being. Teachers were indispensable to the important process of keeping this heritage alive and operative in the community.

The teaching function in Judaism was carried on at different levels and by a variety of personnel. Primary responsibility rested with the parents (see Deut. 6:4–9). The elementary school associated with the synagogue was essentially a place to learn Torah. The synagogue services also furthered this knowledge. But in the forefront of the educational enterprise—in the more technical sense, but with implications for Judaism generally—were the Torah scholars. In the first century these were variously known as scribes (Mark 1:22), teachers of the law (Luke 5:17), and lawyers (11:45–46). The honorific title *rabbi* was also given to them (Matt. 23:4–5).

Behind this terminology is a long and interesting history. After their return from exile in Babylon, the Jews placed emphasis on the knowledge and practice of the Torah, in the hope of averting a future catastrophe such as had befallen the nation in 587 BC. In the time of Ezra and for a considerable period after that, the priests carried special responsibility for interpreting and applying the Torah in the Jewish community. Ezra was both a priest and a scribe (Neh. 8:1–2). A scribe, who gave time to copying the Torah from scroll to scroll, would naturally gain familiarity with its contents. It is understandable that such people would be looked to for direction with regard to its proper meaning and correct practice.

Yet the study of the Torah was an obligation not only for the priesthood but for the community as a whole. Lay Israelites, especially those who had leisure along with their piety, took up such study. The author of the apocryphal book Sirach, who lived in the early part of the second century BC, was a person of this sort. He gives a glowing description of a student of the law, which may well have been autobiographical (Sir. 39:1–11). The importance of leisure for such a pursuit and the respect attached to such study are noted in 38:24–34.

Shortly after Sirach was written, the Jewish community in Palestine fell on difficult times. The Syrian king in Antioch decided to force Hellenistic culture and religion on the Jews in his empire. Many of the leading priests and aristocratic lay people in Jerusalem went along with his scheme, with the result that their leadership as custodians and interpreters of the Torah was seriously compromised. The faithful in the Jewish community found it necessary to look to new spiritual leadership, and they found this emerging in lay people within their ranks who gave themselves to the study and teaching of the Torah. These lay leaders were the forerunners of the scribes and teachers of the law of first-century Judaism.

The role of the scribe at the time of Jesus was essentially threefold. First came the study of the Torah, with a view to developing a system of practical guidelines that would provide direction for life under God in the Jewish community. This study involved an ever-growing body of oral law that came to have an authority equal to that of the written law. Second was the teaching of Torah to students so that as many people as possible might gain expertise in the law. Some of these teachers had many students on whom two demands were made: they were expected to remember everything they were taught, and they were not to alter any teaching they had received. Third, scribes were expected to participate in the administration of justice. Because they had detailed knowledge of the law, they would logically be qualified to pass legal judgment on cases brought before the courts for decision. The great Sanhedrin in Jerusalem thus had scribes on it.

> The greatness of Jesus as a teacher lay ultimately not in his pedagogical skill, significant as that was, but rather in his message and the way he embodied what he taught in his own life. In him word and life coalesced: "The Word became flesh."

The scribes were held in high esteem by the Jewish community. They were addressed by such reverential titles as *rabbi* ("my lord"), *father*, and *master* (Matt. 23:7, 9–10). Students were expected to revere their teachers above their own fathers. The scribes were permitted to wear the dress of the priesthood and the aristocracy. The best seats in the synagogue and the places of honor at feasts were reserved for them (Matt. 23:6).

It is against this background that we must look at Jesus as a teacher. In some respects he resembled the scribes. He regarded himself as a teacher (Mark 14:14) and was addressed as rabbi (Mark 9:5; John 1:38). Jesus had disciples both in a general and in a more intimate sense. He taught in the synagogues. He was concerned with the meaning of the Torah (Mark 12:18–34), and on occasion he used typical rabbinic methods of exegesis (Mark 12:24–27; John 10:31–36). There were times when he was asked to make legal decisions (Mark 10:2–12; 12:13–17) and to pass judgment on supposed offenders (Luke 12:13–17; John 8:3–11). The latter, however, he refused to do.

On examination, however, the similarities turn out to be rather superficial. More impressive are the differences. Martin Hengel has noted that "Jesus was not at all like a scribe of the rabbinical stamp." Let us observe some of the distinctive features in Jesus as a teacher. First, although he was addressed as teacher by both friend and foe, he did not have rabbinic training. He had not been a student of a recognized scribe, and this lack of formal training was a bone of contention between him and the traditional scribes (Mark 11:27–33; see John 7:15). This difference is also reflected in the absence of appeal to earlier scribal authorities to support his teachings. Nowhere in the Gospels does the name of a single scribe occur to accredit his pronouncements. Indeed, the scribes as a whole are viewed rather unfavorably.

Second, unlike the scribes, Jesus manifested an attitude toward his disciples that was anti-hierarchical. Although he accepted the title and the role of teacher in relation to them, there is no indication that he demanded or expected the traditional services from them. He did not come to be served but to serve (Mark 10:45; Luke 22:27). The disciples were not his slaves but his friends (John 15:15). He could even perform the menial service of washing their feet (John 13:2–16). This act was distinctly uncharacteristic of a typical rabbi.

Third, while scribes might travel, they did not engage in the itinerant style of ministry so characteristic of Jesus. They did not wander around the countryside with their disciples, nor did they normally address crowds in the open air. Even more striking was the character of the audience that Jesus spoke to on those occasions. By and large they were the so-called "people of the land," that is, Jews who were lax in religious observance according to the standards of the Pharisees. He mingled freely with tax collectors and sinners. He had women in his entourage (Luke 8:1–3) and related publicly to some of questionable character (Luke 7:36–50; John 4:7–30). Unlike other teachers, he did not advise his disciples to seek fellowship and discussion with other students and like-minded people.

Fourth, the scribal teachers normally did not take the initiative to gather students but responded to those who sought them out. Jesus, on the contrary, was more aggressive. He summoned people to become his disciples, indeed, to follow him. There appear to be no rabbinical stories of teachers calling and of disciples following after the rabbi such as occur in the Gospels (Mark 1:16–20; Luke 9:59). The teacher-student relationship in Judaism was normally put in terms of "learning Torah." Jesus, however, enlisted disciples for service in his mission.

Finally, the Torah theoretically was the authority on which scribal teaching rested. The rabbis believed that what they were doing was in essence an exposition and restatement of the Torah itself. Their attempts to demonstrate the connection between specific rulings and the biblical text in many cases appear strange to us, but the exercise was necessary because the scribes had no independent authority. With Jesus it was different: the people perceived him to teach with an authority unlike that of the scribes (Mark 1:22). This authority was expressed in a variety of ways. For example, he not only criticized some of the laws that the Jewish teachers had developed supposedly on the basis of the written Torah, but he was critical of certain provisions in the latter itself (Matt. 5:33–48; Mark 7:14–23; 10:2–6). Again Jesus' use of the phrase "truly I tell you" to introduce a pronouncement has no parallel among the rabbis (Mark 3:28; 8:12; 9:41). Scholars regard this as a replacement for the prophetic formula "thus says the Lord." It suggests a claim that surpasses that of the prophets.

The preceding observations support the conclusion of Martin Hengel: "Quite certainly Jesus was not a 'teacher' comparable with the later rabbinical experts in the law, and he was a great deal more than a prophet. . . . He remains in the last resort incommensurable, and so basically confounds every attempt to fit him into the categories suggested by the phenomenology or sociology of religion."

Even if the title *teacher* is not adequate to express the full significance of Jesus (apparently the early Christians did not use it), an outstanding teacher he was! He knew how to communicate effectively—likely not without conscious effort on his part. It has been suggested that perhaps when Jesus sought to be alone, the time was not only for the purpose of prayer but also to prepare *what* and *how* he would teach. Attention may be called to some of the more prominent features that characterized his teaching style.

Jesus used picturesque speech that arrested attention and was readily remembered. It took a variety of forms. He majored in concrete terminology rather than abstract. His was language drawn from everyday life familiar to the family, the farmer, the merchant, the shepherd, the vinedresser, the day laborer. He used simile and metaphor extensively. He likened people to "whitewashed tombs" (Matt. 23:27). He sent his disciples on their mission "like sheep into the midst of wolves" (Matt. 10:16). He called Herod a "fox" (Luke 13:32) and spoke of "the yeast of the Pharisees" (Mark 8:15). Particularly memorable were the parables, which have retained their freshness and power across the centuries. His speech was studded with proverbs (Luke 4:23; 9:62), paradox (Mark 4:25; 8:35), overstatements (Matt. 7:3–5; Luke 14:26), puns (Matt. 16:18, where the same Aramaic word can mean both "Peter" and "rock"), and irony (Mark 4:12).

Furthermore, many of Jesus' utterances were cast in the form of Semitic poetry, which is characterized by a rhythmic balance of thoughts. One line may essentially repeat another (Mark 3:24–25), stand in contrast to the preceding (Matt. 7:17), or build on it (Matt. 10:40). Such structuring of thoughts aids greatly in retention.

Jesus also made liberal use of questions. They served a variety of purposes. Sometimes they elicited information (Mark 8:27–30); again, they were a weapon of counterattack (Mark 3:1–4). More frequently, however, they were a rhetorical device designed to stimulate thought (Mark 3:33; 12:35–37). Jesus as well made rather common use of a fortiori type of argument: here a generally accepted fact or conclusion is made the basis of appeal to recognize something regarded as still more certain. The earmark of this logical instrument is the phrase "how much more" (Matt. 6:28–30; 7:9–11).

The greatness of Jesus as a teacher lay ultimately not in his pedagogical skill, significant as that was, but rather in his message and the way he embodied what he taught in his own life. In him word and life coalesced. To put it into New Testament phraseology, "The Word became flesh" (John 1:14).

Reflections on the parables of Jesus

A famous American preacher of the nineteenth century, Horace Bushnell, once preached a sermon entitled "Our Gospel, a Gift to the Imagination." The point he made was that the gospel of which the New Testament speaks is cast in the language of imagery, and imagery is addressed to the imagination. The first part of his thesis would not seem to need much proof: the evidence is spread out in rich abundance in the New Testament, particularly in the four Gospels. It was the significance of this observation that Bushnell was eager to stress.

Imagery addresses the imagination. It is picture language that is anchored in the concrete and ordinary experience of human life; for example, "Joseph is a fruitful bough, a fruitful bough by a spring; his branches run over the wall" (Gen. 49:22). Often it opens windows on a more or less unfamiliar landscape. Imagery does not define with logical or mathematical precision. It stimulates the imagination; it is an invitation to adventure. Within limits, one may say, it is open-ended.

Bushnell lamented that the church, through most of its history, has been too eager to change the lively picture language in which the gospel was first expressed for the lifeless categories of abstract speech. While he was willing to allow for theological formulations, these should not displace the primary language of religion, which is of another kind. Theological statements tend to shut out more of the reality of religion than they shut in. The truth of the gospel can be adequately grasped only by the imagination, claimed Bushnell, who spoke of Christ as God's great and final metaphor—a word that literally means one thing but that can be made to represent values and ideas. God's message to us in Christ can never be exhaustively contained in theological statements, although, to be sure, they may and do serve a useful purpose. In a profound sense Christ is a gift to the imagination—which is perhaps what Paul had in mind in Ephesians 2:9.

Our purpose is not to discuss Bushnell's suggestion as such, but rather to focus on the parables of Jesus as one of the most distinctive and significant forms of his picture language. His parables are not only unique in the literature of the New Testament but are not as a whole really matched in the teachings of the rabbis. They are among the best known and most loved of Jesus' utterances.

We may begin by noting the relation between the literary form known as parable and the nature of the good news or the gospel. From a literary point of view, the parable is an extended simile, a "like" blown up into a story. It is a comparison that has been expanded by details to make a meaningful narrative.

Interest in the parable often centers on its effectiveness as a means of communication. A story can often do what pages of non-story material cannot do. An idea is more likely to spring to life, the truth to take on recognizable shape, or understanding to emerge out of confusion, when a story is pressed into the service of illuminating a difficult matter. It is frequently the high road to comprehension that remains open when the others for one reason or another are blocked.

Less generally recognized is the fact that the story form of the parable is in keeping with the very nature of the gospel as story. The gospel is not a timeless idea or a collection of general truths: it is essentially a story of God in action seeking to win people into fellowship. It involves the particularities of times, places, people, events, purposes, feelings, responses, and other such factors—the stuff of which stories are made. The parables, too, belong to the realm of event. They do not report actual occurrences, but they are intimately related to the happenings of ordinary human existence.

The worldview of a people and their understanding of the nature of human existence are reflected in their literary forms. The story character of biblical faith bears witness to a view of the world in which the individual and history have meaning. The parables, likewise, point to a similar understanding of reality; they are little stories that have their place in the big story. They point to the dynamic character of human exist-ence. Parables highlight the importance of the particular (events, persons, places, times), of personal decisions and conduct, and of specific consequences that flow from such actions. The parable form thus is congenial to the Hebraic-Christian understanding of reality.

> A story can often do what pages of non-story material cannot do. An idea is more likely to spring to life, the truth to take on recognizable shape, or understanding to emerge out of confusion, when a story is pressed into the service of illuminating a difficult matter.

A second observation, closely related to the first, is the secular character of the parables. Very few of them have to do with religious personnel or functions in the technical sense. For the most part they are concerned with ordinary people in the varied experiences of common life: the farmer who goes out to sow seed in the field, the housewife who puts yeast in the dough to make bread, the father who waits for the return of a prodigal son, the vineyard owner who employs laborers to harvest the crop, the fisherman who casts his net into the sea, the shepherd who has lost a sheep and goes in search of it, the guests who are summoned to a feast, the widow who pleads her case before an insensitive judge, the rich man who goes his way oblivious to the needs of a poor man at his gate. This list might be extended considerably. In short, the parables are a transcript of the broad range of normal Palestinian life in Jesus' day.

What is the meaning of this observation? The worldly dress of the parables should not be viewed merely as an unimportant means to accomplish an important end—the communication of a spiritual truth. There is an intimate tie between what makes up the form of the parable and the message conveyed by it. Jesus did not sharply distinguish between the secular and the sacred; he did not find value only in the one and despise the other. The world in its wholeness and concreteness is the arena where he works. It is in the ordinary pursuits and experiences of daily life that God encounters us with his offers and demands. It is in the everyday world that we make the choices that give character to our lives and shape our destiny. The very nature of the parables should not allow us to forget this fact.

In the third place, the parables are not concerned with trivial matters. On first encounter with them, some may appear to be little more than delightful entertainment. But in fact, the parables as a whole are designed to illuminate the basic issues of human existence. To give serious attention to them is to open windows on life that may result in revolutionizing our experience.

Some of the parables speak to the character of God and God's attitude toward us. Others have to do with the certainty, the manner, or the direction of God's workings in the world. But a great many focus on individuals and their attitudes, their sense of values and the character of their relationships both with God and with their fellow humans. The parables raise basic questions, such as: Am I confusing possessions with real living? Do I share God's attitude toward the lost? Do I say "yes" to God and then do not do what God says? Am I asking, "Who is my brother?" or "Am I a brother to the person in need?"

The parables, however, do more than identify or sharpen issues. They elicit response; they call for action. They may begin with a question (Matt. 18:12–14; Luke 11:58) or end with one (Matt. 21:28–30, 33–43). But the questions are not meant for mental amusement or endless debate. They are to trigger appropriate conduct. "The parables are told," says Gunther Bornkamm, "in order to deny to the hearer the attitude of a spectator."

Finally, the parables of the Gospels are not anonymous stories: they are the parables of Jesus. They bear witness to his unique ability in storytelling. Beyond that, however, to see the parables in relationship to Jesus is to bring into view two important additional considerations for their proper under-standing. For one, they provide insight into the way Jesus saw God and human beings and what it means to live as a person in God's world. They have a certain autobiographical reference: they indicate something of his own sense of values, his faith, and his commitment to the will of God—which helps us understand him as a person.

In addition, the parables must be seen in the context of the crisis that Jesus' mission precipitated and still precipitates in people. Jesus saw his ministry as decisive for human well-being;

to ignore or reject him was to invite judgment. To respond positively to him and to his message was to build life on a rock that is firm and abiding. The parables were meant to highlight the critical situation the coming of Jesus brought about.

This situation is ours as well. The Jesus of the parables is our contemporary. The options and their consequences that were open to men and women as they confronted Jesus back then remain similarly valid for us today. To hear again his parables in our context is to be addressed by the gospel that is at once a message of judgment and of grace. If we do not see this reality, we have not really understood Jesus' parables.

The Pharisees:
Saints or sinners?

Perhaps to most readers of the New Testament the answer to
the question "Were the Pharisees saints or sinners?" is
obvious. Of course they were sinners! The evidence is accumu-
lative. One cannot forget that unlovely figure of a Pharisee at
prayer in the temple: he thought he was worshiping God, but
he was only congratulating himself. He went to his home as he
had come from it, a sinner (Luke 18:9–14). Again, we recall
those repeated references to the Pharisees scheming in one way
or another to entrap Jesus in order to destroy him (for example,
Mark 3:1–6; 12:13–17; Luke 11:53–54). Were they not his
determined enemies? Above all, some of the most scathing
words Jesus ever uttered were spoken against these people. To
be called "hypocrites," a "brood of vipers," and "whitewashed
tombs" (Matt. 23:27; Luke 11:37–52) is to be on the receiving
end of less-than-complimentary language!

Yet in spite of this strong evidence, it surely is unfair to the
Pharisees to regard all of them as sinners. Like most move-
ments, they had both good and bad in their ranks. The Acts of
the Apostles records that some Pharisees became Christians
and entered the church (Acts 15:5; 21:20). Even during the
ministry of Jesus, we learn of the Pharisee Nicodemus who was
attracted to Jesus and apparently became a secret disciple
(John 3:1–21; 4:50–51; 19:39). The Jewish Talmud also
distinguishes between Pharisees who deserved to be condemned and others who merited approval. Especially com-
mended are those who love God and joyfully devote themselves to serving God. We may conclude, therefore, that both
sheep and goats were among them. Those denounced in
Matthew 23 were the goats; the harsh judgment pronounced
there need not be extended to cover all members of the
movement.

Who then were the Pharisees? How did they come into existence? What did they stand for? How could a person join their ranks? How shall we assess the movement? If we are to understand them properly, we need answers to such questions.

The origin of the Pharisees is not entirely clear. The name means "separated," but separated from what or from whom? Probably we should see the beginning of what later became the Pharisaic movement in the work of Nehemiah and Ezra. These men were instrumental in helping the Jews who returned from exile in Babylon in the sixth century BC to establish a distinctly Jewish community in Judea. The people bound themselves in a covenant to separate themselves "from the peoples of the lands to adhere to the law of God . . ., to observe and do all the commandments of the LORD" (Neh. 10:28–29). The separation was both negative and positive: they were separated from sinners and for God.

> The Pharisees represented the progressive wing of the Jewish community. Unlike the Sadducees, who favored freezing the ancient text, the Pharisees stood for its modernization: the text of the law had to speak meaningfully to the problems at hand.

Now the ideal of obedience and purity set for the community was a high one, and it obviously would be put to a test in the years that followed. One such severe test came in the first half of the second century BC, when the Judean Jews were living under Syrian control. Antiochus Epiphanes, who was on the throne in Antioch, was determined to integrate the Jewish community in Palestine into his Greek kingdom. He set out to break down Jewish religion and to put in its place Hellenistic culture and religion.

The king found collaborators among some of the high-ranking priests and the rich aristocracy in Jerusalem, but many of the peasants and the priests of lower standing were opposed to the Hellenistic king's policies. The crisis came when the king ordered that a statue be erected in the temple to the Greek god Zeus and that swine's flesh be offered to it. This demand led to what is known as the Maccabean revolt in 167 BC, led by a priest who refused to bow to the king's demand. To his side rallied many of those who were zealous for the law of God and willing to die rather than surrender their faith.

There was now a definite division not simply between Jew and non-Jew but within the Jewish community itself. Those who chose loyalty to their religious heritage, even if it should mean death, were known as the Hasidim ("pious ones"). Likely we should see some relationship between these people and the Pharisees; not only does the name first occur in history shortly after the Maccabean revolt, but they shared a common deep devotion to the law of God.

At the heart, then, of the Pharisaic movement when it emerged into the clear light of history was an intense desire to be faithful to God's law. The goal of the movement was to preserve the Jewish community as the people of God. Certain things were necessary in order to achieve this objective.

A first task was to apply the law to the whole range of contemporary life. This called for an updating and an extension of the Mosaic law. The law originally was given in quite different historical circumstances: it envisioned a free people controlling their own community affairs. That had changed, for from the fall of Jerusalem in 587 BC through New Testament times, the Jews lived under foreign domination—except during the century of independence ended by Rome in 63 BC. This new situation posed many problems not encountered in earlier days and to which the law did not explicitly speak. A need existed, therefore, for spelling out in some detail what shape obedience to the law would take in the new circumstances. What, for example, was the meaning of the prohibition on work on the Sabbath day when the country was controlled by rulers who were not Jews?

In order not to transgress the law, its demands needed exact definition in every situation. The implications and applications of the ancient code needed to be drawn out and made clear. The Pharisees, therefore, represented the progressive wing of the Jewish community. Unlike the Sadducees, who favored freezing the ancient text, the Pharisees stood for its modernization: the text of the law had to speak meaningfully to the problems at hand.

This first task entailed a second—to train and provide competent teachers. Traditionally the responsibility for interpreting and teaching the law rested with the priests. But during the difficult years under the Syrians in the second century BC, many priests yielded to pagan pressure. They were no longer trusted by the pious of the land. Consequently, a new class of lay interpreters arose alongside the official priestly teachers.

The teachers of the law were called scribes. The Sadducees—centered mainly in the temple and composed of influential priests and the social and economic aristocracy of Jerusalem—had their scribes. In the New Testament, however, we hear mainly of the scribes of the Pharisees. These men developed a considerable body of interpretation referred to as "the tradition of the elders" (Mark 7:3). It was regarded as authoritative. To violate it was as serious as breaking the written law itself. It was at this point that Jesus clashed with the Pharisees.

The third goal of the Pharisees was to establish a faithful, identifiable community with clear requirements for its members. Membership must mean something, and thus an organization was developed with conditions for admission and continuing membership. Full admission into the fellowship was not granted immediately: a period of probation might last from one month to a year, during which time candidates had to prove their ability to live by the ritual laws of the group. This probationary period was followed by a solemn pledge before a scribe in which people bound themselves to obey the laws of purity and the tithe.

No complete uniformity of understanding or practice existed within the Pharisaic movement, and indeed several schools could be found within it. For example, the school of Shammai took a more rigid line than the rival school of Hillel. The movement was organized in small fellowships or associations, each with its own leader and to some extent its own character. The members of these small groups regarded each other as comrades. From time to time they shared together in communal meals, especially on Friday evening at the beginning of the Sabbath. They were known for wearing conspicuous phylacteries (a small case containing extracts from the law) on the upper left arm and tassels on the four corners of their cloaks.

From the prominence given to the Pharisees in the New Testament Gospels, we might conclude that most of Jesus' contemporaries belonged to this class. But the Jewish historian Josephus sets their number at about 6,000 during the time of Herod the Great (37–4 BC). This number, however, may refer only to "card-carrying" members. Loosely attached adherents may have included perhaps another 20,000. In a total Judean population ranging somewhere between 500,000 and 2,000,000, that number would be proportionately small.

The Pharisees, then, began as a noble movement. They proposed to take religion seriously and to bring the whole of life under the will of God. It is clear, however, that by the time of Jesus not all was well with their endeavor. It is sometimes thought that the severe critique of the Pharisees in the Gospels may reflect the bitter tension between the church and the synagogue in the late first century AD when the Gospels were written. But the charge persists that the leadership of the Pharisees appears to have had a significant role in bringing Jesus to his death.

Finally, a question for personal reflection: If I had lived in Jesus' day, would I have been a Pharisee of the kind Jesus condemned? The fear that I might have been one haunts me.

Jesus and the poor

Jesus was not making a profound observation when he said, "You always have the poor with you" (Mark 14:7). He was merely stating what everyone in the ancient world knew to be a fact. The poor were a majority in all the great civilizations of antiquity, and the little country of Palestine was no exception. The poor greatly outnumbered the rich.

Both New Testament and Jewish sources indicate the existence of rich people. Herod Antipas, the ruler of Galilee and Perea from 4 BC to AD 39, had extensive landholdings in his kingdom. The historian Josephus mentions the names of other people who owned large estates. Some of Jesus' parables also reflect this situation (Mark 12:1–11; Luke 16:1–7). In addition to the small group of landlords there were merchants. One such Galilean was John of Gischala, who gained considerable wealth selling grain and oil. Likely Zebedee, the fisherman of whom we hear in Mark 1:20, was a man of modest means. He had a boat and nets and employed men to help him in his business.

Judea also had a landowning aristocracy, rich merchants, high priests, and tax collectors. Zacchaeus was one of the latter (Luke 19:2). Between the rich and the poor in Judea was a middle class. It was largely made up of priests, innkeepers, and others who profited from services related to Jerusalem as a religious center.

But the great majority of the people in Judea, as elsewhere in Palestine, were poor. There were at least two reasons for this poverty. First, the economy was oriented to agriculture. Given the physical features of Palestine, climatic conditions, and the methods of cultivation, the returns were limited at best. A failure in rainfall, prolonged hot winds from the desert, or an invasion of insects could quickly result in crop loss and hardship for many without financial reserves to meet such crises.

Second, heavy taxation was a constant drain on the country's economy. Emperor Augustus allowed Herod Antipas to receive 200 talents in tribute from Galilee and Perea; this today might equal several million dollars. It is likely that the funds for running his government, for his extensive building operations, and for his annual tribute to Rome were raised by taxation over and above the 200 talents Herod Antipas was allowed to receive for himself.

During the ministry of Jesus, Judea was under direct Roman rule. A major function of the Roman procurator was to collect the taxes levied on the province. Some of these were collected by representatives of the procurator, working through local village, town, or city administrations. Others were farmed out in lump sums to tax-collecting companies, who then raised the contracted amounts with liberal additions for their own pockets. The system had built-in temptations to abuse.

Added to these civil taxes were a series of religious taxes. These had their basis in the Old Testament organization of the Hebrew people as a religious community. They included various offerings, tithes, annual temple tax, redemption of the first-born money, and offerings for the poor. Because these taxes were rooted in the Old Testament law, they were obligatory for those who took their faith seriously. But the combination of two extensive taxation programs was a grievous economic burden. It is estimated that it may have amounted to as much as 30 or 40 percent of a Palestinian's income. When that income for many was meager at best, the result is not difficult to imagine.

What was the attitude of Judaism toward the problem of poverty? The response, as in most matters, was not uniform; various opinions and practices prevailed. Let us look first at a quartet of what might be called theological opinions.

In the first place, Judaism in the time of Jesus had inherited the prophetic criticism of wealth gained through oppression of the poor (Amos 8:4–8; Isa. 5:8–10; 10:1–3; see also Deut. 15:7–11). The author of Ecclesiasticus at the beginning of the second century BC has some harsh words for those who extort the poor: they are murderers. This same note is continued in apocalyptic Judaism, which predicts dire judgment for those who have gained riches unjustly.

Second, wealth justly acquired through honest toil was regarded as evidence of God's favor (Prov. 10:22). This view is a continuation of the earlier Old Testament belief that faithfulness to God will result in material blessing (Deut. 28:1–14). The corollary is that poverty might readily be regarded as a sign of God's disfavor. Some rabbis in the period after the New Testament did indeed take a disdainful attitude toward the poor.

Third, some of the literature of Judaism emphasizes the duty and virtue of almsgiving. Giving to the poor is to be motivated by a remembrance of the goodness of God. While almsgiving was praised, there were also attempts to set limits to its exercise. One rabbi said that the most a man was to give was 20 percent of his total income.

Fourth, in some Old Testament psalms the poor are regarded as synonymous with the righteous (Pss. 14:5–6; 132:15–16). This association is also made in the *Psalms of Solomon* (first century BC). In the first century AD, the people at Qumran thought of themselves as "the congregation of the poor." This identification was not merely a socioeconomic description but a religious title designating the community as the true people of God in the end time.

Judaism did not just think about the poor; the faithful took steps to help them. This activity took various forms. There was the dispensing of charity. Almsgiving was practiced personally and voluntarily and was particularly prominent in Jerusalem, where swarms of beggars waited to receive gifts from worshipers at the temple. After AD 70 an elaborate organized program of community charity was developed in Palestine. The community at Qumran followed a plan of communal property. Personal possessions were surrendered to the community on entry into full membership. In this way distinctions between the rich and the poor were erased. An attempt was made to reflect the order of life that they believed God would establish in the age that was coming.

> **The poor were a special concern to Jesus. There is no suggestion in his teaching that material things as such are evil, but Jesus was sensitive to the subtle temptation to make the acquisition of things the goal of life. He was person-oriented: the welfare of people took precedence over interest in material things.**

Such then was something of the character of the world into which Jesus was born. It was a society that knew poverty as a major problem. It had its particular perspectives with regard to poverty and made its own practical responses. What can we say about Jesus in relation to this matter?

We do not know a great deal about Jesus' personal economic situation. There were at least six children in the family besides Jesus (Mark 3:31; 6:3). His father was an artisan who may have died when Jesus was a young man. The Gospels do not suggest that Joseph played an active role in Jesus' ministry. If he died before the children were grown, his death would have had economic implications for the family. In any case, the family apparently was relatively poor. This inference can be drawn from the purification offering Joseph and Mary made in the temple when Jesus was an infant: they could not afford a lamb, so they brought "a pair of turtledoves or two young pigeons" (Luke 2:24; see Lev. 12:6–8).

As far as we know, Jesus did not own property. By his own statement, he had "nowhere to lay his head" (Luke 9:58). He may have stayed with Peter and Andrew when at home in Capernaum (Mark 1:29–34). During his Galilean ministry he was at least partially supported by contributions from grateful beneficiaries (Luke 8:2). Like other Jewish teachers, he did not receive pay for his work as a teacher. The lifestyle Jesus held up for his disciples in Luke 12:22–31 probably reflects his own. When he died, the meager possessions he had—his clothes—were divided among his executioners, and he was buried in another man's tomb (Mark 15:24, 42–46).

Although Jesus directed his mission to the entire nation, it is clear that the poor were a special concern to him. He knew himself to be called "to bring good news to the poor" (Luke 4:18) He said that the poor are blessed, for the kingdom of God belongs to them (Luke 6:20). When a rich man wished to find the way to eternal life, he was told to sell his possessions and give the proceeds to the poor (Mark 10:17–22). Jesus advised a dinner host that he ought to have invited "the poor, the crippled, the lame, and the blind" (Luke 14:13). He noted with deep appreciation the small but meaningful contribution of a poor widow to the temple treasury (Mark 12:41–44). He told a parable about a rich man who ignored a poor man at his gate and after death found himself in torment (Luke 16:19–31). To these explicit references to the poor could be added other materials that more or less directly point to the same concern. Surveying the mission and message of Jesus as a whole, we can make the following observations.

First, Jesus' attitude toward the poor and his perspective more generally toward material possessions must be seen in the context of the kingdom of God. The establishment of this new order was the thrust of his entire ministry. The kingdom represented a radical revision of existing values and loyalties. The neglect or oppression of the poor and the devotion to things were to have no place in the community where God's will is taken seriously.

Second, there is no suggestion in Jesus' teaching that material things as such are evil. Poverty for its own sake is no virtue; it is not in itself a passport to heaven. Jesus was not an ascetic. Unlike John the Baptist, he came "eating and drinking" (Luke 7:34). Jesus affirmed the material order as God's creation and thus good.

Third, Jesus was sensitive to the subtle temptation to make acquisition of things the goal of life. He warned against the dangers of riches and of seeking material possessions (see Luke 6:24; 12:13–34; 16:10–17, 19–31; 18:18–30). He categorically asserted that one "cannot serve God and mammon" (Matt. 6:24). Devotion to things will surely choke the word of the kingdom and make it unfruitful (Mark 4:18–19).

Fourth, Jesus was person-oriented: the welfare of people took precedence over interest in material things. Money and possessions were to be used for the benefit of people rather than people exploited for the sake of things. As Jesus saw it, to be deaf to the cry of the poor and the needy is to give evidence that one has not really understood what biblical religion is about. We hear the echo of his voice in the words of 1 John 3:17: "How does God's love abide in anyone who has the world's goods and sees a brother or sister in need and yet refuses help?" That is a disturbing question!

"Blessed are the peacemakers"

The Beatitudes that introduce the Sermon on the Mount (Matthew 5–7) are too often viewed as individual and independent sayings. Any of them may be treated in isolation from the rest as a gem existing in its own right. Further, any may also be seen as standing apart from the main body of the discourse that follows. But this approach does not do justice either to the Beatitudes or to the sermon of which they are a part. The Beatitudes are not independent descriptive state-ments of eight or nine separate groups of people; on the contrary, they portray one community from a variety of perspectives. The description is diverse but cumulative. The community in view receives the kingdom of heaven (see Matt. 5:3, 10). It is with these people also that the remainder of the discourse is concerned. The Beatitudes, therefore, should not be forgotten when the material that follows is examined.

The word *beatitude* comes from a Latin term meaning "happy" or "blessed" used by Jerome in the fourth century AD in his Latin translation of Matthew 5:3–11. The word, however, has come to designate a literary form usually composed of two parts. The first part ascribes blessedness to a certain type of person or people; the second states the basis or reason for such an ascription. Sometimes the second part is assumed as under-stood and is not expressed. Both of these types are found already in the Old Testament, particularly in the Psalms (41:1; 65:4; 2:11; 34:4).

The Beatitudes of Jesus thus are not formally a novel literary creation. But if the form is not new, the content is fresh and distinctive. Two features characterize these sayings. First, blessedness is no longer tied to material blessings and well-being, as in the Old Testament. The frame of reference is the kingdom of God that Jesus proclaimed as imminent (Matt.

4:17, 23). This association is made explicit in the first and eighth beatitudes (5:1, 10). Second, because the kingdom is a present and a future reality, there is room for paradox in the way the beatitude is stated. For example, blessedness and persecution are not normally regarded as compatible experiences; they cancel each other out. This paradoxical way of speaking can be understood only in the context of the "already" and "not yet" character of the kingdom. Another way of saying this is that the present observable situation of the member of the kingdom is not the total story; it is only part of a larger whole in the light of which the present is transformed.

> The blessedness about which the beatitude speaks resides in knowing that in peacemaking we are sharing in what God is about in the world. To know in our hearts that we are caught up in a transcendent purpose rooted in God is surely to be blessed.

With this introduction, we are now ready to look more carefully at one particular beatitude included in this catalog: "Blessed are the peacemakers, for they shall be called children of God" (Matt. 5:9). Five brief observations are in order.

First, the beatitude presupposes a situation that is not as it ought to be. If peace needs to be made, then it does not exist. Perhaps there is an absence of genuine community. Indeed, in the larger context of the sermon and the Gospel, the situation must be described as the presence of opposition, hatred, and persecution. So the setting of this beatitude, far from being utopian, is one of somber, this-world realism.

Second, the meaning of peace is not exhausted in a negative definition. Peace is not simply the absence of discord or strife; it has a wide and deep positive content. It is not the lack of diversity but the presence of concord. It is not the removal of factors that destroy community but the experience of wholeness, well-being, and richness of life in relationship with others. Peace in its true theological meaning is intimately allied to what the Bible means by the kingdom of God. The close association of these terms in this catalog of beatitudes would also suggest this connection.

Third, the beatitude speaks about peacemaking as an activity. It envisions a task or a vocation for those who would be blessed. Nothing, however, is said in the statement itself about the way peace is to be made—although the materials that follow in the sermon will shed some light on this matter.

Fourth, the phrase "children of God" is not to be understood biologically. It is a metaphor for a moral and spiritual relationship to God, pointing to a family kinship of character. Just as children naturally bear some resemblance to their parents, so peacemakers are recognized as children of the one who in the New Testament is called more than once "the God of peace" (Rom. 15:33; 16:20; Heb. 13:20).

Fifth, wherein then does reside the blessedness about which the beatitude speaks? Is it not in knowing that in peacemaking we are sharing in what God is about in the world? This participation is more than an intellectual idea: it has the dimensions of life. The parent-child relationship is a daily experienced partnership that is lived out in the context of a common mission. To know in our hearts that we are caught up in a transcendent purpose rooted in God is surely to be blessed.

So much for this beatitude as such. We must now explore the way the material that follows further illuminates the meaning of this terse statement. The passage that is of special importance is Matthew 5:38–48. The following observations merit consideration. First, the situation that is addressed is the disciple-enemy relationship. The discussion is not cast in the third person but in the language of direct discourse. The disciples are envisioned as living in a world in which a face-to-face encounter with enemies is anticipated. Who these people were or would be is not made clear, but we may assume that Jesus regarded those who opposed him as foes of his disciples as well. But the identity of the opponents is not of first importance. Rather, Jesus gives attention to the recognition of opposition, and above all, to the pattern of response by the disciples.

Second, the passage portrays several different patterns of response to those who mistreat the disciple. Two texts are quoted from the Old Testament as a basis for Jesus' comments. One (v. 38) is the tit-for-tat principle of retaliation found in various places in the Pentateuch (Exod. 21:24; Lev. 24:30; Deut. 19:21). The purpose of this legislation was to restrain the exercise of unlimited revenge (for example, Gen. 4:24). Nevertheless, this law did permit returning evil for evil. Jesus now withdraws this permission: the law of restrained revenge is replaced by no revenge at all.

The other text (v. 43) is drawn from Leviticus 19:18 and commands love for the neighbor. To this obligation, however, is added another statement not found either in Leviticus 19:18 or elsewhere in the Old Testament. It is the admonition or permission to hate the enemy. Although there is no such explicit command in the Old Testament, some passages might be understood to support or even encourage such an attitude (Deut. 30:7; 2 Chron. 19:2; Ps. 5:5; 139:19–22). According to Josephus, the Essenes, one of the Jewish parties at the time of Jesus, required of their members an oath "always to hate the unrighteous." Firsthand evidence from Qumran now confirms that the community members pledged themselves "to hate all the sons of darkness." This category included not only the Romans but very likely also all apostate Jews and the Sadducean high-priesthood at Jerusalem. (We must, of course, be fair to Judaism, and not draw too many conclusions from this Essene attitude; the command to love the neighbor was not forgotten and a kind of nonretaliatory attitude existed at times.)

Third, not only is there a "plus" element in the way disciples respond to opponents, their conduct is expected to exceed that of other segments of society. If the disciples' treatment of others is wholly determined by others' treatment of them, then how are disciples different from non-disciples? What difference does discipleship make? There is no indication in the teachings of Jesus that he wanted his disciples to differ from others in every aspect of their conduct. But he did expect more than conventional performance in the character and quality of interpersonal relationships.

Fourth, this pattern of treating the enemy is anchored in the Father-child relationship already noted in the beatitude (5:45, 48; see v. 9). While others take their cue for action from the actions of fellow humans, the sons and daughters of the heavenly Father look to him as their model of conduct. Leviticus 19:18 was normally and rightly understood to refer to a fellow Israelite, and the attitude to be taken toward one's enemy was not specified. Jesus left no doubt how he saw the matter. His word is a crisp categorical imperative: "Love your enemies" (v. 44). It has about it a fire, a passion, and an intensity that is fresh and distinctive. The question has been debated whether the enemies in mind were primarily personal or also national foes. Jesus does not explicitly speak to this question, but there is no indication that he intended a less than inclusive reference. Whoever the enemies and wherever they are encountered, love is to be the disciples' attitude.

Fifth, the meaning of love is spelled out in a series of practical and concrete forms of action. Love entails more than passive nonresistance. It calls for turning the other cheek, going the second mile, giving an additional garment (vv. 39–41), and praying for the persecutor (v. 44). To this list are added others in the parallel passage in Luke 6:27–28. Writing about Jesus, with this passage in mind, a noted Jewish scholar has said: "Jesus teaches an excess in virtue, an excess in forbearance, an excess in forgiveness, an excess in gentleness, an excess in giving and yielding. He does—and here there is originality—very often oppose the principle of measure for measure, and it is against this principle that he is speaking here." Conceivably, Jesus might have appealed to Old Testament materials that would have supported a punitive treatment of sinners. But he chose instead to point to the mercy of God revealed in nature: "He makes his sun rise on the evil and on the good, and sends rain on the righteous and on the unrighteous" (v. 45). It is this aspect of the Father's character that his children are called to imitate.

Sixth, associated with the challenge to imitation is the matter of motivation. The incentive for this style of action is no pragmatic promise of success. Disciples receive no guarantee that if they pursue this course, no harm will befall them; Jesus does not suggest that every enemy will promptly be turned into a friend. Rather, the rationale is stated in the form of a purpose clause, namely, "so that you may be children of your Father" (v. 45). Present also is the implicit suggestion of reward for those who act this way (v. 46).

Two things may be said about the motivation that is appealed to here. The purpose clause is not to be understood as indicating a meritorious ground for being a child of God. Disciples do not earn membership in the family of God by virtue of their conduct; it is a gift of grace. But membership is revealed and validated by conduct in keeping with the moral and spiritual character of that relationship. In short, there will be family resemblance. Furthermore, the reward motif, although present, is not prominent. No attempt is made to explain its nature, but the context would suggest that it is intimately related to the privilege of being called the sons and daughters of God. We do not know what joys and blessings are yet to be unfolded in that relationship, but we do know that whatever they are, they are framed by divine grace. That knowledge has a transforming impact on any conception of reward.

Thus far we have noted some of the details of both the beatitude on peacemaking and the passage on loving the enemy closely linked to it. Both focus on the meaning of discipleship in the kingdom. It must yet be said that these materials should be seen in the larger context of Jesus' mission. They speak not only about the disciple but also about Jesus and the way he understood his own mission. In a basic and profound sense, as God's Son par excellence, Jesus came to make peace, to bring wholeness and well-being to men and women. He dealt with his enemies not by retaliatory measures but by absorbing their enmity and hostility and giving back love and acceptance. The ultimate cost was a frightful self-sacrifice. But Jesus broke the cycle of tit-for-tat evildoing that had long reigned in human relationships. He opened doors for us to new life in relationships both to God and to one another. As Paul put it: "He is our peace; in his flesh he has made both groups into one and has broken down the dividing wall, that is, the hostility between us" (Eph. 2:14).

It is to the ongoing mission of peacemaking that his disciples are now summoned in this sermon. This mission is set out in the immediate context under the further imagery of being salt and light in the world (Matt. 5:13–16). Both suggest positive redemptive functions pointing the way to the possibilities of new existence through the Christ-event. If this witness is to remain vital, the salt must not lose its saltiness, and the light must not be put under a bushel.

"Blessed are the peacemakers"

The enigmatic Judas

Charles Lamb, the early nineteenth-century British essayist, once expressed the wish that he might have seen the face of Judas. Despite painter Leonardo da Vinci's portrayal of Judas in *The Last Supper*, he had no conception, he said, of how one would have looked who could dip his hand in the same dish with the Christ and then betray him.

Lamb's wish was not and can never be fulfilled. History has left us no such legacy. Indeed, little is known about Judas. His name is mentioned as one of the twelve people whom Jesus at some point in his ministry chose from the larger group of disciples. He is not again referred to by name in the first three Gospels until the week of Jesus' passion, when he appears as one already intent on betraying Jesus to the Jewish authorities.

The Gospel of John, it is true, gives somewhat more attention to Judas. The formal selection of the twelve has no parallel in this Gospel. However, the call of Judas to be a disciple is referred to when his name first appears in connection with the Galilean crisis at the time of the feeding of the 5,000 (John 6:70–71). Judas is also singled out for special mention in the story of the anointing of Jesus at Bethany a few days before the Passover (John 12:4). In the betrayal story, some detail is given that is not found in the first three Gospels—for example, that Judas was treasurer of the disciple band (John 13:29). Finally, attention may be called to a reference to Judas, without actually mentioning his name, in the prayer of Jesus found in John 17 (see v. 12).

Beyond the betrayal material found in all four Gospels, there is one further reference to Judas in the Gospel of Matthew (27:3–10). It is the story of what happened to him after the arrest of Jesus: he brought the money back to the Jewish authorities and then committed suicide. Although none of the other Gospels report this matter, there is an independent account of Judas's death in Acts 1:18–20.

From this brief survey of the Gospels, clearly the focus of interest in Judas is on his role in bringing Jesus to his death. Not only does he appear most prominently in the events associated with his arrest, but also he is identified as the betrayer both in earlier and later references to him (see Mark 3:19; John 12:4; Matt. 27:3; Acts 1:16). Although the name *Judas* was an honored name in Judaism, deriving as it did from the tribal name of Judah, it has in Christian history become thoroughly stained with infamy. Judas and treachery have become synonymous terms.

> Judas had the potential of becoming a faithful disciple of Jesus. Likely, he entertained wrong expectations of Jesus' mission, and he did not believe deeply enough in Jesus to be open to other options. At some point his disappointment turned to bitterness.

Before turning to the intriguing question of why Judas acted as he did, closer attention should be given to some details in the narrative of the betrayal. First, in all the Gospel accounts Jesus foretold his betrayal to the disciples (Matt. 26:21; Mark 14:18; Luke 22:21; John 13:21). It is clear, however, that the (eleven) disciples did not know to whom Jesus was referring: one after another they asked, "Surely not I, Lord?" The Gospel of John suggests that the beloved disciple was given a sign pointing to Judas, but he did not seem to understand the full significance of the hint. When Judas left the room to implement his dark design, "no one at the table" understood what he was about to do (John 13:21–29). Apparently there were no obvious evidences of Judas's grave disloyalty that alerted the rest of the disciples to what lay in the immediate future.

Second, according to the first three Gospel accounts, Judas took the initiative in contacting the Jewish authorities and offering his services to them (Matt. 26:14–15; Mark 14:1–2; Luke 22:4–6). This understanding is in contrast to a late apocryphal tradition that regards Judas as a recruit by the Jewish authorities to act as a planted spy within the disciple band. It is not entirely clear whether it was Judas or the authorities that first proposed a monetary reward (Matt. 26:51; Luke 22:4–6). If greed was a motive for his deed, then likely Judas made the proposal.

Third, at what point did Pilate become involved in the proceedings against Jesus? Among those whom Judas led into the garden to arrest Jesus was "a detachment of soldiers" (John 18:3). The terminology points to a contingent of Roman soldiers, which would have been secured through an arrangement with Pilate. Thus the Roman procurator may well have had a hand in arresting Jesus. Judas likely had nothing to do with these negotiations.

Fourth, although the Gospel of John makes no mention of Judas kissing Jesus in the garden, this gesture was not an unusual Jewish greeting between disciples and their master. What we do not know, however, is whether it was a common practice for Jesus' disciples. There are no other references to it in the Gospels.

Fifth, what did Judas divulge to the Jewish authorities about Jesus? Was it, as Albert Schweitzer thought, the knowledge that Jesus was the Messiah? If this were the case, we might expect that Judas would have been called on when witnesses were sought against Jesus by the chief priests and the council (Mark 14:55–60). But we have no evidence that he was. More likely, then, Judas told the authorities where Jesus was accustomed to retire with his disciples and where he might be apprehended (John 18:2).

Sixth, the betrayal of Jesus by Judas is linked in the gospel tradition with three motifs: the fulfillment of scripture, the activity of the devil, and greed. Each of these will need consideration in connection with the question to which we now turn: why did Judas do what he did? The answers are not simple but deserve some discussion.

We begin with observations that arise out of the biblical text. First is the matter of greed. Some support for this motivation may be found in Matthew's report that Judas approached the Jewish authorities with the question, "What will you give me if I deliver him to you?" (Matt. 26:15). But interest in financial gain is not explicit in the parallel accounts of these negotiations. It does surface in a rather forthright manner in

John's version of the anointing of Jesus at Bethany. Not only is Judas identified as the critic on that occasion, but his criticism is attributed to avarice. He had no genuine concern for the poor, but as treasurer he was also a thief who helped himself to the common funds (John 12:4–6). The text makes it clear that such theft was his habitual practice. It may, therefore, have been one strand of motivation, although perhaps not the most significant.

Next is the activity of the devil. He is said to have put the thought of betraying Jesus into the heart of Judas (John 13:2). Later Satan is represented as entering him (John 13:26–27). Elsewhere in the Gospel of John, Judas is also linked with the demonic world (6:70–71; 17:12). Surely Satan was at work in the life of Judas. It does not follow, however, that responsibility for what Judas did can be loaded entirely on the devil. What was it that led Judas to make himself available as the devil's agent to bring Jesus to his death?

Finally, the Gospels make repeated reference to the fulfillment of scripture in relation to Judas and what he did. An interesting example of this matter is some words spoken by Jesus to his disciples at the Last Supper. "I am not speaking of you all," he said, excluding Judas; "I know whom I have chosen. But it is to fulfill the scripture, 'The one who ate my bread has lifted his heel against me'" (John 13:18). The Old Testament passage referred to is Psalm 41:9. The appropriateness of this scripture to describe the intimate relation of Judas to Jesus and his subsequent betrayal of his master is evident. What is not so clear is whether Jesus chose Judas knowing what sort of person he would become. The statement in John 6:70–71 suggests that by the end of the Galilean ministry, Jesus was aware that Judas was not giving him full support. But does either of these passages require the conclusion that Jesus, in his original choice of Judas, was acting in complete knowledge of a predetermined, divine plan that only awaited Judas's implementation?

Before answering this question, other passages that link Judas and his conduct to the fulfillment of scripture may be noted. The prayer of Jesus in John 17 includes the statement that "not one of them"—referring to the disciples—"was lost except the one destined to be lost, so that the scripture might be fulfilled" (v. 12). Again, the saying, "All this has taken place, so that the scriptures of the prophets may be fulfilled" (Matt. 26:56), is a summary statement that includes the betrayal of Jesus by Judas described earlier (26:14–16, 47–56). Furthermore, the use of the betrayal money to purchase a burial ground, "the Field of Blood," is said to have fulfilled Old Testament prophecy (Matt. 27:3–10). Finally, in Acts 1:16–26 we find a more general reference to Judas's conduct and the subsequent necessity, after his death, to replace him in the apostolic band as necessary to fulfill scripture.

What can be said about all this data? Was Judas somehow programmed by Old Testament prophecy to do what he did? What is the meaning of this fulfillment language? One answer is that the Old Testament passages in question do indeed speak about Judas and were spoken in foreknowledge of what he in freedom would do later. To many students, however, it is not evident that this is a likely understanding of these passages in their Old Testament setting.

Another approach is to regard the fulfillment language as meaning that certain passages in the Old Testament are now filled full of meaning in light of what has just happened. These Old Testament statements were not, in the first instance, made with Judas in mind but had a more immediate reference. But the language did provide a suitable medium for the expression of what actually happened later in the case of Judas. He did, for example, eat of Jesus' bread and then indeed lifted his heel against him (see Ps. 41:9).

But more can be said. Jesus and the early church believed that God had a finger in what happened in the events of the passion week. The divine role, however, was not such that reduced Judas to the status of a puppet. If this were true, it would be hard to understand Jesus' repeated bids—up to the very end—for the loyalty of Judas. On the contrary, it was believed that God could make good come out of even this inexcusable conduct on the part of Judas.

On the assumption that Judas voluntarily chose to betray Jesus, another explanation for his action is sought in disappointed dreams. Judas was initially attracted to Jesus in the expectation of fulfillment of Jewish hopes for the coming of the kingdom. These anticipations may well have taken the form of the expulsion of the Roman presence and the reestablishment of the Jewish state. Increasingly, however, it became clear to Judas that Jesus' utterances (about dying) and his conduct (refusal to respond to popular interest in making him king after the feeding of the 5,000) were not consistent with such hopes. In bitter disillusionment, then, he turned against Jesus.

A final and more positive interpretation of Judas's motivation has also been suggested: Judas did not act out of malice but in the belief that Jesus needed to be goaded to action. He expected that when confronted by a crisis Jesus would openly vindicate his messianic claims. When he did not, Judas's world caved in and in remorse he committed suicide. This proposal helps explain the stricken conscience of Judas, but it hardly does justice to other data already noted in the text.

In conclusion, perhaps the best we can say is that Judas—no less than the rest of the twelve—had the potential of becoming a faithful disciple of Jesus. Likely, he along with his associates entertained wrong expectations of Jesus' mission, and he did not believe deeply enough in Jesus to be open to other options. At some point his disappointment turned to bitterness. This disillusionment was the devil's opportunity to fill his heart with greed and his mind eventually with thoughts of betrayal. On these impulses he ultimately acted.

Judas betrayed Jesus and so brought about his death. That is hard to believe. But what is even more mysterious is the thought that came to Malcolm Muggeridge one day as he sat looking at what purports to be the Field of Blood where Judas met his end. It was that Jesus died for Judas. "The thought so delighted me," he wrote, "that I kept on repeating to myself: *Jesus died even for Judas!* as though I had made some extraordinary discovery. Perhaps in a way I had."

The crucifixion of Jesus

A mong the ruins of ancient Rome is a building now called the Paedagogium. It apparently belonged to the imperial palace. Some of the rooms seem to have been used as prisons. On the walls can still be seen roughly sketched drawings and various inscriptions. One such drawing of interest to Christians is the famous caricature of the crucifixion, portraying the body of a man with an ass's head, hanging on a cross. Beneath the feet is a platform supporting the body; the outstretched arms of the man are fastened to the transverse bar of the cross.

To the left is the smaller form of a boy or young man. One hand is raised in a gesture of salute to the crucified figure. Under the drawing is the inscription in large letters: "Alexamenos worships his god." Likely this graffito represents the ridicule to which some unknown Christian in the imperial palace was subjected in the late second or early third century AD. It is a vivid reminder that the Jesus whom we love and worship was indeed crucified.

Although the crucifixion holds a very important place in the Christian faith, the New Testament Gospel records provide us with a minimum of details. We know that prior to his crucifixion, Jesus was scourged. We know that he was made to carry his cross part of the way to Golgotha, that he was offered a narcotic drink to deaden the pain, that he was stripped of his clothes, that he was nailed to the cross, that a plaque bearing the charge against him was placed over his head, that he experienced thirst, and that he died earlier than was expected. The apocryphal gospels (not found in the New Testament) often fill in gaps in the canonical accounts with imaginative details, but they do not choose to do so here. One small touch is added by the *Gospel of Peter*, which suggests that Jesus seemed to suffer no pain while he was being crucified; this surely reflects a theological interest that had difficulty reckoning seriously with the humanity of Jesus.

The brevity of the Gospel accounts of the actual act of crucifixion may be the result of a reverent desire to hide those gruesome details from our view. Or the evangelists may have wished to focus on other matters both leading up to and growing out of the crucifixion as such. More likely, however, the Gospel writers felt no need to supply their immediate readers with a detailed description of what occurred because these readers were already familiar with such proceedings. Crucifixions were not uncommon in the Roman world of the first century.

> The brevity of the accounts of the crucifixion may be the result of a reverent desire to hide gruesome details. More likely, the Gospel writers felt no need to supply a detailed description, because their immediate readers were already familiar with such proceedings.

The Romans did not invent crucifixion as a form of punishment. It was practiced by other peoples of the ancient world, including the Persians, Phoenicians, Greeks, and Carthaginians. The Romans used it primarily to punish slaves, foreigners, and criminals of the lowest class. Theoretically at least, a Roman citizen was to be spared the indignity of this sort of punishment. This statute helps us understand why according to tradition Paul (a citizen) was beheaded, while Peter (a non-citizen) was crucified.

The Romans saw in this form of capital punishment an effective way to maintain order in the provinces. The Roman writer Cicero speaks of this punishment as "the most cruel and frightful sentence." The Jewish historian Josephus refers to it as "the most wretched of all ways of dying." Crucifixion was meted out especially to rebels against Roman rule. One might suppose that people would think twice before they risked facing this fate.

But in a province such as Judea feelings against Rome could not be controlled even by the threat of crucifixion. We have no way of knowing how many Jews were put to death in this manner during the first century. Josephus makes repeated references to such occurrences. In some instances, large numbers of people were involved. Therefore it is not surprising that Roman sources should take no particular interest in the crucifixion of Jesus, or that Christian sources should find it unnecessary to give a detailed report on how it was carried out.

We are able from various literary sources to supplement the information that the Gospels provide. We know, for example, that there were various types of crosses; the form depended on the way the two wooden beams were put together. The crossbar might be placed atop the upright beam, or it might be attached to it at some lower point. Because the inscription was attached to the upright beam above Jesus' head, we surmise that in his case the second type of cross was used (Matt. 27:37).

The height of the cross also varied. Most often it was only high enough to ensure that the feet of the victim were off the ground, thus leaving the person exposed to easy abuse by enemies or possible attack by hungry wild animals. But a somewhat taller cross was also occasionally used, either to guard against a premature death by animals of prey or to make it possible for more people to see the criminal. The cross of Jesus seems to have been of the taller type: the soldier could not lift the sponge to Jesus' lips without putting it on a reed (see Mark 15:36).

The common opinion—that the cross was already put together before the condemned person was attached to it and subsequently erected—is a misconception. The "cross" that was borne by the victim to the place of execution was only the crossbeam. At the place of crucifixion the upright beam was first firmly secured in the ground. Then the person was made to lie on the ground while his outstretched arms were fastened to the crossbeam. The beam with the body attached to it was then raised and fastened to the upright pole.

Various methods were used to hold the body to the cross. Sometimes the person's arms and legs were tied with ropes. At other times nails were used. In the case of Jesus nails were employed (John 20:25). Midway on the upright post was a projecting peg or block of wood which provided some support for the suspended body; otherwise the weight of the body would have torn it away from the nails. Despite what the later drawing referred to above portrays, there seems to have been no support under the feet.

How long a person could live after being crucified depended on various factors such as the severity of the prior scourging, his age and general health, the method used to attach the body to the cross, and additional abuse suffered while he was suspended on the cross. As Josephus was leaving the city one morning during the siege of Jerusalem in AD 70, he saw some newly captured Jews being crucified. When he returned in the evening he discovered three of his friends among them. He promptly went to the Roman commander and got permission to take them down. Under medical care one recovered, but the other two died.

Thus far we have been relying on information provided by ancient literary sources. Our knowledge of this cruel practice now has the additional support of a twentieth-century archaeological discovery. In the summer of 1968, four cave-tombs were discovered just north of the city of Jerusalem, part of a large Jewish cemetery that existed in the time of Jesus. Within the caves fifteen limestone ossuaries (urns) were found which contained the skeletons of thirty-five people. A careful study of these remains has shown that nine of them met a violent death. Among these nine was one of particular interest. One ossuary contained the bones of a man somewhere between twenty-four and twenty-eight years of age. He was of slight build, about five feet six inches tall. There are clear indications that he died by crucifixion, probably sometime between AD 7 and 66. It was the first certain archaeological evidence of a crucifixion in antiquity to be found in our time.

A detailed examination of the skeleton has led scholars to a number of conclusions about the manner of his death. First, the man was nailed to the cross rather than tied with ropes. Moreover, the nails were driven through the lower forearms and not through the palms of his hands. If this procedure was customary, then the reference to Jesus' nail-pierced hands in John 20:20, 25, 27 may really indicate his arms; the Greek word used in this passage and in Luke 24:39 can carry such a meaning.

Second, the body rested on a small block of wood attached to the upright beam. The legs apparently were drawn up under the thighs but pressed together and turned to the left side so that the thighs were almost parallel to the crossbeam at the upper end of the post. Thus, contrary to the usual paintings, the body was not extended in a straight vertical position.

Third, the feet were placed sidewise, the right one on top of the left, and fastened to the cross by a single iron nail through both heels. To make certain that the feet could not be slipped over the head of the nail, it was first driven through a small piece of wood placed against the top foot. When the skeleton was found, small bits of this piece and of the upright post still adhered to the nail.

Fourth, the shinbones of both legs were fractured, giving evidence of what is known from literary sources to have been a Roman practice to hasten death by breaking the legs of the criminal. Jesus escaped this treatment by an early death (John 19:31–33).

From the Gospel accounts, it is evident that Jesus died before the two men who were crucified with him and apparently earlier than expected (Mark 15:44; John 19:32–33). What caused his early death? The following opinions have been advanced during the last century: a rupture of the heart because of intense mental agony; an embolism or blood clot; asphyxiation brought on by the twisted position of the body on the cross which would have made breathing difficult as he grew weaker; acute dilation of the stomach, a complication which can follow surgery or severe injury and which if not treated can be fatal; a deliberate act of the will—he died because he willed to die (see Matt. 27:50; John 19:30).

With the data available to us, it is not likely that a specific medical cause of Jesus' death can be identified with any degree of certainty. A significant factor in his early death may well have been a particularly brutal pre-crucifixion scourging as one accused of sedition against the Roman state. Simon's conscription to bear Jesus' crossbeam (not a heavy burden) on the way to execution might well point to a condition of great physical weakness. The added torture of crucifixion, the possibility of further abuse while he hung on the cross, and the spiritual agony of the ordeal (Mark 15:34) serve to make an early death credible.

Some thoughts about Good Friday

ESSAY
37

Good Friday is partly shrouded in mystery. We will never be able to banish all of it. What our hearts know to be true will always exceed our ability to explain. But try we must for two reasons: the stark fact of the cross and our incurable curiosity.

Of course, we do not begin from scratch. We are Christians. We have long been familiar with the symbol of the cross in Christian art and liturgy. The story of the passion has been rehearsed many times in Sunday school literature and in sermons. While such conditioning may give us a head start in our quest, there is also the danger that it may make the discovery of fresh insights difficult.

The passion story is found in each of the New Testament Gospels. Although the accounts vary in detail, the basic story is marked by simplicity, forthrightness, and power; if read with attention and imagination, it can scarcely fail to move us. But the passion story has a setting that must not be neglected if we would understand it, and it also has a sequel that is equally important. Torn from its context, the story is exposed to whatever meaning we might wish to bring to it.

What then is the meaning of the cross when seen in proper perspective? In this brief discussion no more than a few comments can be offered. These are not so much decisive conclusions as they are basic considerations that must enter into the process of reaching conclusions. They are intended to be helpful guidelines in your own personal study of the biblical materials.

The cross should not be detached from its immediate setting in the life and ministry of Jesus. It might be possible, if we fix on a few texts in the New Testament Epistles, to suppose that the death of Jesus alone was significant for our redemption. But this conclusion would do violence to much else in the New Testament. The Gospels make it clear that the cross was not an isolated boulder on a barren desert but an event intimately related to the total landscape of his life. A redemptive note of loving, sacrificial self-giving runs throughout the entire story of his ministry; the cross is merely the supreme expression of this spirit. It was only because Jesus lived as he did that the cross, historically speaking, happened at all.

On the other hand, it was the death of Christ that gave supreme meaning to his life. It was sacrifice to the uttermost that stamped as genuine every lesser sacrifice he made. Or, to approach it from the standpoint of Christ's obedience to the divine intention to save humanity, it was only complete obedience to the very end of the quest that validated his mission as a whole. The life and the death form an indissoluble unity that cannot be fractured without serious loss to each.

In the Old Testament, the purpose of human existence is interpreted in the framework of fellowship with God. Sin is a refusal to fulfill that purpose; it is not so much the breaking of laws as the rupture of a relationship. Human denial of God's intention is seen to have serious consequences. Attempting to get out of life what God has not put into it can only spell frustration and, in the end, tragedy.

But tragedy is not the last word. The Old Testament knows a system of offerings and sacrifice that was meant to aid men and women in expressing penitence for their sin, gratitude for God's mercy, and devotion to God's service. Sacrifice was not a magical rite bestowing automatic benefits; the prophets vigorously condemned such a conception of sacrifice. H. H. Rowley has said that Old Testament sacrifice had to bear "a two-way traffic or none. . . . It could not be charged with power to bless the offerer unless it was also charged with his surrender of himself in humble submission and obedience to God." The emphasis on the personal and spiritual elements for which the sacrificial system stood is seen in such passages as Psalm 40:6–8 and Isaiah 53. Both of these passages are applied to Christ in the New Testament (see Heb. 10:5–9; Acts 8:32–35; 1 Pet. 2:22–25). It is also important to note that in Isaiah 53 sacrifice is not only thought of in personal terms; it also has vicarious significance, for others benefit from the self-offering of the servant.

Although the cross is not left uninterpreted in the New Testament, there is no one consistently formulated and logically developed theory of the atonement such as are found in later Christian thought. The diversity of approach may be illustrated by the variety of images that are employed to portray the significance of the cross.

> **The Gospels make it clear that the cross was not an isolated boulder on a barren desert but an event intimately related to the total landscape of Jesus' life. A redemptive note of loving self-giving runs throughout his ministry; the cross is merely the supreme expression of this spirit.**

Let us look at only two passages. In Romans 3:24–25, three images are found in rapid succession: acquittal in a law court ("justified"), release from slavery ("redemption"), and ritual sacrifice ("expiation by his blood"). Three additional images occur in Colossians 2:13–15: raising the dead to life (v. 13), the cancellation of a debt (v. 14), and a military victory over an enemy (v. 15).

Such diversity of imagery—and more images might be cited—does not mean that there is hopeless confusion in the way the early church understood the death of Christ. They were certain of its basic meaning. They were sure that God was acting in and through that death to bring people to God. But they were equally aware that no one category or image is completely adequate to express the total meaning of the cross. Each image was a window through which people might glimpse some aspect of the reality.

But the part must not be taken for the whole. We are sure to sacrifice some of the richness of the New Testament view if we confine our attention to only one image. Indeed, we are likely to distort the truth if we unduly press one figure without the balance or corrective that is provided by other images. This distortion has happened repeatedly in the history of theology.

We must keep God closely tied to what happened at Calvary. We should not pit God and Jesus against each other, as though Jesus by his death made it possible for God to love us. To see the cross as God exacting the last pound of flesh in retributive justice before the floodgates of mercy could be opened is to misunderstand the New Testament. Calvary is no less a revelation of God's love than it is of Jesus' love (see Rom. 5:8; John 3:16; 1 John 4:9–10). Paul affirms that "in Christ God was reconciling the world to himself" (2 Cor. 5:19).

An artist has painted a picture of the crucifixion that hangs in the National Gallery in London. Behind the face of Jesus is the outline of another face; behind the outstretched arms and the nail-pierced feet are other hands and feet. This portrayal is the artist's way of saying that God was not on a holiday in the hinterlands of the universe on that first Good Friday.

I do not mean to say that the sufferings on the cross were not in some sense penal. But they were not penal in the sense that they were inflicted on Jesus as the personal object of an angry God. They were penal only to the extent that by Jesus' complete identification with humanity in our sin, he realized to the full the divine reaction against sin.

We should recognize the firm bond that exists between sin, love, suffering, and redemption. That suffering should be associated with our redemption from sin is not the result of an arbitrary arrangement: it is inevitable in the very nature of the problem. Sin as the refusal of a personal relationship of fellowship with God came home to the divine heart as "the sorrow of a defeated purpose." God, of course, might have reacted to the pain which our sin inflicted on him in one of two ways. He might have risen up in wrath and utterly destroyed humanity from the face of the earth. Such a course would have made our redemption an impossibility.

God chose, on the contrary, to set about salvation for all people. God chose to bear the sufferings that human sin entailed. Before Christ came, we already catch a glimpse of the pain in God's heart in such utterances as Hosea 11:1–9. But it was in Christ that God entered into the sin problem in a unique and decisive way. In Christ God took to God's own heart the full consequences of the bitter enmity of humanity as we lashed out against God. But when sin did its worst, Jesus quietly prayed, "Father, forgive them," and sealed that prayer with his death. His was the voice of divine love that knew experientially the full measure of the painful cost of forgiveness. Love that can take on itself all the worst consequences of human sin and still go on loving—indeed forgiving and accepting men and women into its fellowship—such love has reconciling power.

In the end, nothing reconciles but love. And when God so loves that Calvary is the manner and the measure of its expression, then from God's side no more can be done to open the door for the possibility of a new relationship based on the miracle of grace. Whether reconciliation actually follows depends on our response to such grace. God has acted. Now we must act. "Love so amazing, so divine, demands my soul, my life, my all." This is the ultimate meaning and challenge of Good Friday.

The gospel of the resurrection

In the last chapter of *The Work and Words of Jesus*, A. M. Hunter deals with the resurrection of Jesus. He reports that when the Queen of England read the book, she wrote to him as follows: "I am sorry to say that I read the last chapter first, which is, I know, dreadful cheating; but it makes a wonderful and hopeful background to the rest of the book, and I do not regret it at all."

The queen was right. The resurrection does make a wonderful and hopeful background, not only to Hunter's book, but to the entire story told in our Gospels. And it would not be amiss—at least occasionally—to read the last chapter(s) of any of the New Testament Gospels before reading the remainder, and then to read the rest of the book with that event fixed firmly in mind. This approach might enable us to put new questions to the story as it unfolds and to ponder it with fresh excitement.

In any case, what should be clear to us is this: the account of the resurrection is no mere last event in the remarkable tale that the evangelists tell. It is the presupposition of their story. In *The Founder of Christianity*, C. H. Dodd has written: "The resurrection is not a belief that grew up within the church; it is the belief around which the church itself grew up, and the given upon which its faith was based." This is not to say that the resurrection can be detached from the rest of the story and made, in itself, to be the gospel. But if the account of Jesus' life had ended with his death and entombment, the four books in our New Testament that tell his story could hardly have been called Gospels ("good news"). Paul was speaking not only for himself but for the entire early church when he wrote, "If Christ has not been raised, then our proclamation has been in vain and your faith has been in vain"(1 Cor. 15:14).

It is not sufficient, however, merely to affirm the significance of the resurrection of Jesus for the Christian faith; we must seek to understand its centrality. To find an answer to this question, we need to explore the setting of the resurrection both in the proclamation of the early church and in the Jewish beliefs regarding the end time. Because the church emerged out of Judaism, and because many early Christian understandings can only be comprehended against a Jewish background, we need to begin with the Jewish context.

The account of the resurrection is no mere last event in the remarkable tale that the evangelists tell. It is the presupposition of their story.

It is well known that the Old Testament has very little to say about the resurrection of the dead. There are two passages that may be cited as witnesses to this belief: Isaiah 26:19 and Daniel 12:2. For the most part, however, the Old Testament is concerned with life before death rather than with what happens afterward.

But in the last two centuries before the Christian era, for various reasons that we cannot fully explore here, Jewish thought increasingly gave attention to human destiny beyond death. But when serious thought did turn to life beyond the grave, Jewish theology in the main could not be satisfied with belief in the immortality of the soul. The body was an essential part of the person. For personal existence to be meaningful after death, the body is necessary.

The resurrection of the body, therefore, came to be part of the Jewish expectation about the end time in at least certain quarters of Judaism. This hope is expressed in various Jewish writings produced from the second century BC through the first century AD. The last two centuries before the coming of Jesus were very difficult years for the Jewish people in Palestine. In the midst of their fears, frustrations, and sufferings, the vision of a future day when the books would be balanced, the world cleansed of its wickedness, and the dead (some or all) restored to life (either for punishment or bliss) became more or less clear to some of them. The Pharisees in particular believed in the resurrection of the dead, but the Sadducees did not; what the people of Qumran thought on this subject is not entirely clear.

During his ministry, Jesus restored a few people to life. Such raisings were followed in time by another victory of death. At best these resuscitations were few in number and raised more or less immediate excitement. But the end—the general resurrection and the new order—had not come. It tarried beyond the horizon; it was still a matter of hope. Then Jesus himself was put to death at the end of a most remarkable ministry. But the cross had a sequel in the discovery of the empty tomb, the encounters with the living Lord, and the resultant firm conviction that Jesus had been raised from the dead.

Now it is clear, not only from the New Testament Epistles but also from the Gospels themselves, that the resurrection event was no mere resuscitation of the dead body. The Gospel accounts provide certain links with the pre-passion physical presence of Jesus, but they also include new elements. The living Lord cannot be wholly described simply in the terms of his earlier mode of existence among them. Easter was not so much a return to life as it was a victory over death and the entrance into that life where death has no power. Indeed, the forces of unbelief, hatred, and opposition continued to be strong: the kingdom of God apparently had not come in its fullness.

To put it briefly, for the early Christians eschatology had been fractured: certain end-time events had happened, yet in other respects the old age continued much as usual. The end had come, and yet it had not fully come. The full theological and ethical significance of the conviction that experience had forced on the early church was not immediately worked out. But in due time the task was undertaken, and the literary deposit of this activity is found in our New Testament materials. What are some of the features that marked this product?

The significance of the resurrection for the early Christians can be expressed in two ways. First, it was seen as God's reversal of the judgment that the Jewish leaders had passed on Jesus. This turnabout is made very clear in Peter's sermon at Pentecost: "This man . . . you crucified and killed by the hands of those outside the law. But God raised him up. . . . God has made him both Lord and Messiah, this Jesus whom you crucified" (Acts 2:23–24, 36).

Second, the resurrection of Jesus demanded a revision of Jewish thinking about the end time. In order to understand why this was so, we must recall what was said earlier about the nature of Jesus' resurrection. The disciples sensed that it was of a different order than a mere resuscitation of a dead person to mortal life. It was rather passage to life on the far side of death in which death had been overcome. Jesus was truly alive!

Along with this unique experience that had come to them was another: the advent of the Spirit on the day of Pentecost (Acts 2). Peter recognized this sudden flooding of their very beings with a presence, life, and power from beyond themselves to be the fulfillment of the prophecy of Joel 2:28–32. The renewal of the Spirit's presence that Judaism looked forward to in the end time had now occurred. Both the resurrection and the coming of the Spirit followed hard on the heels of Jesus' preaching about the coming of the kingdom of God. The kingdom to which he made reference was not the timeless sovereignty of God: it was the fresh and powerful manifestation of God's rule in the end time.

Coupled with this preaching were claims for Jesus as a special representative of God among God's people. At Caesarea Philippi, Peter ventured the belief that Jesus was the Messiah (Mark 8:29). But what was spoken there in privacy—and probably subsequently doubted when death overtook Jesus—was confidently proclaimed in public after the resurrection and the coming of the Holy Spirit. Jesus was the Messiah (see Acts 2:36). The long-awaited figure of the end time had come.

Thus there were three interlocking events that had come into the purview of the disciples: the advent of the Messiah, the resurrection, and the coming of the Spirit. In Jewish theology, all of these events belonged to the end time. But it soon became evident that the end time had not fully come. Although Jesus had been raised from the dead, there was no general resurrection of the dead. And while some Jews were now prepared to recognize Jesus as the Messiah, many still did not.

From a theological point of view, New Testament writers attempted to bind firmly together the "already" and the "not yet" elements of end-time happenings. They did so in a variety of ways. In Hebrews, for example, the imagery of the Jewish ritual of the Day of Atonement is used to tie the two together. Jesus, who has offered the ultimate and perfect sacrifice on earth, is now behind the veil in the presence of God on our behalf, but in due time he will return to us to complete his ministry of salvation. In the letters of Paul, other images are used to bridge the gap between what has happened and what is still anticipated. There is the military imagery that represents Christ as one exalted to the place of supreme authority in God's world. But his foes are not yet fully subdued: he must exercise his lordship until the last enemy is conquered. Again, there is the imagery of the "first fruits," which finds its point in the solidarity of the part with the whole. Christ's resurrection is thus made to carry the promise of the resurrection of the dead that is still future. Likewise, the gift of the Spirit is tied to the final redemption of our bodies by the imagery of first fruits.

So the formal representations of the tie between the past and the future may vary. But what is important is the uniform certainty of the linkage. What has happened becomes a base for affirming what will happen. Conduct in the time between the beginning of the end and the end is to be oriented toward the newness that has come in Christ. We are to live as sons and daughters of the day that has already dawned and will soon come in its full eschatological splendor. To this end the Spirit has been given to help illumine the meaning of that norm and to implement it in life.

What happened at Pentecost?

The story of Pentecost is the gateway into the book of Acts. Chapter 1 is introductory material, some of which is another version of Luke's conclusion of his Gospel. Already in this initial material the reader's attention is directed toward the coming of the Spirit in chapter 2 (see 1:4–5, 8). What follows the event of Pentecost in the remainder of the book cannot really be understood unless it is seen in the light of this incident. Indeed, it is doubtful whether Luke would have written a sequel to his first book if the Spirit had not come. Likely there would never have been a Christian church or a New Testament apart from Pentecost. "In Acts as elsewhere in the New Testament" says James Denney, "the reception of the Spirit is the whole of Christianity. . . . To understand what is meant by the Spirit is to understand these two things—the New Testament and the Christian church."

If the Pentecost event is as crucial as Denny has suggested, then it is important that we try to understand as fully as possible what actually happened. The scriptural account is brief. It has a setting, there are certain secondary or associated features, and then there is the core reality itself. Some attention will need to be given to the first and second of these items. But it is the third that demands primary consideration.

The festival of Pentecost has an Old Testament background. There it is variously known as "the festival of harvest" (Exod. 23:16) and "the festival of weeks" (Exod. 34:22). It was to be celebrated seven weeks after the beginning of barley harvest (Deut. 16:9–10). The term *Pentecost* comes from the Greek word meaning "fiftieth" and designates the festival as occurring on the fiftieth day after the first sheaf of barley was offered to the Lord. A description of the ritual to be followed in the celebration of the festival is found in Leviticus 23:15–21.

Originally this festival was an agricultural one. In the course of time, however, it was also related to the history of salvation and came to memorialize the giving of the law at Mount Sinai. This connection was probably suggested by the time of its celebration early in the third month of the year, which roughly corresponded to the traditional time of Israel's arrival at Mount Sinai (Exod. 19:1). How early in Jewish history this historical association was made is not entirely clear; the first unambiguous evidence post-dates the New Testament. But some scholars think it may have been made in certain Jewish circles already before the time of Jesus. In any case, in first-century Pharisaic Judaism the festival of Pentecost does not seem to have enjoyed the prominence that was accorded to the other two pilgrimage festivals, Passover and Tabernacles.

It was what happened in connection with the first celebration of Pentecost after the death of Jesus that has given this festival a place of enduring significance in the Christian calendar. The disciples of Jesus, badly shaken and bewildered by what had recently transpired in their experience, gathered in Jerusalem with other Jews to keep the festival. They had no way of knowing what was to happen to them on that occasion. The interval between the ascension of Jesus and Pentecost was given, among other things, to corporate prayer (Acts 1:14). Doubtless this activity was accompanied by much reflection on what lately had happened in Jerusalem. Probably the disciples engaged in intensive study of the scripture following the clue that the resurrected Jesus had provided (Luke 24:25–27, 44–47). Surely they would have recalled and pondered many of the sayings of Jesus during his ministry. Then there was the command not to leave Jerusalem until the promise of the coming of the Spirit should be fulfilled (Acts 1:4–5).

In spite of the words of Jesus, the disciples could not have anticipated what actually happened to them. Associated with the coming of the Spirit were sensations of sight and sound. The language of analogy is used: the sound was not produced by a mighty wind but was "like the rush of a violent wind"; what they saw were not tongues of fire but "tongues as of fire." The reality was something other than that which could be described in a straightforward, literal manner. It was akin to a vision. This acknowledgement in no way detracts from the meaningfulness of the experience; it is simply a way of identifying its nature.

The analogies of wind and fire were not ordinary symbols for the disciples: they had religious significance drawn from their Jewish heritage. Scholars have called attention to passages in rabbinic literature where the symbols of light and sound indicate the presence or activity of the Spirit. Beyond these were the Old Testament materials where God's presence is frequently associated with noise or wind (Ezek. 3:12; Job 38:1), or with fire (Gen. 15:17; Exod. 3:2; 13:21–22; 19:18). Thus the symbolism accompanying the Pentecostal experience is suggestive of its inner and real meaning: a divine visitation.

> What follows the event of Pentecost in the remainder of the book of Acts cannot really be understood unless it is seen in the light of the coming of the Spirit. Indeed, it is doubtful whether Luke would have written a sequel to his first book if the Spirit had not come. Likely there would never have been a Christian church or a New Testament apart from Pentecost.

The advent of the Spirit was attended by glossolalia, or speaking in tongues. This happening has been the subject of much discussion and considerable diversity of opinion. What was the nature of the experience? How should the tongues at Pentecost be related to the tongues described in 1 Corinthians 14? What particular significance did Luke see in the phenomenon? Is speaking in tongues in some sense prophetic of the universal intention of the gospel? These questions are interesting but cannot be pursued here. It is sufficient to note that tongues are neither the essence of the Pentecostal experience nor the most significant consequence.

What then really happened at Pentecost? The narrative of Acts 2 answers the question in a simple, forthright manner: "All of them were filled with the Holy Spirit" (v. 4). What had been promised (Acts 1:4–5; Joel 2:28–32) was now fulfilled. The Spirit had indeed been poured out, and this was the solid core of the experience on that day. This mysterious, marvelous, and memorable event has forever stamped Pentecost as unique in the annals of God's people. It marked the birthday of the Christian church.

To say, however, that "the Spirit came" on that occasion is likely, on a little reflection, to raise some difficult problems. Such language suggests that the Spirit was entering human experience, if not the world, for the first time in history. This impression may indeed be made by a passage such as Acts 2:33—if taken literally and in isolation from other biblical materials. But the rest of scripture contradicts such an opinion. Luke already has made clear in his Gospel that the Spirit came upon Jesus at his baptism (Luke 3:21–22). Prior to that, the Spirit was active both in the conception of Jesus (Luke 1:35) and in the various figures associated with the infancy narrative (Luke 1:15, 41, 67; 2:25–27). And behind the Gospel, the Spirit is repeatedly referred to in one way or another in the pages of the Old Testament. Surely the Spirit was in the world before Pentecost. The evidence is overwhelming.

How then should we understand the language of the Spirit being "poured out" or "coming" at Pentecost? Perhaps we should begin by asking what is meant by the term *Spirit*. One way of understanding this word is to say that the Spirit is used in the Bible to describe God's presence and activity in the world. God is not only the creator and Lord of creation who as such stands over against it; God is also present and active within it. Note, for example, how in Psalm 139 spirit is a synonym for God's presence. Again, Ananias's lie to the Spirit was a lie to God who was present and active in the Christian community (Acts 5:3–4). God is both transcendent over and imminent in the world; God's Spirit is one way of speaking about the latter.

Now the human scene has never been without the presence and activity of God; in this sense we can speak about the continuity of God's working in the world from the very beginning. The presence of the Spirit in both the Old and the New Testaments has this significance. But continuity does not mean unrelieved sameness. There must be room for the element of novelty. The history of God's saving activity in the world is a story of successive acts in which the continuity of God's purpose is carried forward in new and fresh happenings. So in speaking about the Spirit at Pentecost, it will not do to emphasize the matter of the continuity of God's working to the point of obscuring the element of novelty. Conversely, novelty must not be stressed at the expense of denying the previous ministry of the Spirit in the world.

The chief problem is to define the element of novelty. What was really new about the Pentecostal Spirit? This question has been answered in a variety of ways. Some would find the newness in a wonderfully fresh awareness of the Spirit's timeless presence and work: there was no new coming of the Spirit, but rather a new perception of the Spirit's presence. To use an image from photography, there was no increase of light, but the shutter was now more widely open to let more light in. The emphasis is placed on what happened in the disciples rather than on some objective change. Others would locate the element of novelty in a new inwardness of the Spirit's presence and work versus a more external relationship in the Old Testament; or in a present permanence of dwelling versus a former spasmodic or temporary coming of the Spirit; or in a communal experience of the Spirit versus a privilege enjoyed by relatively few individuals in earlier times.

The most helpful way to deal with this question is to see Pentecost against the backdrop of the person ministry, death, and resurrection of Jesus. The Spirit "came" successively upon persons in the Old Testament, upon Jesus, and upon the disciples at Pentecost. This is a metaphorical way of speaking of fresh divine encounters with people along the time line of history. In this series, Jesus stands out above all others. Not only was he brought on the human stage through the activity of the Spirit, but his life was fully and constantly open to the Spirit in a way earlier people were not. He was uniquely God's agent for the execution of God's purpose in bringing people into fellowship with God and with others. The Christ-event was God's fresh and decisive engagement with the age-old human predicament.

To speak of the coming of the Spirit at Pentecost is to say that a new chapter was beginning in the story of salvation. That day must be interpreted against the background of the pivotal person and work of Christ. In the New Testament the new terminology for the Spirit—"the Spirit of Christ" (Rom. 8:9; see Gal. 4:6; Phil. 1:19; Acts 16:7)—has this significance:

God's ongoing presence and work are now newly conditioned by the Christ-event. The implications of this great truth are profound and far-reaching both theologically and experientially. Pentecost in AD 30 is not only historically significant; it is also contemporarily relevant. Only as we come to terms with this fact can we claim to be Christian in person and in conduct. This relevance must be our agenda not only for today but also for every day that God grants us to live.

Acts: The church in conflict

The early church was a child of Judaism. Its parental home was first-century Palestine. Jesus grew to adulthood as a Jew in a small hill town in lower Galilee. He directed his brief public ministry to his own compatriots. As a result his disciples were Jews mainly from Galilee. Some of these were in Jerusalem during those eventful days, probably in the spring of AD 30, when Jesus was crucified and soon after raised from the dead. The Spirit that had earlier been bestowed on him was subsequently poured out on them at Pentecost

The birthday of the church saw these disciples and the newly won adherents from the festival throng in Jerusalem united in a fellowship of common life and devotion (Acts 2:42–47). All were Jews by birth or were proselytes to Judaism. Although there were special ties between them, their rapport with the larger Jewish community was good. Luke reports that they were "having the goodwill of all the people" (Acts 2:47).

The situation was quite otherwise at the end of the century, seventy years later. Church and synagogue had become two distinct communities. The final stage in the separation process was set in motion some years earlier. It was out of the anguish at the heart of any church split that a prayer invoking a curse on Christians was added to the series of prayers used in the synagogue: "For apostates let there be no hope, and the kingdom of arrogance do Thou speedily uproot in our days; and let Nazarenes [Christians] and heretics perish as in a moment; let them be blotted out of the book of life and not be enrolled with the righteous. Blessed art Thou, O Lord, who humblest the arrogant." Thus the child was disowned by its mother. No Christian Jew, obviously, could join in such a prayer.

If the separation was complete by the end of the century, it did not occur suddenly. Difficulties between the followers of

Jesus and the rest of the Jewish community began to emerge already in Jerusalem soon after Pentecost. Conflict repeatedly punctuates the story that is spread out for us in Acts. Active opposition begins with the arrest of Peter and John by the temple authorities in chapter 4. The book concludes in chapter 28 with a scene in far-away Rome: Paul is now a prisoner because of charges brought against him by fellow Jews. He is in dialogue over the gospel with the leaders of the Roman-Jewish community. Their response led Paul, again out of the pain of a church split, to quote the words of Isaiah 6:9–10 as finding fulfillment in their rejection of the gospel. Then he added: "Let it be known to you . . . that this salvation of God has been sent to the Gentiles; they will listen" (Acts 28:28).

The presence of conflict between church and synagogue in Acts should not surprise us. It is a continuation of a struggle between Jesus and the synagogue found already in Luke's first volume. Although the birth of Jesus is heralded by the angels as tidings of "peace on earth," the unfolding story is heavy with conflict. The initial scene in the Galilean ministry concludes with an attempt to destroy Jesus (Luke 4:16–30). At midpoint in the Gospel, Luke reports Jesus as saying: "Do you think that I have come to give peace to the earth? No, I tell you, but rather division" (Luke 12:51). Then at the end there is a cross. It is a stark reminder of the opposition to Jesus by the leadership of his own people as well as the Roman authorities. As that final conflict was gradually taking shape, Jesus informed his disciples that the road ahead would also involve suffering for them (Luke 9:23–24; 14:26–27; 21:12–19). What was foretold in Luke's first volume found fulfillment in the second.

How shall we account for the tension that developed between the church and the synagogue? The answer cannot be a simple one. Many factors were involved, some of belief, others having to do with conduct. But no explanation is adequate that does not see the figure of Jesus as central to the problem. It was the way that the thought and life of the Christians were polarized around him that more or less put them at odds with the patterns of life and thought in other segments of Jewish society. To get in step with Jesus was to get out of step with those who were marching to other drummers.

The early disciples were thoroughly convinced that Jesus was not dead but alive. The sermons in Acts 2–5 and 10 highlight this conviction. It was a matter of profound significance for them. The verdict of the Jewish leadership in Jerusalem had been decisively reversed by this happening. Some Jewish leaders regarded the death of Jesus as apt punishment for his sin. But the disciples viewed the resurrection as God's vindication of Jesus: God had accredited him as God's true servant. The appearances of the living Christ, followed by the experience of the outpouring of the Spirit, led the disciples to the unshakable belief that Jesus was indeed Messiah and Lord (Acts 2:36).

> What was being challenged was a mode of existence, an identity. In Palestinian Judaism there was a measure of latitude, but toleration had its limits. Jesus, in his attitude toward such symbols of ethnic solidarity as Torah, temple, Sabbath, food laws, and ritual purity, was a threat.

This firmly held conviction was destined to have far-reaching implications for them. It meant that what Jesus said about God, about God's purposes for his people, and about the piety and practices of Judaism provided a pattern for their thinking. Jesus' conduct in relation to the institutions and traditions of the day offered guidance for their style of life. The creative and dynamic Spirit that once dwelt in fullness in him was now in them also to carry forward what Jesus "began to do and teach" in his earthly ministry (Acts 1:1–8).

A by-product of the early Christian confession of Jesus as Messiah and Lord was the process of a gradual reevaluation of various aspects of contemporary Judaism. This reassessment did not happen in any systematic way. Basic questions were raised: How should the scriptures be understood? What was the significance of the temple and the sacrificial system? Of what importance was Jerusalem and the land of Israel? Was it necessary to observe the food taboos and the ritual laws of purity? What was the meaning of circumcision? How was the Sabbath to be observed? What authority did the priesthood, the scribal teachers, and the Sanhedrin have? What stance was to be taken toward the Gentiles? If Gentiles had a role in the salvation purpose of God, on what conditions might they participate?

The early Christians, of course, were not the first in Judaism to raise these questions. But they did insist on dealing with these issues in the light of the Christ-event; their point of reference was new. Moreover, the freedom with which they dropped or modified accepted answers or formulated new ones tended to identify them as a sect or party within Judaism. When we add to this dynamic the enthusiasm with which early Christians pressed their claims for the significance of Jesus, it is not difficult to understand the tension that developed between them and their non-Christian Jewish compatriots.

At stake was a basic question: How were the true people of God to be identified? It is clear that the community that gathered around Jesus did not regard itself as a splinter group whose existence was problematic. On the contrary, they thought of themselves as the authentic people of God. Jewish peoplehood was to be defined in terms of adhering to Jesus. There was salvation in "no other name under heaven" than his (Acts 4:12). Fleshly Israel was a "crooked generation" from which men and women needed to save themselves by joining the messianic community through repentance, baptism, and the reception of the Spirit (Acts 2:38–40). Indeed, the experiential hallmark of membership in the true Israel came to be seen not as circumcision but as the possession of the messianic Spirit (Acts 8:14–17; 10:44–48; 11:17; 15:8–9; 19:1–6).

It is important to see this conflict in more than purely spiritual terms. What was being challenged was a basic self-understanding, a mode of existence, a sense of identity. In Palestinian Judaism as a whole, there was a measure of latitude in the way these understandings were formulated. But toleration had its limits. To defy these limits was to attack what gave structure and cohesion to the Jewish community. Jesus, in his attitude toward such symbols of ethnic solidarity as the Torah, the temple, the Holy City, the Sabbath, food laws, and ritual purity, was such a threat.

Jesus' disciples and the Christians in the early church who followed in his steps were subsequently seen in the same light. Their willingness to admit Gentiles into full membership in the community of God's people without circumcision was regarded as undermining Jewish peoplehood. Their utter allegiance to

Jesus was seen as a weakening of devotion to the Jewish nation and its political destiny. The later refusal of Jewish Christians to join in the rebellion against Rome in the great war of AD 66–73 was probably interpreted by their compatriots as national treason. The Christian movement was seen as subversive to the continued existence of the Jewish community.

The tension between Christian and non-Christian Jews was expressed in a variety of ways and in differing degrees of intensity. Luke records several instances of violent death: Stephen probably was lynched (Acts 7:54–60); James, the brother of John, was killed by Herod Agrippa I (Acts 12:1). The king intended to dispose of Peter also, but his plans were thwarted. There is some evidence in Acts that Paul's persecution of Christians may in some cases have involved death (Acts 22:4; compare 9:1), although his letters make no mention of this fact.

In two passages Luke refers to Jewish floggings. The apostles were so treated in Jerusalem by the Sanhedrin (Acts 5:40). Saul also meted out this punishment to Christians (Acts 22:19); later, according to his own testimony, he himself suffered five such treatments (2 Cor. 11:24). Jewish law set the limit of strokes in such beatings at thirty-nine. Paul also suffered the Roman punishment of being beaten with rods on three occasions (2 Cor. 11:25); Luke reports one of these incidents (Acts 16:22). There are various references to the apostles being imprisoned by Jewish authorities (Acts 4:3; 5:18; 12:4). Saul too used this procedure against Christians (Acts 9:2, 14, 21; 22:19). It was probably a matter of detention with a view to trial rather than of punishment as such. Paul also suffered imprisonment at Roman hands in Philippi (Acts 16:23–24). Luke reports other forms of persecution: the stoning of Paul at Lystra (Acts 14:19), the expulsion of Paul and Barnabas from Antioch in Pisidia (Acts 13:50), and two instances of verbal abuse against Paul (Acts 13:45; 18:6). No reference is made to formal excommunication of Jewish Christians from the synagogue.

Acts represents the persecution of Christians as arising for the most part from Jewish initiative. There are a few exceptions, such as at Philippi (Acts 16:16–24), at Ephesus (Acts

19:23–41), and the joint attack on Paul and Barnabas at Iconium (Acts 14:5). Where Gentiles took the initiative, economic interests appear to have been prominent. When Christians were brought before Roman authorities, they were invariably cleared of any punishable charges. There were some imperial persecutions of Christians under emperors Nero (AD 54–68) and probably Domitian (81–96), but these fall outside the period covered by Acts.

Although conflict is a prominent theme in Acts, the mood of the book is not somber. The Christians who fill its pages are not a mournful lot. They exhibit no self-pity or of pessimism in outlook. On the contrary, they display a pervasive sense of commitment, enthusiasm, joy, and certainty. They are convinced that something utterly wonderful has happened in their midst. God has met them in Jesus, and life can never again be the same for them. If following Jesus means suffering, they are not left to their own resources in such moments. They experience the mysterious presence and sustaining power of the living Christ. This is the secret of the paradoxical union of joy with suffering that marks the Acts of the Apostles.

James: From skeptic to martyr

Artists have portrayed Jesus' family as consisting of three people: Mary, Joseph, and Jesus. There are understandable reasons for this portrayal. For one, the nativity narratives in the Gospels of Matthew and Luke represent the family in this way. Again, the story of Jesus' attendance at the Passover at the age of twelve speaks of Jesus as if he were the only child in the family (Luke 2:41–51). Furthermore, the Christian church early developed a special veneration for Mary. It became difficult to imagine that Mary would have had children by Joseph after the unique manner of Jesus' conception. Finally, the religious significance of Jesus has tended to focus attention on him to the point where the thought of other children in his family becomes unimportant—or even a distraction.

There is, however, ample positive evidence in the New Testament that the family to which Jesus belonged did consist of more than three people. There are repeated references to Jesus' brothers (see Mark 3:31; John 7:3; Acts 1:14; 1 Cor. 9:5). We know the names of four: James, Joseph, Judas, and Simon; in addition, the family included at least two sisters, whose names we do not know (Mark 6:3). So the family circle included no fewer than nine. The small, simple house of the carpenter in Nazareth in the early years of the first century must have been a place alive with children's voices and full of youthful enthusiasm and incessant activity.

James, then, was one of that group of siblings. Likely he was next to Jesus in age, for he is mentioned first in the list of Jesus' brothers (Mark 6:3). Probably he was not much younger than Jesus. We know more about him than about any of the other children because of the role that he later played in the early church. Even so, our knowledge of him is limited. None of the authors of the Gospels, Acts, or the Epistles had a biographical interest in Jesus' kin: they focused on Jesus and the new community that took its rise with him. The people who find a place in the pages of the New Testament are related in one way or another to him or to the Christian movement.

Although James eventually came to prominence in the early church, he was late in coming to faith in Jesus. Unlike the Twelve and many others who identified with Jesus during his Galilean ministry, James apparently rejected discipleship. Indeed, disbelief seems to have been the stance of all of Jesus' brothers during that period (John 7:5). This lack of family support, to which Jesus may have alluded in a visit to his hometown of Nazareth (Mark 6:4), is attested also in another incident that likely occurred in Capernaum. The passage is Mark 3:19b–35. Of particular interest is verse 21: "When his family heard about this, they went to take charge of him, for they said, 'He is out of his mind'" (NIV). There is some ambiguity in the Greek text, which is reflected in the various English versions. But the people who were unsympathetic to Jesus on that occasion were probably members of his family. The larger context would suggest this situation (vv. 31–35). Here Jesus made it clear that he regarded his true family as those who were related to him by spiritual rather than blood ties.

The reason for the family's opposition to Jesus is not clear. If Joseph died early, Jesus—as the oldest son—would have been expected to assume primary responsibility for supporting the family. His decision to leave the carpenter shop for a vocation without income may have resulted in serious economic hardship for the family. That outcome could have created tension. Perhaps, more basically, the family did not share his clear spiritual vision and deep inner dedication to it.

If—so far as we are permitted to glimpse—this description characterizes the general situation during the Galilean ministry, when did matters change? We know that Mary and Jesus' brothers were part of the disciple band in Jerusalem after the resurrection (Acts 1:14). At that point, the transition to faith and commitment had already occurred. When and under what circumstances the change came about we do not know. Mary apparently followed Jesus to Jerusalem, because she was present at the crucifixion (John 19:26). No mention is made, however, of the presence of Jesus' brothers. We are told of a special appearance of the risen Christ to James (1 Cor. 15:7). We do not know whether James was already a believer at that time or whether he came to faith through that experience, like Paul on the Damascus road. Again, the record does not state whether Jesus appeared to other members of his family. We would like to think that he did.

The first reference to James by name in Acts occurs in 12:17. It follows the unexpected release of Peter from prison after he had been arrested on orders from King Herod Agrippa I (AD 41–44). Herod was intending to kill Peter as he had already killed James the son of Zebedee. But the church prayed for Peter, and he was miraculously delivered from the king's designs. Peter, on his release, went to the house of Mary the mother of John Mark to tell the disciples who were praying there what had happened. Then he requested that they inform James and the brothers of his deliverance. Peter then "went to another place," and we hear no more of him until the Jerusalem conference some years later.

> Jesus' brother James, while giving freedom to Gentile Christians, expected Jewish Christians to continue observing the law. He also was anxious that Paul, the apostle to the Gentiles, give evidence of his respect for and his willingness to practice Jewish ceremonies when in Jerusalem.

The fact that James and certain other Christians were not present at Mary's house may well point to the existence of more than one house church in Jerusalem. As a result of the great influx of people into the church described in the early chapters of Acts, it is likely that more than one place of meeting and more than one leader were required to accommodate the growing numbers. Perhaps James was the leader of a house church other than that to which Peter had gone, which may have been his own group. Peter was eager to have James and those associated with him know of his release. If this understanding of the passage is correct, then James was a leader in the Jerusalem Christian community at a point approximately a dozen years after Pentecost.

How much earlier did he emerge as a leader? The early chapters of Acts do not provide much help to answer this question. However, Paul sheds some light in Galatians 1:18–

19, where he reports that on his first visit to Jerusalem three years after his conversion, he saw Peter but "I did not see any other apostle except James the Lord's brother." This visit may have occurred around AD 35. At that time, then, James was recognized, at least by Paul, as an apostle. Like Paul, he was not one of the Twelve. But he had seen the risen Lord and presumably had received a commission from him. Undoubtedly, James was already a leader in the Jerusalem church at the time of Paul's visit. Whether Paul contacted James on that occasion because of James' importance or whether the meeting was more circumstantial is not clear.

Let us return to Acts. The next reference to James in Acts after 12:17 is in chapter 15 in connection with the Jerusalem conference. Along with Luke's account, we should note the report by Paul in Galatians 2:1–10. The issue on that occasion was the terms on which Gentiles might enter the church. Would they need to become Jews through accepting circumcision? Did they have to observe the Mosaic law? Both accounts clearly indicate that James played the leading role in the consultations. Paul mentions him first among the people of repute, the pillars of the Jerusalem church. Peter and John fall into place after James (v. 9). Luke supports the prominent leadership role of James with more detail. It was James who summed up the sense of the meeting and proposed a policy decision that won approval from the participants: Gentile believers would not need to be circumcised, although they were advised to observe several restrictions (Acts 15:6–29).

It is evident, therefore, that James was the recognized leader of the entire Jerusalem church at the time of the conference, which took place twenty years or less after Pentecost. This influential leadership role is further confirmed by two additional pieces of evidence. The first is the incident in Antioch reported in Galatians 2:11–14. This event apparently took place after the Jerusalem conference. Peter had come to Antioch and joined with the practice of the church there in disregarding table segregation between Jewish and Gentile Christians. Then "certain people came from James" (v. 12) to Antioch and protested this policy. The inference is that these people represented the position of James on this matter. If this conjecture is correct, then we must conclude that James did not intend the decision of the Jerusalem conference to release Jewish Christians from observing the law. They were still obliged to do so, even if Gentile believers were not. The point of interest to us is not primarily the issue in question but the powerful influence that James exerted over Peter, Barnabas, and the Jewish Christians in general at Antioch. They reversed their stand and again took up segregation. Peter and Barnabas were not ready to oppose the leadership of James.

The second incident occurred seven or eight years after the Jerusalem conference, when Paul returned to Jerusalem at the end of his third missionary journey (Acts 21:17–26). He immediately sought out James and reported to him and the elders of the church "the things that God had done among the Gentiles through his ministry" (v. 19). Although the believers in Jerusalem rejoiced over what they heard, they were concerned about the potential negative reaction to his presence in the city. It was rumored that Paul advised Jews "to forsake Moses, . . . not to circumcise their children or observe the customs" (v. 21). The many Jewish Christians in Jerusalem who were "zealous for the law" (v. 20) could be expected to oppose Paul as an enemy of the law. Therefore, James and the elders advised Paul to squelch the rumors by joining with some Jewish Christians in a ritual celebration in the temple (vv. 23–25). Paul agreed, but the outcome was less than desirable: it led to his arrest and two-year imprisonment in Caesarea.

This episode is of interest because it underscores the essentially conservative orientation of James that we have seen emerging. He was prepared to allow Gentiles to become Christians without becoming Jews, but he expected Jewish Christians not to forsake their Jewish religious customs. At the time this course may have appeared as the only practical solution to the relationship between the Jews and Gentiles in the early church. Historically, however, it proved to be untenable, and James's espousal of it may have contributed eventually to his own undoing.

Before pursuing the final fate of James, we may briefly review some of the factors that contributed to his rise to leadership in the Jerusalem Christian community. First, James was a blood relative of Jesus. This is not the most important explanation for his role, but it gave him an initial advantage. That some weight was attached to this factor is suggested by the fact that after the death of James, the church appointed his cousin Symeon to become the head of the Jerusalem church.

Second, James was privileged to have seen the risen Christ and presumably to have received a commission from him. Although Luke does not call him an apostle, as Paul does, James may well have been recognized as such in the Palestinian church (see Gal. 2:9).

Third, if James was already the leader of a house church when Peter was still a dominant figure on the Jerusalem scene, the imprisonment and departure of Peter from the city opened the way for the rise of James to greater influence. His continued residence in the city contributed further to that development.

Last, James was sympathetic with the Jewish loyalties of the Jerusalem church. His piety was beyond question. Later church tradition called him "the Just," and legends circulated about his religious devotion. The ultra-conservatives may well have seen Peter as suspect because of his dealings with the Gentile Cornelius (Acts 10:1–11:18) and his defection at Antioch (Gal. 2:12). James, on the contrary, while giving freedom to Gentile Christians, did expect Jewish Christians to continue observing the law. He also was anxious that Paul, the apostle to the Gentiles, give evidence of his respect for and his willingness to practice Jewish ceremonies when in Jerusalem.

We should not regard James's dedication to his Jewish heritage as playing politics in a difficult situation. It was doubtless a matter of conviction: there is no evidence to indicate otherwise. In the end, however, it was a loyalty that proved to be difficult to maintain fully in the Christian community.

Twelve years after the Jerusalem conference, James was stoned to death by order of the Jewish high priest, who took advantage of the absence of a Roman procurator in the country. The charge against him, according to Josephus, was that he broke the law. The details of the case against him are uncertain. What is clear, however, is that a brother who had once been skeptical of his brother's mission died a Christian martyr.

Paul, citizen of four worlds

To refer to Paul as "citizen of four worlds" might suggest that he was a prominent, cosmopolitan figure in the world of his day. This was not the case. No secular ancient historian as much as mentions his name; there is no clear reference to him in the Jewish Talmud or in any other early non-Christian Jewish writing. It is also quite possible that some Christian enclaves here and there in the Roman Empire in those early decades may not have heard of Paul. Yet in the providence of God he was destined to become the most influential person in shaping the development of the Christian movement in its later history.

For our knowledge of Paul we are indebted to some of his correspondence with early Christian communities and to Luke's account of him, both of which are found in our New Testament. The letters provide an exposure to the mind and heart of the man. The Acts of the Apostles is helpful in reconstructing the external framework of his career as a missionary. But both of these sources of information are at best fragmentary for the purpose of putting together a biography of the man.

As a matter of human interest, we are curious about his personal appearance. We have hints in his letters that he was not a commanding figure; his critics apparently spoke of him as a man whose "bodily presence is weak and his speech contemptible" (2 Cor. 10:10). There is a cryptic reference to a bodily ailment that may have been a cause for the Galatians to despise him, although they did not (Gal. 4:13–15); in the same letter Paul speaks about bearing on his body "the marks of Jesus" (6:17). These were probably physical disfigurements resulting from his being stoned, flogged, and otherwise mistreated in his missionary travels (see 2 Cor. 11:23–27).

It is not likely, however, that one of fragile physique could have endured the hardships attending Paul's extensive missionary journeys and the repeated persecutions inflicted on him. A late second-century description by an unknown Christian from Asia Minor portrays him as "a man small of stature, with a bald head and crooked legs, in a good state of body, with eyebrows meeting and nose somewhat hooked, full of friendliness." We do not know, of course, whether this description rests on some earlier tradition.

To cite another modern curiosity, we would like to know whether at some stage in his life Paul was a married man. Clearly, when he wrote 1 Corinthians 7 he was not married. Celibacy, however, was not a common practice in Judaism and was frowned on by the rabbis. The supposed basis for the view that Paul was at one time married is the Acts 26:10 reference of Paul casting his vote against Christians, implying that he was a member in the Sanhedrin; membership is said to have required marriage. Both of these assumptions, however, are questionable: the reference to voting may mean no more than giving moral approval, and the requirement of marriage for membership in the council dates from the beginning of the second century AD.

It is clear from what we do know of Paul that he was a complex person. He was a diaspora Jew with rabbinic training in Jerusalem who subsequently became a Christian and gave his life to a ministry among Gentiles. Any biography of Paul must bring together many distinct factors. Let us isolate and briefly discuss some of the elements that entered into making Paul the man that he was.

First, Paul was a citizen of the commonwealth of Israel. The symbol of membership in the Jewish community was circumcision, which he underwent on the eighth day of his life (Phil. 3:5). Although his parents lived outside of Palestine, evidently they were deeply devoted to their ancestral faith. They knew their tribal roots (Benjamin) and gave their son the name of the most illustrious member of the tribe, Saul—the first king of Israel. They are further described as Hebrews, which is not in this context merely a synonym for Jews; it indicates that they continued to cling to the national language, either Hebrew or Aramaic, in addition to Greek. They belonged to the Pharisaic wing of Judaism (Acts 23:6). This observation should not be taken to mean that the religious atmosphere of their home was an arid legalism. There is much evidence of genuine warmth and living faith in Pharisaic circles; we have no reason to suppose that the situation was otherwise in Paul's home.

Paul fully accepted his religious heritage and, indeed, took pride in it. According to his own testimony, he achieved renown in his practice of Pharisaic piety: he was both blameless in his own observance of the law and zealous in his persecution of heretics (Gal. 1:13–14; Phil. 3:6; Acts 23:1). Like his parents he also was able to speak Hebrew or Aramaic (Acts 22:2).

Paul was given the opportunity to take advanced religious studies in Jerusalem under the renowned Jewish teacher, Gamaliel (Acts 22:3), a Pharisee and a member of the Sanhedrin. Gamaliel was distinguished not only for his learning and piety but also for his moderate stance in the interpretation and application of the Torah—a quality reflected in his advice in dealing with the apostles in Acts 5:34–40. Sometimes the reliability of the tradition of Paul's training under him has been questioned because of the difference between teacher and pupil in attitude toward the early Christians. Perhaps, however, the occurrence of the preaching of Stephen between Acts 5 and 8:1–4 may account for the difference.

> **Although Paul later became the apostle to the Gentiles, he never repudiated his membership in or lost his devotion to the Jewish community. Paul's indebtedness to his religious heritage and his rabbinical training is evident on virtually every page of his letters.**

Although Paul later became the apostle to the Gentiles, he never repudiated his membership in or lost his devotion to the Jewish community. This continued loyalty is clear in his discussion of the destiny of the Jewish people in Romans 9 to 11 (especially 9:1–5; 10:1–2; 11:1–2, 17–32). Paul's indebtedness to his religious heritage and his rabbinical training is evident on virtually every page of his letters. To try to understand Paul without taking seriously this factor in his background is a dead-end venture.

Second, Paul was a citizen of Tarsus, the city in which he was born (Acts 21:39; 22:3). In Paul's day, Tarsus was the capital of the Roman province of Cilicia in southeast Asia

Minor, and thus no mean city. Two of its industries were linen and the making of tents. Adding to its prosperity was its location on a trade route coming from the east to the Aegean Sea to its west. Beyond its political and economic importance, however, was its fame as a center of intellectual life. Its schools were full of local students. Many Stoic philosophers were born and taught there, and some later migrated to Rome. One such teacher had as a pupil the young Augustus, and later, when Augustus became emperor, was his adviser.

From a cultural point of view, the city represented a meeting of Greek and Oriental streams of thought and life. Its population was a mixture of native Anatolians, Greeks, Romans, and Jews. We do not know many Jews lived there in Paul's day. Tarsus was an appropriate birthplace for a Jew who was to be the herald of a Palestinian gospel to the lands to the west.

How much was Paul influenced by the intellectual life and thought of Tarsus? This question raises another: at what age did Paul leave Tarsus for Jerusalem? The traditional answer has been sometime in his middle teens—when he was ready for advanced studies. More recently it has been suggested that Paul came to Jerusalem as a child and grew up in the city. The crucial text is Acts 22:3: "I am a Jew, born in Tarsus in Cilicia, but brought up in this city at the feet of Gamaliel, educated strictly according to our ancestral law." Are the terms "brought up" and "educated" in this passage used to cover the same period of Paul's life, or are they distinct in meaning—referring to two successive periods? If the latter is the case, then the comma in the text should be placed after the word "city" and not after "Gamaliel."

Regardless of how this problem is resolved, the decisive factor in determining the impact of Greek thought on Paul's letters is not the relative length of such influence. His epistles do reveal some acquaintance with popular Greek philosophical terminology, but Paul's thought basically remained oriented to Palestine rather than to Greece.

Third, Paul was also a Roman citizen. We are dependent again on Luke for this information (Acts 16:37–38; 22:25–29), as Paul does not have occasion to mention it in his letters.

His status as a Roman citizen was not one that he personally acquired. He was born into it; his father was a citizen.

How Paul's family came to hold citizenship we do not know. In the eastern provinces in the early period of the empire, citizenship was conferred on individuals for some service rendered to Rome. The procedure involved a recommendation of a given person to the emperor by a Roman official or some person of note, opening the door to securing such a recommendation through personal influence or bribery (see Acts 22:28). Paul's family may have been granted citizenship for some significant political or, more likely, economic service.

Citizenship carried with it certain privileges. In the provinces, these were mainly legal and social rather than political. They included special privileges in the area of criminal jurisdiction. For one, a citizen was not to be subjected to scourging—which explains the anxiety of the Philippian magistrates when they discovered that the men they had beaten were Roman citizens (Acts 16:37–39). Again, a citizen could appeal over the head of the provincial governor for trial before the emperor: Paul did so as a prisoner in Caesarea (Acts 25:9–12). Furthermore, the property of a citizen could not be arbitrarily disposed of by a provincial governor; it had to be handled according to imperial laws. Citizenship also opened the door to positions of influence and potential wealth in the Roman state or army.

Citizenship also had its obligations. Citizens were expected to know Latin. They could be drafted for military service—although Jews were exempted from such service. Citizens were not allowed to worship foreign deities unless the cult had been officially approved by the emperor, as was the case with Judaism. When the apostles in Acts got into trouble with the Roman authorities, it was not on religious grounds but because they were suspected of causing civil disturbance.

A Roman citizen traditionally had three names: a personal name, a clan name, and a family name. It is not certain whether the Latin *Paulus* was Paul's personal or his family name.

Fourth, finally and above all, Paul was a citizen of the Christian community whose true base is heaven. He employs the imagery of citizenship in this sense in Philippians 3:20. He thought of the church as a colony of heavenly citizens occupying an outpost on earth. It is from this homeland that the citizens await the coming of their Lord who will consummate his kingly purposes with respect both to them and to the world. Meanwhile, the citizens are called to discharge their obligations in a worthy manner (Phil. 1:27), in full dependence on the divine resources at their disposal (Phil. 4:6, 13). This responsibility means that the outpost should faithfully represent to non-citizens what life is like in the commonwealth of heaven. The colony is the homeland in miniature. And what is more, it should serve to recruit new citizens for the kingdom.

For Paul, this citizenship gathered up and refocused the other three. It did not destroy them, but it did profoundly alter their character. Paul first and last was a Christian, that is, one whose life was lived out of and for Christ (Phil. 1:21). This identity was the secret of his amazing life and enduring contribution.

Paul and the way of love

When seeking help on the way of love, we may not on first impulse turn to Paul's writings. Usually Paul is remembered as the great theologian of salvation by grace through faith, or of the Spirit, or of the church as the body of Christ. To be sure, he is the author of the beautiful hymn to love in 1 Corinthians 13, but that does not alter our basic impression of him as a thinker whose thoughts run mainly in channels other than those of love. However, the vocabulary of love—both the verb and the noun—occurs almost as frequently in his letters as do the cluster of words dealing with righteousness and justification. We can learn much from him about the meaning of Christian love and its role in our lives as Christians.

Before focusing on the details of Paul's presentation, let us make a few general observations on the New Testament understanding of love. First, the phrase "the way of love" has been chosen deliberately because it is in keeping with love's dynamic character as portrayed in the New Testament. Love, of course, can be analyzed as a concept, but it is more at home in the practical realm than in the domain of abstract thought. Love is known in the way it behaves in a social context. It lives, if at all, in specific attitudes and deeds. It is a quality of life expressed in the way we relate to and interact with one another.

Second, love in its distinctive New Testament sense is not essentially an emotional sentiment. Although not devoid of emotional content, it is not grounded in the glands but rather in the will. It should not, therefore, be equated with liking. Love is commanded and as such is a summons to the will (Luke 6:27; Rom. 13:9). Love is the determination to seek the well-being of the other person. Perhaps the best equivalent for the word *love* in its Christian sense is the word *care*: to care for another or to refuse to do so is a matter of decision.

Third, the first word of the New Testament is not a demand that we love God or our fellow humans, but the good news that God loves us. Divine love is basic to all else: it precedes and conditions our response to God and our relationship to others. This fact makes the gospel message something other than mere good advice. Because we are the recipients of God's prior love, we are both expected and enabled to love (1 John 4:19).

Fourth, the norm of divine love in the New Testament is the Christ-event. To dramatize God's love one no longer needs to point to the exodus from Egypt, to the covenant at Sinai, to the return from exile, or to any other pre-Christian event. The person, ministry, death, and resurrection of Jesus is that demonstration par excellence, as is asserted repeatedly in a variety of texts such as John 3:16, Romans 5:8, and 1 John 4:10.

Fifth, to speak of being found in the way of Christian love is to express the inner essence of what the Bible means by salvation. Salvation speaks of God's intention to create community between God and us and among us. That intention is rooted in God's love and has as its goal the evoking of love from us. When the seeking love of God finds response in the free offering of the love and devotion of our total selves to God and God's purposes for us, then we are in the way of salvation. Within this framework of happenings, place can be found for those elements traditionally expressed in such terms as *atonement, faith, justification,* and *discipleship.*

Against this background we may now set some specific details from Paul's letters about the way of love. His primary concern was with the internal life of the Christian community. This concern is understandable for several reasons. For one, his letters were addressed to what must have been largely first-generation Christians. Many were Gentiles who needed to understand what it meant to be the people of God, personally and as a group. Paul wanted to spell out the gospel and its implications for the basic shape of the Christian lifestyle. Next, Paul had a sense of priorities. He was aware that if the church internally was what it should be, this fact would condition the whole of the relationship of Christians with the non-Christian community. Finally, the opportunities for a responsible participation in determining the structures of society on the part of

Christians were very limited. No elaborate social ethic to guide Christians as they sought to follow the way of love on this frontier was necessary in Paul's time.

What, then, are some of the major outlines of the way of love in the corporate life of the Christian community? First, love is essential to the maintenance of Christian fellowship. The unity of the body arising out of sharing in the common Spirit can only be maintained as each member is willing to relate to the other in genuine love (Eph. 4:1–3). Love has a way of oiling potential points of friction and reducing tension that might otherwise tear the body apart; it is the supreme grace that binds together all other virtues within the Christian community into a harmonious relationship (Col. 3:14).

> **The way of love in all aspects of the Christian's life— including relationships with enemies—is not peripheral to the gospel but integral to it. To regard it as optional is to misunderstand the nature of God's love and God's strategy for dealing with human sin in Christ and in the contemporary situation.**

Second, love is the prerequisite to a full understanding of the gospel. No single Christian is able to adequately grasp all of the far-reaching and profound dimensions of the gospel: only as we are knit together in love in both sharing and receiving with our brothers and sisters in Christ are we able to make real progress toward understanding the gospel (Col. 2:2–3).

Third, love provides the proper control in the use of Christian liberty that is necessary to the well-being of the body of Christ. This point is made very clearly in 1 Corinthians 8: knowledge without love for the brother or sister in Christ can lead to conduct that will destroy those for whom Christ died. Only as love is wedded to knowledge will conduct be harnessed to build up the Christian community; only as freedom is restrained by love that seeks to serve the welfare of others will it be free from potential destructiveness (Gal. 5:13–14).

Fourth, love is utterly essential to the exercise of spiritual gifts in the church if the church is to profit from their exercise. This is the meaning of the discussion of love in the midst of Paul's treatment of the gifts in 1 Corinthians 12–14: love prevents the gifts from being used selfishly and turns them in the direction of building up the body of Christ.

Finally, love is the guiding principle of all Christian conduct. Paul makes it clear that neither the restraint of traditional Jewish religious culture (represented by circumcision) nor the freedom from such controls (represented by permitting Gentiles to remain uncircumcised) is a guarantee of the conduct for which God is looking. That can result only from "faith working through love" (Gal. 5:6). Elsewhere Paul makes the same point in slightly different words: "Let all that you do be done in love" (1 Cor. 16:14). There is also the memorable passage in Romans 13:8–10: "Owe no one anything, except to love one another; for the one who loves another has fulfilled the law. . . . Love does no wrong to a neighbor; therefore, love is the fulfilling of the law."

Let us turn now to look at the way of love in relation to the non-Christian community. This focus does not involve a new understanding of love but rather an extension of its practice to situations beyond the Christian community.

What does the way of love mean in relation to the state? The important text here is Romans 13:1–7. Although nothing is said within this passage about Christian love, the discussion is framed by references to love (Rom. 12:9–21; 13:8–10). What then is the relationship between the way of love and submission to the state? Two answers have been given to this question. Some scholars believe that Paul wishes to make the point that the state is a legitimate exception to the way of love under which the Christian is called to live. The emphasis then is on the exception.

It is more likely, however, that Paul's interest continues to center on the Christian community throughout chapters 12 and 13. Read in this way, the passage speaks to the temptation to resist the state in ways inconsistent with the ethic of Christian love, and Paul's words forbid such action. Support for the second reading is sought in the historical probabilities that may have given birth to the passage. In the decade prior to this writing, tensions between the Jews and Rome were mounting in Palestine. Jewish Christians in the Roman church, by virtue of their ethnic ties, would have been sympathetic with the anti-Roman feelings of the Palestinian Jewish community. The climate of opinion, therefore, would have been conducive to resistance against Rome. Paul's response to this situation was a counsel of submission to the Roman state.

Whether this reconstruction of the background to the passage is correct is difficult to say. In any case, we should note that Paul counsels submission and not unqualified obedience. Where the demands of the state conflict with the supreme loyalty that we owe to God, submission will take the form of suffering the consequences of necessary civil disobedience. Paul himself was later to suffer martyrdom at the hands of the state to which he here urges submission. The form of resistance, however, must be consistent with the principle of love by which the Christian lives.

Next, there is the way of love in relation to the enemy. The most significant text is Romans 12:14–21. This passage is an expansion of the general exhortation to love in verse 9, but with specific reference to the matter of dealing with an enemy. Several things are worth noting in this discussion. For one thing returning evil for evil is strictly forbidden—in keeping with Jesus' prohibition of retaliation (Matt. 5:38). But the Christian response to evil is not a mere refusal to respond in kind. Christians are called to actively meet evil with positive deeds of good will and kindness: "If your enemies are hungry, feed them; if they are thirsty, give them something to drink. . . . Do not be overcome by evil, but overcome evil with good" (Rom. 12:20–21). This aggressive program refuses to allow evil to shape our response to it. On the contrary, the strategy is dictated by the nature of Christian love itself. This approach to dealing with the enemy opens up the genuine possibility of converting the opponent into a friend.

Paul's formula is not an innovation; he is building on a foundation laid by Jesus. Indeed, we should observe that the injunction to feed a hungry enemy and to give drink to a thirsty one is actually a quotation from Proverbs 25:21–22, and thus is a directive from the wisdom literature of pre-Christian Judaism. Similar expressions of kindness toward the enemy and illustrations of it can be found in other Jewish literature and elsewhere. But this quotation from Proverbs, to say nothing of other analogous materials, is now given a new frame of reference by the life, ministry, death, and resurrection of Jesus. That event was the supreme and decisive confrontation of evil with aggressive love, and it is that victory that is the context and inspiration of Paul's teaching in this passage.

Closely related to what has just been said about the background of Romans 12:14–21 is another passage from Paul's pen, in 2 Corinthians 5:18–21. Here Paul affirms an intimate connection between the unique reconciling ministry that God accomplished in Christ and the ongoing ministry of reconciliation that God has committed to the Christian community. The former determines the latter: the way God once dealt with evil in the Christ-event is the way God proposes now to deal with it in and through the church. The church fulfills the ministry of reconciliation, not only by bearing verbal witness to the decisive action of God in Christ, but also by a particular lifestyle of dealing with the enemy that takes its cue from Jesus. The gospel of reconciliation is implemented when word is fleshed out in spirit and in deed.

The way of love, then, in all aspects of the Christian's life—including relationships with enemies—is not peripheral to the gospel but integral to it. To regard it as optional or as an addition is to misunderstand the nature of God's love and God's strategy for dealing with human sin in Christ and in the contemporary situation.

But if this is God's plan, how can it be made effective? This is the important practical question. The answer is not to be found in any attempt simply to imitate Jesus as a model. The love that God is looking for is, according to Paul, "the fruit of the Spirit" (Gal. 5:22). Paul speaks of God's love being "poured into our hearts through the Holy Spirit" (Rom. 5:5). Only as we are truly open to receive and experience the gift of God's love can we in turn be channels of that love to others, including our enemies.

Spirit and Christian life in Paul's thought

One day long ago Paul encountered twelve people in the city of Ephesus to whom he put a question: "Did you receive the Holy Spirit when you became believers?" The reply was, "No, we have never even heard that there is a Holy Spirit." They were disciples of John the Baptist who promised that the Spirit would be given by one to follow him, but they had not heard that the promise had been fulfilled.

Paul regarded the question as crucial, as may be inferred from Luke's account of the incident in Acts 19:1–7: to be Christian, they needed to be baptized in the name of the Lord Jesus and to receive the Spirit. In his letters, Paul is clear on this matter. To the Galatians tempted to embrace another gospel, Paul wrote: "The only thing I want to learn from you is this: Did you receive the Spirit by doing the works of the law or by believing what you heard?" (Gal. 3:2).

The reception of the Spirit was the experiential hallmark of being Christian; it distinguished the Christian community both from the Jewish synagogue and from other religious groups. Even more explicit is Paul's declaration to the Romans: "Anyone who does not have the Spirit of Christ does not belong to him" (Rom. 8:9). For Paul, there can be no such thing as a Spiritless Christian. Paul regards the Christian dispensation as the age of the Spirit (see 2 Cor. 3:1–6).

These statements are forthright and strong. What is the rationale behind them? Paul does not address this matter in any systematic fashion. He assumes that his readers will understand his premises without any need for formal argument. It is possible, however, to form some opinion of Paul's mind on this matter from hints here and there in his letters.

For Paul, the Spirit brings the Christ-event into the present. Paul regarded Christ as the watershed in holy history.

In 2 Corinthians 4:6, he uses language reminiscent of the original creation to describe the significance of God's new act in Christ. A similar reference occurs in 2 Corinthians 5:17: in Christ "there is a new creation: everything old has passed away; see, everything has become new!" But Jesus' life and ministry already was a matter of history in Paul's day. How could that happening of the past, from which daily he was being separated by a growing temporal distance, be of present significance?

The answer to this question must take into account several things. First, Paul frequently employs the phrase "in Christ" to describe the context of the Christian's life. Christ as resurrected and living is an inclusive personality in whom Christians are caught up in a participating relationship. To say that one person is in another is odd language: it has no precedent in pre-Christian literature. Its oddness can only be accounted for by the strangeness of the reality that lies behind it. But if Christians are in Christ, Paul can also speak of Christ being in Christians. This term, while perhaps less striking than that of Christians in Christ, is also, surprisingly, less common than the former.

Second, parallel to the Christ-Christian phraseology is that describing the Spirit-Christian relationship. Here the conception of the Spirit being in the Christian is of common occurrence. Less frequent, however, is the notion of the Christian being in the Spirit.

Third, the Spirit in Paul's thought, as in the New Testament generally, is closely tied to Christ. This link is indicated by such expressions as "the Spirit of Christ," "the Spirit of his Son," "the Spirit of Jesus Christ." Thus, while the Spirit came after the historical ministry of Jesus, the Spirit did not supersede or eclipse that ministry. The Spirit remains subordinate to Christ.

We may now put these various bits and pieces together as follows: Paul normally thinks of the Christian as being in Christ rather than in the Spirit. But if the living Christ also can be said to be in the Christian, Paul usually prefers the language of the Spirit in the believer; that is, the presence of the living Christ is experienced through the Spirit. The living Christ is brought into the present through the Spirit's indwelling.

The living Christ's and the Spirit's presence in our hearts cannot be distinguished in experience. Theologically, however, the two are not the same: the Spirit is the medium in and through whom the resurrected Christ now lives and continues his ministry in and through the Christian community. Paul's abundant references to the Spirit are not meant to detract attention from his primary interest in Christ and ultimately, of course, the God-focus of his thought. But their importance, for this reason, is in no sense diminished.

Paul is recognized as the great theologian of the Spirit in the New Testament. The Spirit is mentioned in all of his letters except in the brief personal message to Philemon. How shall we account for this emphasis on the Spirit? Was it the product of creative theological speculation? To be sure, Paul had an incisive mind and was able to articulate profound ideas.

> For Paul, all that God has intended for the Christian experience is wrapped up and given in the gift of the Spirit: in fact, Christian experience can be viewed as the progressive unfolding of the rich potential concentrated in the initial bestowal of the Spirit.

But his theology of the Spirit is not abstract. It is rooted in the soil of Christian experience, his own and also that of the larger Christian community. "Long before the Spirit was a theme of doctrine," says Eduard Schweizer, "he was a fact in the experience of the community." Paul's theology of the Spirit is a confession of his experience.

We may now look more carefully at Paul's understanding of the role of the Spirit in Christian life, both individually and collectively. In general, the Spirit is seen as basic to the Christian life in a way that was not understood to be the case in the religious life of Judaism or Hellenism. In Judaism, the Spirit could be thought of as the reward of piety and in Greek culture as the principle at work in the erratic or unusual.

For Paul, the Spirit was the context of the whole of the Christian experience from beginning to end. All that God has intended for the Christian experience is wrapped up and given in the gift of the Spirit: in fact, Christian experience can be viewed as the progressive unfolding of the rich potential concentrated in the initial bestowal of the Spirit. What then is involved in this unpacking process? Let us note several aspects.

First, the Spirit makes membership in God's family more than a matter of formal status: the awareness of God's love is communicated to us by the Spirit (Rom. 5:5). As we address God, the Spirit enables us spontaneously to cry "Abba"—the intimate affectionate term of children for their father (Gal. 4:6). The fear that is characteristic of the slave has been replaced by the love and confidence that belongs to children in the family circle (Rom 8:15–16).

Second, the Spirit is important for the development of Christ-like character. Paul speaks of this reality under the image of "the fruit of the Spirit" (Gal. 5:22–23); the diverse fruits are the virtues of Christ that God intends should also characterize God's sons and daughters. It is not without significance that fruit imagery is used for this process. The reproduction of Christ's character in us is not the product of merely human effort; it is rooted in a vitality imparted by the Spirit. Our task is to allow Christ so to live in us through his Spirit that we will be progressively transformed into his image.

Third, closely related to the Spirit's formation of the Christian's character is the Spirit's ordering of conduct to conform to God's will. "If we live by the Spirit," wrote Paul to the Galatians, "let us also walk by the Spirit" (5:25). *To walk* is a common biblical metaphor for a pattern of conduct or style of life. This walk is to be shaped under the guidance of the Spirit.

Fourth, the Spirit also equips each Christian with some gift for ministry in the building up of the church (1 Cor. 12:14; Rom. 12:6–8; Eph. 4:11–14). These "enablements" differ in character but basically fall into two categories: gifts of word and gifts of deed. Although the gifts are oriented to the internal life of the Christian community, they have implications for the mission of the church in the world. When the church is what it ought to be, it will also be effective in extending the mission of Christ in the larger society.

Finally, the Spirit is related not only to the beginning of Christian experience but is also significant in its consummation. For one thing, the Spirit is the pledge of our ultimate salvation. This promise is expressed in two metaphors: seal and guarantee. The first suggests ownership and security (Eph. 1:13; 4:30); the second portrays the Spirit as the present down payment assuring us of God's intention some day to complete the work already begun in our lives (2 Cor. 1:22; 5:5). But the Spirit is more than a pledge of what is yet to come: the Spirit will be the medium through whom God will effect the resurrection of the body at the end of time (Rom. 8:11).

Clearly from this limited survey of Paul's teachings on the Spirit, ignorance or neglect of the Spirit's role can only mean a greatly impoverished Christian experience. In this context, we may recall Paul's admonition: "Be filled with the Spirit" (Eph. 5:18). The form of the imperative indicates that this experience is ongoing. To be filled with the Spirit is metaphorical language for the Spirit having full control of us through our complete surrender to the lordship of Jesus Christ. Such openness must also be a matter of daily affirmation if we are to live in the fullness of the Spirit.

At the dawn of each day with gladness in our hearts, let us take our stance with the poet John Greenleaf Whittier:

> *And so the shadows fall apart,*
> *And so the west winds play;*
> *And all the windows of my heart*
> *I open to the day.*

Spiritual gifts for mission

We can never regard our consideration of the church as finished if it does not include some word about the church's mission. Indeed, mission is fundamental to the church's being the church. Emil Brunner expressed it well when he said, "The church exists by mission as fire exists by burning." Its mission, of course, is God-given. The church is not autonomous; it is not free to determine its own agenda. As the people of God, the church must be about God's business in the world, and it is the mission of Christ that defines the shape of the church's task. "As the Father has sent me," said the resurrected Christ to his disciples, "so I send you" (John 20:21).

The mission of the church, then, is to extend the earthly mission of Jesus in the first century into our contemporary world. Put more precisely, it is the task of the church so to be the body of Christ that he may again live out his life in it and carry forward his mission through it in every age.

God, who has called the church to mission, has also provided resources for the fulfillment of that mission. One of these is the gifts God gives to his people. We hear about these mostly in the letters of Paul, particularly in four passages: Romans 12:6–8; 1 Corinthians 12 and 14; and Ephesians 4:11–16. Elsewhere in Paul's letters, Acts, and other passages in the New Testament, we find scattered references to the gifts in one form or another.

We will focus attention on Paul's contribution. The terms *gifts, spiritual gifts, manifestations of the Spirit,* and, by implication, *gifts of the Spirit* occur in the passages mentioned above. But nowhere does Paul offer a formal definition of what he means by these phrases; he assumes that his readers will understand. In the four catalogs included in the passages mentioned above, Paul does give illustrations of what he is referring to.

Certain insights can also be gained from the accompanying discussions.

We can make five general observations on these materials that will help us formulate a definition of Paul's understanding of spiritual gifts. First, the items that Paul includes in his lists are abilities for ministry of one kind or another. Sometimes he mentions functioning personalities (apostles, prophets, and teachers in 1 Cor. 12:28) rather than abstract abilities (1 Cor. 12:8–10). But the focus in each case is on service abilities. These ministry abilities contrast with what Paul elsewhere calls "the fruit of the Spirit" (Gal. 5:22–23). The items included in the list of the Spirit's fruit are virtues of Christian character. They are designed to make us Christ-like in the kind of people we are.

> Paul understands spiritual gifts as divinely given and diversely bestowed service abilities in the Christian community for the purpose of ministry with a view to the building up of the church.

Second, the gifts are divinely given abilities. The giver is sometimes said to be God (1 Cor. 12:6, 28), sometimes Christ (1 Cor. 12:5; Eph. 4:11), but more frequently the Spirit (1 Cor. 12:4, 7–11). Perhaps the close tie of the gifts to the Spirit is understandable in light of the Spirit's being the dynamic or energizing principle at work in these abilities for service. Indeed, they are called a "manifestation of the Spirit" in two passages (1 Cor. 12:7; 14:12). The origin of these gifts is heaven, not earth.

Third, the gifts are diversely bestowed (Rom. 12:4–5; 1 Cor. 12:7–11, 29–30; Eph. 4:11). Not all the gifts of the Spirit are given to every Christian; different gifts are given to different Christians. True, some Christians may have more than one gift, as Paul did. But the principle of diverse distribution remains fundamental. This diverse allotment of gifts is in contrast to the fruit of the Spirit, which Paul expects should be manifested in the life of every Christian. No Christian is exempted from the obligation to be Christ-like in character, but Christians are meant to complement each other in service abilities. Paul makes this point effectively in 1 Corinthians 12:14–26 using the analogy of the body. Apart from diversity, there is no body either in the physical or the spiritual sense.

Fourth, the gifts are sovereignly bestowed (1 Cor. 12:11). The decision regarding what gift or gifts a Christian will have is in divine hands. The giver, not the receiver, controls the nature of the gift that is given. Paul does speak about desiring spiritual gifts, especially the gift of prophecy (1 Cor. 14:1), and he writes about praying for the gift of the interpretation of tongues (1 Cor. 14:13); apparently he saw a limited role for certain subjective conditions in the granting of at least some gifts. But even in these instances the ultimate decision to grant remains in the hands of the giver.

Fifth, the gifts are given for a very specific purpose. That purpose is not basically an apologetic one, namely, to prove that the Christian has the Spirit or to authenticate the gospel. To be sure, the gifts may be seen as a "manifestation of the Spirit" (1 Cor. 12:7; 14:12) or as evidence confirming the gospel message (Heb. 2:24). But Paul places the emphasis elsewhere: he sees the gifts as given for the purpose of building up the church. This point is made repeatedly in 1 Corinthians (12:7; 14:3, 5–6, 12, 17–19, 26, 31) and in Ephesians 4:11–16. Indeed, the basis for Paul's preference for the ministry of prophecy over tongues in the public assembly is the greater value of prophecy in social edification. It is likely that tongues is included in the category of spiritual gifts only because the gift of interpretation is joined with it in both lists (1 Cor. 12:10, 30). At least Paul clearly indicates that tongues should not be permitted in church if no interpreter is present (1 Cor. 14:28). He assumes that what goes on in church must edify the congregation, and that edification in the case of a word gift depends on intelligible communication.

In light of these five characteristics of spiritual gifts, we may now attempt a definition of Paul's understanding of spiritual gifts: they are divinely given and diversely bestowed service abilities in the Christian community for the purpose of ministry with a view to building up the church. Perhaps we should note that the building up of the church should not be interpreted too narrowly. It is true that the great majority of the gifts seem to envision a ministry within the gathered life of the congregation. But surely Paul did not think of the function of the church as being exhausted in its corporate fellowship, ministry, and worship. These were ways of preparing the church for its scattered function in the community. The extension of the body of Christ in the world would also have been a part of building up the church.

Turning from definition to the gifts that are included in the four catalogs, several comments are in order. First, no two of the lists are exactly alike in length or in the gifts mentioned. This fact suggests that Paul was not concerned about drawing up a firm, normative list of gifts to serve as an exact standard for his congregations; the lists are illustrative rather than definitive. Probably Paul would have been against the idea of drawing up a normative checklist of gifts to be used by Christian groups, for his concept of gifts was open-ended. The gifts were heaven's response to the needs of the church on earth. As needs to some extent may vary from time to time and from place to place, so also the gifts may vary.

Second, the four lists include about twenty different entries. Broadly speaking, the various gifts fall into two general classes: gifts that relate to the ministry of word and gifts that have to do with the ministry of deed. Each of these two groups can be further divided into two. Under gifts of word are those that have to do with the intelligible word—for example, prophecy and teaching—and those that are related to unintelligible utterance—tongues and the interpretation of tongues, for example. Included in gifts of deed are those concerned with working miracles (for example, faith, healing, working of miracles) and those having to do with practical service and leadership (for example, administrators, helpers, leaders, sharing, showing mercy).

These two broad types of gifts correspond to the two aspects of the church's life. As a human, historical community the church has needs akin to those of any other group or organization: organization, leadership, health, and care of the needy. The gifts of deed are designed to meet such needs. The church, however, is more than just another social institution; it is the community of God's people. It owes its existence to God's creative act in Christ, and it is God's will that is to shape its life. Its distinctive existence in history depends on its being continuously nourished by resources from beyond history. To this end a ministry of the word is necessary; the various gifts of word are expected to fulfill this need.

Third, included in the various catalogs are gifts of an ordinary kind and also some quite unusual gifts. The gifts of administration and teaching are not confined to the church; they are also known in the wider secular society. The gift of being a helper is a sort of catchall for those whose abilities cannot be classified more specifically. On the other hand, there are the extraordinary gifts such as prophecy, working miracles, and tongues. These are often thought of as supernatural gifts over against the so-called natural abilities just listed.

Paul, however, makes no such distinction. He lumps all of them together and calls them gifts of the Spirit. How can he do that? The clue seems to be in Paul's religious perspective. He views the Christian from the standpoint of the revolutionary experience of having become a person in Christ. That is the red-letter day that marks the beginning of a new existence (see 2 Cor. 5:17). To be sure, the new person has links with the old. If a person is a good administrator before meeting Christ, he or she does not cease to have that ability after becoming a Christian. Paul surely would have known that. But he was not interested in tracing the roots of spiritual gifts in the pre-Christian past. The whole of a Christian's personality, with all of its actual and potential powers, has been touched by the cleansing, renewing, and energizing Spirit, purifying and strengthening one's native gifts—and in some cases calling into being abilities not previously in evidence. Thus all of the Christian's abilities for service can be regarded as gifts of the Spirit.

What are some of the practical implications of Paul's conception of spiritual gifts? To begin, his understanding of gifts provides a helpful perspective for viewing ourselves. Whatever abilities we have should be viewed as gifts given to us by God for the purpose of ministry in building up the church. Because they are gifts, we can take no credit for them. Any pride in whatever shining gifts we may have is thus completely out of place. If, on the contrary, our gifts are ordinary, we should not depreciate them. These too are God's gifts intended for ministry. We are thus freed "to think with sober judgment" about ourselves (Rom. 12:3) and to serve with freedom and joy in ways consistent with our gifts.

Next, Paul's concept of gifts provides a basis for the enlistment of every Christian in the task of building up the church. None of us is without some gift or gifts equipping us for service. Each person needs to discover what those gifts are and how they can best be used. The help of fellow Christians is essential in this process.

Finally, if personal gifts are to be used to edify the church, the exercise of the gifts cannot be carried on apart from the expression of "the fruit of the Spirit." Paul's great hymn of love in 1 Corinthians 12–14 in the midst of his discussion of the gifts has this significance. Love alone sets the exercise of the gifts free from selfish exploitation for ministry to "the common good" of the Christian community (see 1 Cor. 12:7). If this aim had always been kept steadily in view, the history of many churches and congregations might well have been different.

The Lord's Supper

The Lord's Supper is one of the few rites observed almost universally among Christians. Although details of practice and ways of understanding its significance vary, the celebration in one way or another has been part of the church's tradition from the very beginning of its existence. This fact is evident not only from the pages of the New Testament but also from other early Christian literature such as the *Didache*, the letters of Ignatius, and Justin Martyr's *First Apology*.

In the contemporary church, various names are used to designate the rite. Among these are the Lord's Supper, (Holy) Communion, and the Eucharist. The last two are not found as names for the rite in the New Testament; the first does occur in 1 Corinthians 11:20. In Acts, the phrase "the breaking of bread" describes the communal meal of Christians at which there was undoubtedly some remembrance of the meals that Jesus had shared with his disciples, including the one on the last night of his life (Acts 2:42, 46; see also 20:7). Jude (v. 12) makes reference to Christian "love feasts," which may designate meals similar to those in the Corinthian church during which the Lord's Supper was celebrated (1 Cor. 11:17–34).

Evidence indicates that during the period covered by the New Testament, the Lord's Supper probably was not separated at any time from the framework of a full meal. In the New Testament the phrase "the Lord's Supper" is thus not a technical term for the Eucharist proper within the communal feast, but has a more inclusive reference. By the middle of the second century, the rite as such was separated from the fellowship meal and given an independent status. How much earlier this separation happened is not known.

The Lord's Supper began as a graft on an earlier institution, the Passover feast. Passover was one of the great annual festivals of the Jewish calendar. It was held in the spring. The first three New Testament Gospels clearly identify the meal that Jesus and his disciples shared together in an upper room somewhere in Jerusalem as a Passover feast (Mark 14:12–16; Matt. 26:17–19; Luke 22:7–16). Some difficulty is created by the account in the Gospel of John, which places the Last Supper on the evening prior to the slaying of the lambs for the Passover celebration; Jesus' death thus coincided with the death of the lambs (John 18:28; 19:14, 31, 42). This dating might explain the absence of any reference to the lamb in the accounts of the Last Supper. The difference between John's account and that of the first three Gospels is a problem for which various solutions have been offered, none having won general support.

> **In the Passover Jesus and his disciples celebrated, the focus was no longer on memorializing a past redemption or on rekindling hope in deliverance to come. Jesus directed the disciples to lay hold of what God was doing in their midst through him.**

But whether Jesus observed the Passover at the regular time or in anticipation of it, paschal thoughts appear to have been in his mind as he gathered with his disciples for a final meal together. It was not to be just another Passover festival: his conduct on that occasion meant that the supper was destined to live not only in the memory of his disciples but also in the hearts of countless Christians since that night.

From ancient Jewish sources we can reconstruct the probable outlines of the first-century Passover celebration. For our purpose eight elements may be identified: the first cup of wine over which two blessings were spoken; the homily in which the meaning of the feast was explained; the singing of Psalms 113 and 114; the drinking of a second cup of wine; a blessing spoken over the unleavened bread; the eating of the meal proper; the offering of a prayer of thanksgiving for the meal just finished over a third cup of wine; the singing of Psalms 115 to 118.

Jesus presided over the feast. At certain points in the traditional celebration he added his own distinctive contribution. Three are particularly significant. First, at some point in the supper (Mark 14:25, but see also Luke 22:17), Jesus announced that he would not drink wine again until the kingdom of God comes. This comment suggests he was aware of the crucial character of this feast: he anticipated the advent of the kingdom. Second, instead of distributing the bread in silence, as was customary after the blessing had been pronounced over it, he said to his disciples, "Take; this is my body" (Mark 14:22). This statement must have been startling to them. Third, in a similar way after the prayer of thanksgiving over the third cup of wine, Jesus broke the traditional silence with his words, "This is my blood of the covenant, which is poured out for many" (Mark 14:24). These words are also remarkable, indicating that Jesus attached unusual meaning to what was happening.

How then shall we understand the bread and cup sayings? Obviously Jesus was speaking metaphorically rather than literally: the bread and wine were not transformed into the body and blood of Jesus. But these physical elements were now to carry symbolic significance. They pointed to profound realities that lay beyond ordinary sight and touch. Jesus was concerned that his disciples understand the more-than-sensuous character of the supper.

The Passover, to be sure, was always intended to carry a symbolic meaning. The homily spoken by the leader during the feast was supposed to make this significance clear. It was a recitation of the deliverance God had wrought in bringing God's people out of Egyptian slavery (Exod. 12:24–27). The lamb, the unleavened bread, and the bitter herbs eaten during the meal also carried historic meaning (for example, Deut. 16:3). The feast was designed to memorialize a great event in the past that was never to be forgotten by God's people. Indeed, their present experience could only be understood properly if the history was duly remembered.

But the Passover was more than a memorial celebration: it was a time for the renewal of hope. The several cups of wine used at the feast were interpreted in terms of the promise of redemption set forth in Exodus 6:6–7. While this reference is to the redemption from Egypt, first-century Judaism gave the promise a contemporary application. Just as God had once acted to free his people from bondage at the first Passover, so

God might be expected to act again at Passover time to deliver them from their present plight. The traditional prayer associated with the third cup of wine may well be an index to their thoughts on that occasion: "May the All-Merciful One make us worthy of the days of the Messiah and of the life of the world to come. He brings the salvation of his King. He shows covenant-faithfulness to his Anointed, to David, and to his seed forever. He makes peace in his heavenly places. May he secure peace for us and for all Israel."

It is understandable, therefore, that the disciples in this Passover season would have been talking about the restoration of the kingdom to Israel (see Acts 1:6). Jesus' thoughts were moving in directions other than the traditional ones, as is clear from the symbolic significance he attached to the bread and the wine. The bread was no longer to recall the hurried exodus from Egypt, but was now to point to him. In effect, he was saying, "This is I" or "Think of me as you eat this broken bread." The broken character of the bread is not explicitly stressed in the first three New Testament Gospels but is implied in the action of Jesus. The point is made clearly in Paul's version (1 Cor. 11:23–24): Jesus is directing the attention of the disciples not only to himself but also to the broken form of self-giving in which he will soon be known to them.

In a similar manner, Jesus reinterpreted the symbolism of the wine. When he passed the cup to his disciples, he was not referring to the expectation of national deliverance stimulated by the memory of the exodus from Egypt. His mind was occupied with covenant-making. The covenant God made with Israel at Mount Sinai after Israel's deliverance from Egypt was sealed with sacrificial blood thrown on the book of the covenant, the altar, and the people (Exod. 24:3–8). Now, once again, God was about to seal a covenant with sacrificial blood.

Most likely, Jesus was thinking of the new covenant of which Jeremiah spoke centuries earlier (Jer. 31:31–34). The best text of Mark 14:24 does not include the adjective *new* before covenant; it is found, however, in the longer text of Luke's account (Luke 22:20) and in Paul's version representing early Christian tradition (1 Cor. 11:25). Just as Jeremiah envisioned the new covenant based on God's forgiveness of

Israel's sin, so the covenant about to be made would provide for forgiveness of sins (Matt. 26:28). Just as the Mosaic covenant was ratified with sacrificial blood, so the new covenant was about to be sealed with blood, the blood of Jesus. Such was the significance that Jesus attached to the wine as he gave it to his disciples to drink.

With these shifts of meaning in mind, it could be said appropriately that this last supper has become the Lord's Supper. The focus of attention in the Passover being celebrated was no longer simply on memorializing a redemption in the distant past or on rekindling hope in an expected national deliverance to come. The disciples were directed to fix their thoughts on Jesus and to lay hold of what God was then doing in their midst through him. He was more than the host at the meal—the feast found its true significance in relation to him. "This is my body," said he; "this is my blood."

We may summarize four distinctive features of this celebration as represented in the first three New Testament Gospels. First, there is a sacrificial reference: the death of Jesus is obviously in view. The bread and the wine speak of life offered in sacrifice. The passion predictions found earlier in Mark's Gospel prepare us for this understanding of the paschal symbolism (Mark 8:31; 9:31; 10:33–34; see also 10:38–39).

Second, to the sacrificial note must be added the vicarious. The self-sacrifice of Jesus symbolized by the bread and the wine is not for his own benefit but for the welfare of others. The bread was given to them to eat. The wine they drank spoke of blood "poured out for many for the forgiveness of sins" (Matt. 26:28).

Third, covenant-making is clearly in view. This action involves the establishment of not only a vertical relationship but also a horizontal one. The disciples were bound together as well as to God. This one-to-another dimension is symbolically implicit in the distribution of the broken bread to all the disciples and in their drinking from the same cup. Paul draws out the implications of this bond for the quality of interpersonal relationship in 1 Corinthians 11:17–32.

Fourth, although the words of Jesus in connection with the bread and the cup call attention primarily to his forthcoming death and its meaning, the expectation of the future coming of the kingdom is also present in this celebration (Mark 14:25; Matt. 26:29). This supper is a prelude to that day of perfect fellowship in the new order beyond the dark night of suffering and death. The consummation of that hope was not to come soon, but the expectation was not lost from sight as the New Testament church continued in later years to celebrate the Lord's Supper (see 1 Cor. 11:26). Remembrance of the past and anticipation of the end are thus tied together firmly by this rite.

Undoubtedly in the years that followed that supper in the upper room, the disciples must have returned often in memory to that occasion as they broke bread and shared a common cup in many Christian assemblies. But it was not merely a matter of historical memory which too often fades with the years. "To recall, in biblical thought," says R. P. Martin, "means to transport an action which is buried in the past in such a way that its original potency and vitality are not lost but are carried over into the present." This approach to the past is aided, of course, by the very act of performing the rite. Beyond that, however, is the experienced presence of the living Christ, contemporized by the Spirit, as host at the table whenever and wherever his disciples gather to celebrate again that ancient supper.

The early church and the Roman state

On January 23, 1945, James von Moltke, a German noble man and jurist, was executed by Nazi officials after a year's imprisonment. In a letter to his wife written shortly before his execution, he referred to the trial proceedings that had led to his condemnation. He was not accused of any act of violence against the state but simply of refusal to give absolute allegiance to Hitler. One of the men who tried him said, "We Nazis and Christianity resemble each other in only one respect: we claim the whole man. . . . From whom do you take your orders? From the world beyond or from Adolf Hitler? To whom do you owe loyalty and faith?"

This incident dramatically focuses an issue that is as old as the church itself. The church was born in the bosom of the Roman Empire; Pilate was Rome's procurator in Judea on the church's birthday. And when the church moved beyond its Palestinian homeland it did not escape from Roman jurisdiction, for Rome was everywhere. The world into which the gospel spread was divided into several dozen Roman provinces, each with its own governor, and over all was the emperor on the throne in Rome. How was the church that worshiped one God and honored Jesus Christ as the only Lord to get along with the mighty and ever-present Roman state? Was the state to be its friend or foe?

The Roman state, of course, had its official religion, with its deities, temples, and religious ceremonies. The traditional worship had been somewhat undermined during the last century before the founding of the empire (in 31 BC) by the criticism of the philosophers and the introduction of foreign cults from the east. With the formation of the empire under Augustus, an attempt was made to revitalize Roman religion, but the policy of the government was a reasonably tolerant one. In the lands the Romans conquered, the traditional religious cults were respected. In general the Roman state tolerated non-Roman religious cults so long as such worship did not interfere with the celebration of the official religion and did not disturb the general peace. Although in theory Roman citizens or provincials might be tried for atheism if they forsook the traditional cults and adopted foreign ones, such prosecution rarely occurred.

How was the church that worshiped one God and honored Jesus Christ as the only Lord to get along with the mighty and ever-present Roman state? Was the state to be its friend or foe?

The Jews, however, were a special subject people. Unlike other peoples whom Rome conquered, they refused to worship the Roman gods either instead of or alongside the worship of their God. Rome early decided not to force conformity but to grant religious liberty to the Jews. Julius Caesar, with the confirmation of the Senate, guaranteed religious freedom to the Jews (48 BC), and Augustus later renewed this decree.

The earliest Christians were Jews and therefore enjoyed the religious freedom accorded to Jews. There is no clear evidence that the Roman authorities distinguished Christians from Jews until the beginning of the second century. We should not conclude, however, that Christians knew no persecution until the beginning of the second century: the note of suffering is too well attested both in the New Testament and in other early literature to draw that conclusion.

In its various strands of literature (Gospels, history, Epistles, and Apocalypse), the New Testament both anticipates and reflects the persecution of the church. Many of these references to persecution are quite general and the source of the attack is left unspecified. Some of the conflict was intra-Jewish, tension between groups of Jews who thought differently about Jesus. Some of the conflict occurred because Roman officials became involved at the point of the public disturbance of the peace. Sometimes the Christians encountered opposition from their Gentile neighbors; doubtless to many Greeks the Christians appeared antisocial. They did not participate in many of society's functions, which they saw as idolatrous and immoral. The perplexity that this problem occasioned for Christians is reflected in 1 Corinthians 8 to 10. The Christians likely were viewed as holding dangerous social ideas; for example, the church taught a doctrine of fraternity that brought slave and master together on a plane of common fellowship.

The relationship between the Roman imperial government and the first-century church was marked by several more or less serious crises. First, there was the attempt of Emperor Caligula in AD 40 to have a statue of himself erected in the temple at Jerusalem. These plans were never executed because of his early death a year later. The persecution of Jews (including Jewish Christians) in Palestine that could have resulted from his decision did not develop. But the occasion certainly must have vividly brought to the minds of many the latent possibilities of conflict between emperor and church.

Second, the first major crisis developed under Nero in AD 64. In July of that year, a large part of the city of Rome was destroyed by fire. Rumor had it that the emperor himself was responsible for the fire; he wanted to clear space for a new building project. But in order to shift attention from himself, he accused the Christians of the crime and began to persecute them. As the persecution got under way, the charge of arson was dropped and a more general accusation of "hatred of the human race" was brought against them.

The suffering was intense. Some Christians were dressed in animal skins and then thrown to wild dogs to be torn apart; others were crucified and burned in Nero's gardens. The persecution was limited to Christians living in Rome; it was not empire-wide and did not represent a settled state policy. How many Christians perished in this outburst of violence is not known. According to Christian tradition, both Peter and Paul were victims.

Third, according to Tertullian near the end of the second century, Domitian (AD 81–96) was the second Roman emperor to move against the church. Tertullian speaks of Domitian as "a replica of Nero's cruelty." The evidence in support of this statement is not substantial. The author of 1 Clement, which was written from Rome about AD 96, speaks of "the sudden and repeated misfortunes and calamities which have befallen us." Yet this reference is not very specific. It is known that Domitian had difficulty with various groups and individuals in Rome; in AD 89 he ordered all philosophers and astrologers to leave the city.

Six years later, he accused many individuals of godlessness—of forsaking the worship of Roman gods. By his order, Flavius Clemens (whose son was heir apparent to the throne) was executed and his wife Domitilla banished on the same charge. It is likely that both were Christians. The book of Revelation is usually assigned to the closing years of Domitian's reign. While the book certainly anticipates conflict and persecution, we lack clear evidence that it has already occurred. It is possible that the expected clash did not actually come off and that Domitian's bad reputation among Christians of a later age was attributable more to his intentions as a persecutor than to any considerable accomplishment.

Fourth, there is solid evidence from the early part of the second century that under Trajan (AD 98–117) Christians no longer enjoyed legal protection. Pliny the Younger, a lawyer and financial expert, was sent out to Asia Minor as imperial legate around AD 110. When he needed help on difficult problems, he wrote to the emperor. One such problem was how to deal with Christians who had been brought to his attention. In the correspondence that passed between these two men, it is clear that, while Christians were not to be sought out for punishment, they were to be punished when accused of being Christian by another person before the legate. Christians brought to trial had the option of renouncing their faith, worshiping the Roman gods and going free, or refusing to do so and suffering death. It was at this time that Ignatius, bishop of Antioch, was arrested and taken to Rome for execution.

In Pliny's handling of Christians we hear of emperor worship. One way to determine whether people were Christians was to bring a statue of Trajan into the court and ask them "to make supplication with incense and wine" to it. This, of course, Christians could not do. Such worship developed gradually in the empire and had an uneven history. The worship of a king as a god or the descendant of deity was long common in the Hellenistic kingdoms to the east. When Rome fell heir to these lands the practice naturally was directed to

Roman kings. Most of the emperors during the first century, although willing to be accorded divine status by the senate after their death, did not regard worship while they were living as politically expedient in Rome. In the eastern imperial provinces, however, emperor worship was allowed. Indeed, it was regarded as a useful device to strengthen loyalty to the emperor. During this period three emperors—Caligula, Nero, and Domitian—broke with this general policy and openly encouraged or demanded divine honors for themselves while they were still alive. Such conduct could only invite immediate and absolute resistance from the church.

In summary, it may be said that in the first century there were times of ominous danger for Christians and of actual suffering at the hands of the Roman state. But there was no official and settled Roman policy to destroy the church. On the whole Rome was tolerant of the church as it was of other religious groups, so long as the famed Roman peace was not jeopardized.

What then was the attitude of the church toward the Roman state? The answer involves both positive and negative elements. On the one hand, there was an appreciation of the state's useful services in the maintenance of law and order. This appreciation may be the meaning of 2 Thessalonians 2:3–8; it is clearly reflected in such passages as Romans 13:1–7, 1 Peter 2:13–14, 1 Timothy 2:1–2, and Acts 25:10–11. On the other hand, Christians displayed a consistent refusal to give absolute obedience to the state. Its claims were to be judged in the light of God's claims on Christians. When the two were opposed, there could be no question where the Christian's loyalty belonged. A certain tension, therefore, was felt then, and it will continue to be experienced by the church until the day when "the kingdom of the world has become the kingdom of our Lord and of his Messiah" (Rev. 11:15).

Romans, a Christian classic

Although it stands first in the collection of Paul's letters in the New Testament, his epistle to the Romans was written near the close of Paul's active missionary career. Why it was given pride of place is not clear. Was it because it is the longest of his letters? Or was the importance of the church to which it was addressed a factor? Probably a more important consideration was the character of the letter itself: although it is not a comprehensive statement of Paul's theology, it more nearly approaches a systematic presentation of the gospel than any of his other letters. As such, it serves as a good introduction to Paul's thought.

This characterization of Romans, however, is much too prosaic. New Testament scholar C. F. D. Moule has said that Paul's letters are "among the most intoxicating parts of the whole New Testament." Many Christians would regard this appraisal as preeminently true of Romans. With an eye to the influence that Romans has exerted in shaping the history of the Christian church, Professor John Knox has forthrightly expressed the opinion that it is "unquestionably the most important theological book ever written."

Such a strong claim needs supporting evidence—and evidence is not in short supply. We may begin the selection with the testimony of Augustine regarding his encounter with Romans in Milan in the summer of AD 384. As a man of thirty he was struggling desperately with the passions and desires of a sinful nature too strong for him to subdue. In desperation he cried out to God for help as he lay weeping under a fig tree in the garden adjoining his house. At that moment, he heard the voice of a child at play in the neighboring house repeating in a chant-like way the words, "Take and read, take and read." When he could not remember any children's game with such a refrain, it occurred to him that it might be a word from the Lord to open the Bible and read the passage on which his eyes would first fall. He quickly found a Bible and opened it to Romans 13:13–14. This experience marked a turning point in Augustine's life: "As I reached the end of the sentence," he said, "the light of peace seemed to be shed upon my heart, and every shadow of doubt melted away."

Some 1100 years later, a German monk named Martin Luther set out to lecture on Romans in the university in Wittenberg. Writing about that experience later, he said, "I greatly longed to understand Paul's epistle to the Romans and nothing stood in the way but that one expression, 'the justice of God,' because I took it to mean that justice whereby God is just and deals justly in punishing the unjust." He knew himself to be a sinner deserving judgment. Night and day he earnestly pondered the connection between God's justice and Paul's statement that the just shall live by faith (Rom. 1:17). Eventually it dawned on him that "the justice of God is that righteousness by which through grace and sheer mercy God justifies us through faith. Thereupon, I felt myself to be reborn and to have gone through the open doors into paradise. The whole of Scripture took on a new meaning. . . . This passage of Paul became to me a gate to heaven." This discovery not only transformed Luther's life but radically altered the course of later Christian history.

More than two centuries after the beginning of the Protestant Reformation, John Wesley, a priest of the Church of England, had his life-changing engagement with Romans. It was an indirect contact by way of Luther's preface to his *Commentary on Romans*, which Wesley heard read at a London prayer meeting in May 1738. He recorded what happened to him in his journal: "About a quarter before nine, while [Luther] was describing the change which God works in the heart through faith in Christ, I felt my heart strangely warmed. I felt I did trust in Christ, Christ alone, for my salvation; and an assurance was given me that He had taken away my sins, even mine, and saved me from the law of sin and death." Out of that experience came new life for untold multitudes around the world.

Finally, we may refer to the Swiss theologian Karl Barth, trained in a liberal theological tradition in the early part of the twentieth century. But as a pastor during World War I he was searching for a relevant word to speak to his people. It was then that he discovered what he called "the strange new world within the Bible." It was "the mighty voice of Paul," primarily in the book of Romans, that opened his eyes to the profound dimensions of that new world. He came to the firm conclusion that "if we rightly understand ourselves, our problems are the problems of Paul; and if we be enlightened by the brightness of his answers, those answers must be ours." Barth's discovery sparked a theological revolution, the effects of which were long felt in classrooms and pulpits in many parts of our world.

Why has Romans exercised such power and influence across all the centuries? The answer appears to lie in its penetrating analysis of the human predicament and in the adequacy of the answer it offers to the problem. The appeal and power of Romans lie in its magnificent exposition of the gospel.

The question may well be asked why Romans has exercised such a tremendous power and influence across all the centuries. The answer appears to lie, as Barth saw, in two features that characterize this letter. One is its penetrating analysis of the human predicament, which is our situation; the other is the adequacy of the answer it offers to the problem. Perhaps these two observations can be stated really as one: the appeal and power of Romans lie in its magnificent exposition of the gospel.

From the letter itself, we learn that it was written shortly before Paul's departure from Greece (see Acts 20:2–3) for Jerusalem to take financial aid for the poor of that church (Rom. 15:22–29). According to Acts, this mission to Jerusalem concluded his third missionary journey (Acts 24:17). Following the visit to Jerusalem, Paul planned to return west, stopping at Rome on his way to Spain. Paul had not yet been able to visit the Christians in Rome, although he had long wished to do so (Rom. 1:9–13). The letter served as a contact with the church in advance of his projected arrival. However, these plans were later altered by Paul's arrest and detention for two years in Palestine; when he did eventually arrive in Rome, it was as a prisoner of the Roman state (Acts 28:14–16).

We know little about the church in Rome prior to Paul's visit. Who first brought the gospel to the capital and when can no longer be determined. The purpose of the letter, beyond informing the Roman Christians of his plans, also is not clear. Was Paul primarily interested in setting down a reflective statement regarding the gospel out of his extensive missionary experience as a way of introducing himself to the church? In particular, was he eager to formulate somewhat systematically the more universal implications of the gospel as an apostle to the Gentiles? Or, on the contrary, was Paul addressing some particular need in the Roman church of which he may have had some knowledge?

The latter suggestion is an intriguing possibility, and various attempts have been made to identify such needs. Is the note of dissension treated at length in 14:1–15:13 (see also 16:17–20) a clue to a major concern in writing the letter? Again, is it possible that Paul's purpose was to deal with the problem of the relationship between Jew and Gentile in the plan of God? This subject is discussed in some detail in chapters 9–11 and may well have occupied Paul's thoughts as he prepared to take the offering of the Gentile churches to Jerusalem.

Another proposal is to understand Romans against the backdrop of Paul's ministry at Corinth, where Christian liberty was being abused; the result may have been that more conservative communities, including the Roman church, viewed Paul as a libertine. Did he write this letter with the hope of commending the gospel to them as not promoting irresponsible conduct but as sensitive to Jewish interests? If the Christians at Rome accepted Paul's statement, his chances of being accepted in Jerusalem might then be strengthened (see 15:30–32).

However Paul's purpose in writing Romans may be reconstructed in detail, the document remains a finely crafted legacy of a mature Christian statesman. We would be much the poorer in our understanding both of Paul's own mind and of the gospel if we did not have it. Careful study of the book will make this fact increasingly evident. I can do little more in this essay than make several general comments about the form and content of the letter to stimulate further attention and study.

First, the general structure of the letter is not difficult to detect. There is an introductory unit (1:1–17) and a conclusion (15:14–16:29). The heart of the book falls into three sections. The first deals with the universal human predicament and God's response to it (1:18–8:39). The core of this response is set out in 3:21–31. God's action in the Christ-event is then related to the Old Testament in chapter 4. Other theological and experiential facets of the gospel are then dealt with in chapters 5 to 8. The second section, chapters 9 to 11, builds on the first; if the gospel is God's answer to the human problem, why were some Jews rejecting the gospel? This question, thrown up by history, is addressed from the angles of divine sovereignty, human freedom, and the solution ultimately anticipated. A third section is devoted to the practical implications of the gospel for conduct (12:1–15:13). It is a reminder that theology and ethics must not be kept apart; thus there is a return at the end of the letter to the point of departure in 1:18–3:20, namely, the arena of human conduct. But the perspective now is radically different because of the impact of the intervening Christ-event on the human scene.

Second, turning to the message of Romans, the well-known passage in 1:16–17 is frequently regarded as the key text of the letter. The basic term here is *gospel*, a word already introduced in the salutation (1:1, 3). The "gospel of God," which is "the gospel concerning his Son," is now further elaborated.

The goal envisioned by the gospel is the salvation of men and women. This word, found already in the pages of the Old Testament, may suggest a rescue operation. The thrust, however, is not basically salvation *from* but salvation *to* something. The term points to a condition of wholeness or well-being. In its religious sense it is primarily a relational term: to be saved is to be in a right relationship with God and with others. As a relational term, it designates an open rather than a static situation. It can indicate a past, present, or future reality. The remainder of the letter pours rich content into our understanding of this concept.

But the gospel not only points to God's intention for us; it also speaks of God's power to achieve that goal. This empowerment is what makes the gospel "good news." The power of the gospel is said to reside in its revelation of "the righteousness of God." The meaning of this phrase is not commented on here but will be in 3:21–26. No mere passive attribute of God's character is in view; rather, it is God in action in Christ to bring people into a right relationship with God.

Although God's saving intention is inclusive of all people, its effective fulfillment is conditional on faith. The reason is not arbitrary: it grows out of the nature of salvation as a personal relationship, which necessarily involves the element of response. Faith as response is much more than mental assent to an idea; it is the orientation of the total person to God in Christ in surrender, trust, and obedience. This understanding of faith is made abundantly clear in the remainder of the letter.

Third, Paul focuses on the shape of God's saving activity that forms the heart of the gospel in another significant passage: 3:21–31. This passage is set against the backdrop of the portrayal of all humanity's involvement in sin (1:18–3:20). The focus of God's saving activity is the Christ-event and specifically the cross. It is not restricted to the death of Jesus, as is made clear elsewhere in the letter. That action, however, is most dramatically and climactically seen in the cross. But the cross should not be sundered from either the life or the resurrection of Jesus.

Three images are employed to illuminate the nature of the saving activity. *Justification* is courtroom terminology and speaks to sin as guilt. *Redemption* is drawn from the institution of slavery and speaks to sin as power. *Expiation* is a cultic word and speaks to the removal of sin as a barrier to fellowship.

The saving activity of God is rooted in God's own gracious will. Our dependence on God removes once and for all any ground for meritorious boasting. At the foot of the cross the ground is level. The only appropriate response to such grace is gratitude expressed in a life of trust in and commitment to the Savior (see 12:12).

This brief peek into a few of the riches of Romans should make more understandable the testimonies with which we began. But better still, do countersign them with your own explorations!

Is James "a right strawy epistle"?

In the introduction to the first edition of his German New Testament published in 1522, Martin Luther wrote these words: "In brief, St. John's Gospel and his First Epistle, St. Paul's Epistles, especially those to the Romans, Galatians, Ephesians, and St. Peter's First Epistle—these are the books which show you Christ and teach you everything that is needful and blessed for you to know even though you never see or hear any other book or doctrine. St. James' Epistle is a right strawy one in comparison with them, for it has no gospel character to it."

"Give a dog a bad name and hang him," goes the old proverb. "Luther once gave the Epistle of James a 'bad name,'" says A. M. Hunter, "and nearly succeeded in hanging it." Luther's estimate of James has often been quoted and doubtless has influenced the attitude of many Christians toward this book. They may not bother to read it, or if they do, they may have difficulty giving it a fair hearing.

What shall we say about Luther's verdict? First, it should be made clear that Luther did not mean that the letter contained *only* straw and therefore is worthless; he recognized that "there is many a good saying in it." But Luther missed Christ in its pages. To be sure, there are a few occurrences of his name (1:1; 2:1) but no exposition of his real significance for Christian faith and experience. For Luther, this was a fatal flaw. "What does not teach Christ," he said, "is not apostolic, even though St. Peter or Paul taught it; again what preaches Christ would be apostolic, even though Judas, Annas, Pilate and Herod did it." For this reason, Luther, although not dropping James from his New Testament, assigned it to a sort of appendix status.

It must be admitted that the book of James does not major on the great notes of the gospel that are so clearly heard in Paul's writings. It is likely, however, that there are more references to Jesus than the two explicit ones already noted. For example, "the excellent name that was invoked over you" (2:7) probably refers to the name of Christ. Again, the anointing of the sick with oil "in the name of the Lord" (5:14) may well point to the name of Jesus. Furthermore, the several references to "the coming of the Lord" (5:7–8) likely are to be understood in the sense of Christ's return. A reference to the passion and resurrection of Jesus may be presupposed in the description of Christ as the Lord of glory (2:1) or in the hope of his return in the passages just noted. But at best these are only veiled hints of what elsewhere in the New Testament—the Gospels, the letters of Paul and Peter, Hebrews, and Revelation—is made explicit.

In defense of the Christian character of the book, we may call attention to two additional features. One of these is the way James appears to echo certain teachings of Jesus in the first three Gospels. There is the promise of the kingdom to the poor who are rich in faith (2:5; see Matt. 5:3; Luke 6:20). The work of peacemaking is recognized as having divine approval (3:18; see Matt. 5:3). Divine judgment is pronounced against the rich (1:10–11; 5:1–6; see Luke 6:24; Matt. 19:23–24). Most striking, however, is the prohibition of the oath and the commendation of simple honest speech (5:12; see Matt. 5:36–37).

The other feature worthy of notice is the way the kind of conduct called for in the letter is grounded in a new order or quality of existence. The language used to describe it has Christian overtones. There is, for example, the reference to the reception of "the implanted word that has the power to save" the readers (1:21). From the context, it is clear that the word in view is "the word of truth" (1:18), which seems to be another expression for the gospel. At the root of this life that stands in sharp contrast to "all sordidness and rank growth of wickedness" (1:21) is a power that is not our own.

This power is a gift that we must "welcome with meekness" if we are to be saved (1:21). Those who are thus "given birth by the word of truth" are further described as "a kind of first fruits of his creatures" (1:18). This language is at home in the "already-not yet" framework of New Testament thought. The church is a sort of advance exhibit now of the community that is yet to be when God's purposes some day will be brought to final fulfillment.

Let us now move on to a second comment on Luther's evaluation of James. It has to do with his belief that James contradicts Paul's doctrine of salvation by grace through faith. In its place, he believed, James put a "works salvation." He was unable to reconcile James 2:16–26 with passages such as Romans 3:28, Galatians 3:10–14, Ephesians 2:8, and Philippians 3:7–9. Faced with an either-or decision, Luther's choice was clear: Paul won, James lost.

> **Do Paul and James cancel each other out? Must we choose between them? Did Luther truly understand James? Is it possible that he also misunderstood Paul?**

But do Paul and James cancel each other out? Must we choose between them? Did Luther truly understand James? Is it possible that he also misunderstood Paul?

A quick survey of the above passages will indicate that both Paul and James use such terms as *faith*, *works*, and *justify*. But a more careful study will show that each writer uses them in distinctive ways. Perhaps we may summarize the difference as follows. When Paul speaks of justification, he has in mind God's action in Christ by virtue of which God now sets us in a right relationship with himself. The works that he criticizes as having no value for establishing this relationship are acts done out of a meritorious purpose or spirit. The faith on which Paul insists as the condition for God setting us in the right with himself is the total commitment of the self in trust and obedience to God in Christ; Paul can speak of it as obedient-faith or faith-obedience in Romans 1:5.

Turning to James, the faith that he condemns is a sterile intellectual belief that springs from the top of the head. It has no effect on conduct; it lives in empty words that are un-hooked from action. The works that he commends are those acts of love and service that flow out of a renewed inner life; they are not unrelated to what Paul would call living by the Spirit (Gal. 5:16–26). The justification of which James speaks is not just the present act of putting people into a right relationship with God, but it includes the final verdict on the person's life. It partakes of the nature of vindication.

Is James "a right strawy epistle"?

Can we understand the book of Revelation?

Although the title would hardly suggest it, Revelation is the most difficult book of the New Testament to understand. Ambrose Bierce's comment that it is "a famous book in which St. John the Divine concealed all that he knew" has a ring of truth for many who have tried to read it. Many Christians promptly run aground when they encounter the imagery of the book and never again manage to get afloat for further exploration.

If in their helplessness they put out an SOS call in the direction of commentaries, they soon discover that they are being pulled in opposite directions on almost all questions having to do with the book. Obviously, this discovery does not do much to lift their hopes of success. Their despair is final when they learn that no less a theologian than Martin Luther said that if people are not crazy before they begin to study Revelation, they probably will be before they have finished. Who wishes to run such risks?

Clearly the book of Revelation is difficult, although the point should not be unduly pressed. Certainly even after diligent effort, obscure passages and debatable opinions will remain—biblical scholars are the first to admit this fact. But the landscape need not remain completely shrouded in fog. The lay person who is willing to expend some energy in serious Bible study may well discover this book to be one of the most exciting in the New Testament. In any case, it merits more respect than Luther gave it when he put it into the appendix of his New Testament.

One fundamental cause for much of the difficulty with this book is the lack of any acquaintance with the background and character of the type of literature it represents. It obviously is different from that of the Gospels, the Acts, or the Epistles. It has a parallel, however, in the Old Testament book of Daniel and in much Jewish and in some early Christian literature that did not get into the Bible. To try to understand Revelation apart from the larger body of literature to which it belongs is like trying to understand a branch in isolation from the tree. Some attempt, therefore, must be made to fill in this background.

> **Although the notes of conflict and suffering are heard repeatedly in Revelation, the basic mood is lyrical, resting in hope. Whatever perplexities particular passages may present, the impression made by the document is one of immense buoyancy, because of the faith that shines through it.**

An alternate title for the book is the Apocalypse of John. The word *apocalypse* is the English transliteration of the Greek word meaning "revelation." The word, of course, can be used in a non-technical sense. But in the study of the theological development and literature of inter-testamental Judaism, the word has a rather precise meaning. An apocalypse is a revelatory writing that discloses the secrets of the future, especially the end time. The adjective *apocalyptic* may also be used of this literature or of the way of thinking from which these writings sprang. Since the apocalyptic mentality was prior to its literary expression, we should begin with this theological perspective.

The high point of Old Testament prophecy was the period between the eighth and the sixth centuries BC. After the exile in Babylon and especially after the time of Nehemiah and Ezra, prophetic activity declined. No figures in this period are comparable to the great prophets of earlier times. The conviction gradually grew up that the Holy Spirit ceased with Ezra and that the day of prophecy was now a memory of the past and a hope for the future end time. In the place of the prophet came the writer of apocalyptic and the legalist.

The precise relationship between prophecy and apocalyptic is a matter of dispute among scholars. Some would simply regard apocalyptic as prophecy in a new key; others would stress the differences between prophecy and apocalyptic and find no real continuity between the two. T. W. Manson put forward an interesting theory: that apocalyptic and legalism (as embodied in the rabbinic tradition) were two parallel attempts to deal with life's fundamental problems in the light of prophetic revelation that embodied the notes of both demand and promise.

While legalism focused on the demand element in prophetic thought and developed and codified it, apocalyptic chose to give primary attention to the promise aspect of prophetic thought. It rationalized and systematized the predictive side of prophecy. It stressed the certainty of God's action in the future as the great hope of the Jewish community. The split, of course, was not absolute but was rather a matter of emphasis.

If apocalyptic does have roots in prophecy, there are distinct features that mark out this movement. The first is the doctrine of the two ages or the division of time into "this age" and "the age to come." The prophets, of course, had already looked forward to a new day beyond the time of judgment that would befall a disobedient nation. But the connection between the present and the future was not really broken: the new was more or less continuous with the old. In contrast, with apocalyptic the break is sharp. The new age is not an outgrowth of the old but a new creation. It is a new order that breaks in from beyond and puts an end to the old. It is not merely temporally distinct but different in quality.

Second, corresponding to the doctrine of the two ages is a pronounced pessimism with regard to the present age and a concentration of hope on the coming age. For the prophets, there was still hope in the present if Israel would repent; for the writer of apocalyptic, forces of evil dominated the present. No improvement could be expected—only a progressive worsening of the situation until God would intervene to put an end to evil. The present had little significance; the eye was fixed on the horizon of tomorrow.

Third, in apocalyptic literature the divine drama has a cosmic setting. Prophetic thought, to be sure, is not restricted to Israel but does reach out to the nations and in this sense has a universal cast to it. But apocalyptic has the universe—the earth, the heavens, and Hades—as its stage and all human and superhuman beings as its actors. Special interest is taken in the superhuman world of angels and demons. God's judgment, too, is world-inclusive.

Fourth, a certain determinism marks apocalyptic thought, tending to make belief in the sovereignty of God less dynamic than was the case with the prophets. The future is no longer contingent on human response, but all is fixed in the plan of God and will be played out as determined. History is pre-recorded in heaven, and God may grant knowledge of the future course of events to elect servants on earth. It is no longer a question of *what*, only of *when*.

While the foregoing features are characteristics of apoca-lyptic thought, there was no one fixed scheme. There was great diversity of opinion on the way the apocalyptic mind worked out the particulars of its belief about the future. Apocalyptic was more a temper of mind than a rigidly prescribed body of dogma.

This outlook on the world developed gradually in the difficult years after the Babylonian exile. The frustration of Israel's national hopes helped focus attention on the future and on God's plans for the world. Historical experience helped shape the forms in which Jewish faith was expressed. The apocalyptic perspective was not limited to one party or institu-tion within Judaism; it found expression in a more or less pronounced way in a considerable body of literature produced between 200 BC and AD 100.

This material has certain literary features in common. While prophets spoke or wrote under their own names, the apocalyptic writer used the name of a respected Old Testament figure. For the prophet, the media of vision and audition were genuine personal experiences; for the apocalyptic writer, they are for the most part literary devices for the communication of a message. While the prophet made occasional use of symbol-ism, the apocalyptic writer not only majored in this type of language, but much of his symbolism is quite bizarre. Some of it is rooted in ancient mythology. Considerable use is made of animal figures to portray leaders and nations. Great interest is shown in numbers that seem to carry a symbolic or allegorical meaning. The prophets made genuine predictions about the future; the apocalyptic writer frequently wrote history under the form of a future prophecy. This approach is understandable if the writer used the name of an earlier Old Testament character. Other features might be noted that distinguish this type of literature, but perhaps these are sufficient to provide some feel for its content and tone.

The book of Revelation belongs to this general movement of thought known as apocalyptic and to the literary deposit that it left. To be sure, not everything that has been or might be said about Jewish apocalyptic applies equally to Revelation, for this book is a Christian production. The author does not write under an assumed name; he does not borrow the halo of a great figure in antiquity in order to enhance the authority of his message. He writes as the servant and prophet of the Lord who is a contemporary of those whom he addresses. He does not survey history under the form of future prediction. The mode of revelation is not the common apocalyptic device of dream but rather that of ecstatic vision and audition. Angels, which are common mediators of heavenly or future secrets in Jewish apocalypses, appear only rarely in this capacity in Revelation. Likewise the avid apocalyptic interest in cosmology is not a major concern of this book.

Obviously no detailed, exhaustive guidance can be given here for understanding the content of Revelation. We must be content with a few general remarks.

First, it is evident that the author is steeped in the imagery of the Old Testament and Jewish apocalyptic. The more familiar we are with these sources, the more we understand the pages of this book. It will not do to impart all sorts of possible meanings into the book's word pictures. We must seek their rootage in historical usage at the time the author wrote.

Second, it is not enough to trace backgrounds. It cannot be said too strongly that this is a Christian book. It bears the imprint of the Christ-event and its far-reaching implications for the understanding of all reality. The historical advent, life, death, and resurrection of Christ are the great facts that have refocused the apocalyptic perspective of this author. This reality can be illustrated in various ways. Take, for example, the way the conception of the messiah is transfigured by what happened in history. Judaism had expected a messiah who would be the lion of Judah but he now is seen to be a lamb who bears the marks of sacrifice. This messiah conquers not by the methods of Maccabean militarism, but by his cross and the martyrdom of his followers. Here is one of the most radical recastings of conventional apocalyptic thought in the book. It is attributable to the impact of a historical event. It is so startling that many Christians today have difficulty accepting it.

Third, while the scope of vision in this book is cosmic with a multiplicity of strange details passed in review, this imagery should not be allowed to obscure the ultimate focus of the vision: the creation of a community in which God and humans dwell together in perfect fellowship. This community is the ultimate end of the purpose of God in history. It may seem like a wishful dream in a world now full of bitter tensions and bloodshed. But the city of Revelation 21 is not a human creation. Its advent is not out of the historical process; it descends from heaven. It is a new creation of God's own making.

Finally, although the notes of conflict and suffering are heard repeatedly in the book, the basic mood is lyrical, resting in hope. This anticipation should not be missed, for it provides a genuine insight into the message of the book as a whole. Whatever perplexities particular passages may present, the impression made by the document is definitely one of immense buoyancy. It is because of the faith that shines through it—the conviction that in the cosmic chess game that is now being played out, the figures move on squares that may be dark, but they are set against a background that is light.

Scripture index

About the author and editor

Howard H. Charles (1915–2002) taught New Testament from 1947 to 1989 at Goshen Biblical Seminary in Goshen, Indiana, and at Associated Mennonite Biblical Seminary in Elkhart, Indiana. A native of Lititz, Pennsylvania, and pastor of Lititz Mennonite Church from 1943 to 1947, Charles graduated from Goshen College and later earned advanced degrees from Union Theological Seminary (Virginia), Princeton Theological Seminary, and the University of Edinburgh. He was a long-time regular contributor to *The Herald Teacher* and *Builder*, resources for adult Sunday school teachers produced by Mennonite Publishing House, and the author of *Alcohol and the Bible* (Herald Press, 1966) and *God and His People* (Herald Press, 1969). He also served as the first New Testament editor of the Believers Church Bible Commentary series and on year-long teaching assignments under Mennonite Board of Missions in Japan and Ghana. In 1947, Charles married Miriam Stalter of Elida, Ohio. They are the parents of two sons and five grandchildren.

J. Robert Charles, son of Howard and Miriam Charles, is director for Europe at Mennonite Mission Network. A graduate of Goshen College, Associated Mennonite Biblical Seminary, and the Fletcher School of Law and Diplomacy at Tufts University, he with his wife Sylvia Shirk Charles served eight years in Belgium with Mennonite Board of Missions. He has been co-leader of international study programs in Haiti, Ivory Coast, and Mali and has taught history and political science at Goshen College. He lives in Goshen, Indiana, and is the father of three young adult children: Laura, Daniel, and Sophie.